DEADLY DECEITS
My 25 Years in the CIA

DEADLY DECEITS

My 25 Years in the CIA

By

RALPH W. McGEHEE

Sheridan Square Publications, Inc.
New York

Publisher's Note: This book represents the first of a series of in-depth studies of current intelligence issues. For details, write to Sheridan Square Publications, Inc., P. O. Box 677, New York, NY 10013.

ISBN: Hardbound: 0-940380-03-X
         Paperback: 0-940380-02-1

Library of Congress Cataloging in Publication Data:

McGehee, Ralph W., 1928-
    Deadly deceits.

    Includes index.
    1. United States. Central Intelligence Agency.
2. McGehee, Ralph W., 1928-   . 3. Intelligence
officers--United States--Biography. I. Title.
JK468.I6M43 1982   327.1'2'06073   82-19627
ISBN 0-940380-03-X
ISBN 0-940380-02-1 (pbk.)

DEDICATION

This book is dedicated to all those hurt
by CIA covert operations. It is especially
dedicated to the Vietnamese and the Americans who served in Vietnam.

ACKNOWLEDGEMENTS

I wish to acknowledge the assistance of the staff of the Center for National Security Studies. I especially want to commend the former librarian of the center, Monica Andres, for her frequent encouragement and assistance. Mark Lynch of the American Civil Liberties Union, who represented me so well in my numerous legal battles with the CIA, deserves heartfelt thanks. Zachary Sklar, my editor, who helped shape an inchoate mass into a unified whole, has been of special assistance. I particularly want to thank Michael Ratner, William Schaap, Ellen Ray, and Louis Wolf for their courage in fighting for what they believe to be right and for making this book possible. Special acknowledgment is due my children, Peggy, Jean, Scott, and Daniel, who, while not necessarily sharing my views, gave moral support. Lastly, I wish to acknowledge the assistance of my wife, Norma, who shared and endured my personal strife, and whose unwavering loyalty made this project possible.

CONTENTS

Author's Note viii

Introduction ix

1. Gung Ho ! 1
2. Japan and the Philippines: Innocents Abroad. 17
3. Washington: Fun in the Files .34
4. A Company Man in China 44
5. Life at Langley 54
6. North Thailand: Saving the Hill Tribes 66
7. Headquarters: Duping Congress 81
8. In Search of Reds 87
9. Headquarters: Ghosts in the Halls 117
10. The CIA in Vietnam: Transforming Reality 125
11. Coming Home 160
12. Down and Out in Thailand .163
13. Light at the End of the Tunnel 178
14. Conclusion 192

Appendix: This Book and the Secrecy Agreement 196

Sources 204

Glossary 211

Index 215

AUTHOR'S NOTE

Because of the secrecy agreement I signed when I went to work for the CIA, this book had to be submitted to and approved by the CIA's Publications Review Board. It required that the names of various people be removed from the text. In those cases I have used fictitious names, which are noted the first time they appear in the text. The board demanded that I alter the names and the descriptions of a few specific locations. This I have done. In addition, the board made a number of deletions in the manuscript. I have indicated in the text where these deletions have been made and how long they were. For a full discussion of the Agency's review of the manuscript, a long and difficult process, please see the Appendix.

INTRODUCTION

IT was late one night in December 1968 in Gia Dinh province near Saigon. Angered and miserable, I was sitting alone in the living room of a villa sparsely furnished with standard government-issue rattan tables and kapok-cushioned sofa and chairs. A bare coffee table and empty book shelves signaled the recent transition from one CIA occupant to another. A framed picture of artificial-looking flowers broke up only slightly the monotony of the harsh yellow walls. The lone tape left by my predecessor played on the stereo and Nancy Sinatra sang for the hundredth time "Such a Pretty World Today," soon to be followed by "End of the World." Outside, helicopter gunships circled and off in the distance B-52s dropped another string of bombs on South Vietnamese men, women, and children.

I sat there in agony thinking about all that had led me to this private hell. My idealism, my patriotism, my ambition, my plans to be a good intelligence officer to help my country fight the Communist scourge — what in hell had happened? Why did we have to bomb the people we were trying to save? Why were we napalming young children? Why did the CIA, my employer for 16 years, report lies instead of the truth?

I hated my part in this charade of murder and horror. My efforts were contributing to the deaths, to the burning alive of children — especially the children. The photographs of young Vietnamese children burned by napalm destroyed me. I wanted out of this massacre. Angrily I thought back to the year before in Thailand when I had worked in the rural villages and learned some painful truths about the nature of an Asian revolution. I had faced the undeniable evidence that the Communists had infiltrated much deeper into Asian society than we had ever imagined or reported, and I had devised what I thought was a humane way to beat them. Why had the Agency first accepted that information and then, in spite of countless proofs of its accuracy, denied it? When presented with a viable alternative, why was it following the same old methods that resulted only in more killing and more futility?

I wanted to end this maddening turmoil. I thought about the loaded AR-15 by my bed upstairs and the small loaded pistol in my nightstand. I could kill myself. It would be easy. But if I did, I rationalized, my death should accomplish some purpose, like those of the monks who burned themselves in downtown Saigon. Maybe if I made a huge banner saying "THE CIA LIES" or "FUCK THE CIA" and hung it from the roof of the Agency's Duc Hotel and then jumped off. . . . I hated my inaction and myself, but to die in those circumstances would only bring shame to my family — and poverty, for the Agency was vengeful and would withhold the death benefits. Even if I could hang the banner and jump, the Agency would quickly cover up what happened and issue a statement saying that I was crazy. There seemed no way.

I wondered if I was merely making excuses. Did I lack the guts to do it? Why not just quit the Agency? But then how could I support two children in college and two more at home? In my mental state it would be impossible to find a new career. Anybody in their right mind would send me to an institution, not hire me. No, quitting was out: either I would kill myself, or stay and struggle and suffer. There were no other paths. I stared at the bare light bulb on the ceiling. Outside there was a pause in the bombing and for a brief moment all was peaceful, silent. My hand trembled, I gulped down my drink, and then broke down in tears. Here I was, a former Notre Dame football player, now a macho CIA case officer, weeping like a baby.

It was at this moment of utter despair back in that ugly room in Gia Dinh in 1968 that the seed of this book was first planted. For I realized then that if I stayed I had to do something to fight the terrible things I had seen the CIA do. I knew then that the United States and the CIA had gone very wrong. Killing myself was not the answer. I had to stay alive and tell what I had found out. I owed that much to the American and Vietnamese people — and to myself.

This book is a journey through my 25 years in the CIA. I worked from 1952 to 1977 in many places, including Japan, Taiwan, Thailand, the Philippines, Vietnam, and Langley, Virginia. I had a range of jobs, both in cities and rural areas, working as a case officer on covert operations, as a paramilitary operator, as a liaison officer with foreign police and intelligence agencies, and as an intelligence analyst. I also studied the CIA for years after I retired. This range of experience and research has led me to realizations and conclusions, many of which are unpleasant and painful to me. I choose now to share these experiences and conclusions for two main reasons.

The first is political. I want to reveal to those who still believe in the myths of the CIA what it is and what it actually does. My explanation will not include the usual pap fed to us by Agency spokesmen. My view backed by 25 years of experience is, quite simply, that the CIA is the covert action arm of the Presidency. Most of its money, manpower, and energy go into covert operations that, as we have seen over the years, include backing dictators and overthrowing democratically elected governments. The CIA is not an intelligence agency. In fact, it acts largely as an anti-intelligence agency, producing only that information wanted by policymakers to support their plans and suppressing information that does not support those plans. As the covert action arm of the President, the CIA uses disinformation, much of it aimed at the U.S. public, to mold opinion. It employs the gamut of disinformation techniques from forging documents to planting and discovering "communist" weapons caches. But the major weapon in its arsenal of disinformation is the "intelligence" it feeds to policymakers. Instead of gathering genuine intelligence that could serve as the basis for reasonable policies, the CIA often ends up distorting reality, creating out of whole cloth "intelligence" to justify policies that have already been decided upon. Policymakers then leak this "intelligence" to the media to deceive us all and gain our support. Now that President Reagan, in his Executive Order of December 4, 1981, has authorized the Agency to operate within the United States, the situation can only worsen.

But beyond contributing to the political dialogue about the CIA, I want to understand my own life, to try to adjust to the world as it is, not to the fairy-tale world I was led to believe in. I write with the knowledge that my experiences reflect, at least to a degree, those of the more than two million Americans who served in Vietnam and millions of others at home who idealistically believed, as I did, in the American dream. If this book helps some of them to understand how they were misled and how that dream was shattered, and to adjust, then it will have achieved its goal.

1.
GUNG HO!

BEFORE I went to work for the CIA I believe I was a typical American, if there is such a creature. My family goes back three generations in Louisiana and many of the Scotch-Irish McGehees lie buried in the East Fork Baptist Church cemetery near Kentwood. My father, as a teenager, moved north to make his fortune and after several years returned to marry his childhood sweetheart, a neighboring girl from Osyka, Mississippi. I was born in Moline, Illinois in 1928. Shortly thereafter my parents, my older sister, and I moved to the South Side of Chicago, where my father worked long, hard hours as a janitor to support us. Despite the Depression, my family prospered.

I grew up in the lower middle class all-white South Side neighborhood and after graduating from grammar school attended Tilden Technical High School, located several miles away in a racially and ethnically mixed area. A serious student, I earned membership in the honor society and was elected class president. I also won All State and All City awards as a tackle on our city championship football team. Though I remained an ardent Baptist, two of my teammates persuaded me to go to college at Notre Dame with them. We roomed together and played on four undefeated football teams that won three national championships in the years from 1946 to 1949. I won an award one year as the best blocking tackle and played in the North-South All Star game another year. In 1950 I graduated cum laude in Business Administration.

I was raised to believe in the American dream — the Protestant work ethic, truth, justice, freedom. I had lived through World War II with its clear black-and-white heroes and villains

1

and the stirring messages of fighting for God, country, and democracy in the world. I and my whole generation shared an innate feeling of accomplishment. The satisfaction in victory, the reawakening economy, the Marshall Plan for Europe, and our government's attempts to rebuild a world made safe for mankind had made all of us proud, patriotic and, I suppose, a little smug.

I believed in the basic lessons of life that my legendary Notre Dame football coach, Frank Leahy, had drilled into us — work hard, do your best, and victory in the game and in the larger game of life will be yours. "Oh, lads," I can still hear him saying, "you have to pay the price, but if you do, you can only win." My proudest, happiest, most patriotic moments came before the games as the starting teams lined up in the kick-off formation in the center of the stadium, surrounded by Notre Dame's loyal fans. Standing there in the crisp bright sun, gazing fervently at the flag as the national anthem resounded, I was filled with emotion. Each time I dedicated myself to do my best for myself, my family, my school, and my country.

After college I failed a try-out with the Green Bay Packers. A one-year stint as line coach at the University of Dayton convinced me I needed to change fields. I moved to Chicago and got a job with Montgomery Ward as a management trainee. After all of the glory days, this job seemed unendurably prosaic. But as if out of a chapter of the American dream as taught to me by my parents and Coach Leahy, a telegram arrived: "Would you be interested in an important government position? The duties include foreign travel and involve procedures similar to those of the Department of State. . . ." Suddenly the adrenaline was pumping and I could hear the crowds cheering again.

In mid-January 1952, after a brief interview with a quiet man in the Chicago courthouse, and after several well-dressed young men had invaded my neighborhood asking questions about me (the local druggist stopped my father and asked if I were in trouble with the government), I was called to

Washington, D.C. The man in the courthouse had made vague references to fighting communism but had imparted little additional information. He didn't tell me what I would be doing or what agency I would be working for, but I assumed it would have something to do with foreign diplomacy. Intrigue, danger, adventure, travel to exotic places, and possibly even a mysterious Mata Hari or two might be in my future. I visualized myself at a sidewalk cafe in Paris, sipping Pernod while discussing important foreign affairs with a diplomat.

I boarded the afternoon train for Washington. To prepare for a possible test of my knowledge of world events, I brought with me *Time* magazine and several copies of *The New York Times*. As soon as the berths were made up and after a quick sandwich, I retired to digest the latest news.

The headlines reflected the atmosphere of the time in which I was setting out on my new career. Our courts were processing cases against domestic Communists, and to keep track of all of them it was necessary to designate the cases by city and group number. The Senate Subcommittee on Internal Security was holding hearings as yet another person denied Senator Joseph McCarthy's charges that he was a Communist. Indeed, this was the second anniversary of Senator McCarthy's announcement that he had the names of 205 card-carrying Communists who were working in the State Department. The House Un-American Activities Committee (HUAC) was continuing its attack on the reds in Hollywood. The Soviet foreign minister accused the United States of transporting Chinese Nationalist troops to Thailand and Burma. In Korea the fighting raged, while the peace talks at Panmunjom stalled. President Truman in his State of the Union message before Congress warned that the "world still walks in the shadow of another world war."

These realities were a part of me. My professors at Notre Dame, the news media, public officials, and my friends all discussed the danger and viciousness of communism and the despair behind the Iron Curtain. No one doubted or questioned our government's statements; we all believed. It was obvious to me that the monolithic international communist conspiracy was attacking our way of life, our religion, and our allies overseas. Ralph W. McGehee, Jr. was proud and happy to be on his way to help his government.

I arrived at Washington's Union Station mid-morning. It was a sunny, bright, cold, invigorating day. A recent snowfall had laid a blanket of pure, virginal snow over the capital. I took a cab from the station up Constitution Avenue. On the right stood the National Archives building with its towering Corinthian columns and its huge bronze doors. On the left the glorious Capitol dominated its hilltop site and that tall proud obelisk, the Washington Monument, aimed its adoration straight at God. He, in His infinite loving wisdom, I was sure, pointed His benevolence back at this great country. It was truly an emotional moment for me. I thought back to my history class where I learned of Nathan Hale regretting that he had but one life to give to his country. Sir Walter Scott said it best: "Breathes there a man with soul so dead who never to himself hath said, this is my own, my native land. . . ."

The cab pulled up at the circle at the Washington end of the Arlington Memorial Bridge. I had been told to report to K Building, one of four dirty, gray, wooden structures that had been erected near the Lincoln Memorial during World War II. They looked as if they had not been painted since that time. A formidable eight-foot-high steel mesh fence surrounded the buildings, broken only by a couple of entrance gates. There were no signs to give me any clue about what organization was working inside. I entered at the second gate and the guard directed me to a poorly furnished, rundown waiting room. In about 10 minutes a harried, bespectacled man somberly greeted me, had me fill out some travel forms, and advised me to report the next day to the 9th Street personnel pool. He helpfully suggested that I might find acceptable lodging at the 17th Street YMCA.

The next day I checked in at the personnel pool located above a large store halfway between Ford's Theatre and the building that served as the FBI's headquarters. The head of the pool, whom I shall call Mr. Munson, was a middle-aged, small, thin, kindly man. He at once put me at ease and explained that there were generally about 40 people in the pool at any one time and that they were scattered in four different rooms. They and I were awaiting security clearances, while going through necessary processing. He advised that this was all he could tell me and warned that I should not discuss the tests during the processing since this would be considered a breach of security. Later, various candidates couldn't resist talking and speculating about why we were there. One person mentioned the possibility of our working for the CIA. I had never heard of it.

Mr. Munson seemed to take an instant liking to me and asked if I would like to be his assistant. I, of course, accepted and worked in the "front" office. As his aide, I kept a daily attendance log and had the pleasant task of running occasional batches of typing over to the women in the typing pool around the corner.

About once a week we were shown training films. They puzzled me, as none depicted the lifestyle of a foreign service officer that the telegram had led me to believe would be in my future. One movie was about Navy frogmen and how they operated. Another was an FBI training film that we all quickly labeled "White Shoes" because the tyro G-man wore those conspicuous shoes on what was supposed to be a discreet surveillance mission directed against a communist spy. Another movie dealt with picking a lock.

I flunked the first test, the medical examination. The doctor discovered a small benign nodule on my thyroid. Fortunately the condition was correctable, and after an operation I went back to the processing. Some others, not so fortunate, failed the medical and were dismissed.

Everyone whispered about the dread Building 13, where the lie detector test was administered. Speculation and rumor were held to a minimum by threats to fire anyone who revealed details of the tests. I am still forbidden to reveal those details, but Victor Marchetti and John D. Marks stated in their book, *The CIA and the Cult of Intelligence*, that through the lie detector test "the CIA . . . finds out nearly everything imaginable about the private lives of its personnel. . . . Questions about sex, drugs, and personal honesty are routinely asked along with security-related matters such as possible contacts with foreign agents."[1] One of my roommates — by this time I had moved into a small apartment with two other candidates from the pool — confessed to me that he knew his close friend had committed a murder. He had pledged to his friend he would never tell this to anyone. He agonized about what to say when questioned by the lie detector operator, but he apparently passed, for he was taken on board shortly after his examination. Still, many other candidates were dismissed following lie detector tests.

During this period of testing and processing, a group of young people held a party and invited many of us to attend. One pleasant young man at the party seemed intent on cornering me and asking difficult questions. Whom was I working for? Why had I come to Washington? Where was my office? My intuitive sense immediately sent out warnings. I gave him all the answers prescribed in Mr. Munson's briefing or, as we later called it, our cover story; i.e., one that was plausible, but had nothing to do with the truth. However, several days after the party various other members of the pool were fired.

The most revealing test we had to take was the personality/intelligence test. The Agency used this test to identify the basic Externalized, Regulated, Adaptive individual — the ERA personality — that it prefers to hire. Years later I was able to get a copy of the test. If you read it carefully, you begin to see that the strengths and weaknesses of the CIA start with the selection of its people.

Basically, the test analyzes three different aspects of personality — intellectual, procedural, and social. In the intellectual mode the Agency is looking for an externalizer rather than an internalizer. This individual is active, more interested in doing than thinking. He must exert considerable effort when compelled to work with ideas, to be self-sufficient, or to control his natural tendencies towards activity. He is practical and works by "feel" or by trial and error. In the procedural mode, the Agency prefers a rigid (regulated) person to a flexible one. This person can react only to a limited number of specific, well-defined stimuli. Such a person learns by rote because he does not insist upon perspective. He is psychologically insulated and his awareness is restricted, making him self-centered and insensitive to others. In the social mode the Agency wants the adaptive rather than the uniform individual. He is magnetic, charming, captivating, a person who moves easily in a variety of situations. He has an awareness of and the ability to express conventional or proper feelings, whether they happen to be his true feelings or not. He is chameleon-like, for he tends to be all things to all people and has the ability to spot weaknesses in others and use these to his advantage.

According to this personality portrait, the CIA wants

active, charming, obedient people who can get things done in the social world but have limited perspective and understanding, who see things in black and white and don't like to think too much. The personnel selection process the CIA has set up has its advantages, of course, but it also has disadvantages. It tends to reject those who have perspective, those who can see subtleties, those who think before they act, those who remain true to themselves no matter what the outside social pressures. If we reflect on some of the ways the CIA has done itself in, it is clear that with more people who possess the qualities it has sought to weed out, it might have done better.

I don't believe that my profile was the type the Agency was looking for. I scored 143 on the IQ test, which was fine, but my personality test left much to be desired. It turned out I was far too flexible. This probably would have been enough to end my chances, but the hiring crush for the Korean War, my high school and collegiate academic and football credentials, plus a strong boost from Mr. Munson got me through. A few days after finishing the tests, I was told to report for the orientation course.

More than 100 of us young men and women who had completed all the processing attended the month-long orientation course designed to acquaint us with the structure of our employer, its role in the government, and its attitude toward communism. The course was held in a building not far from the Lincoln Memorial. We were tightly packed into a small auditorium, sitting four persons to a table in two long rows.

After greetings and opening remarks by a dignified older man who was the head of the training office, a man in his early thirties mounted the stage. With a flourish he lifted a cloth covering a large organizational chart. He proudly announced that we would be working for the CIA. Most of us by this time had figured that out, but few knew just where we would be placed organizationally, or just what we would be doing. The instructor explained that the Agency consisted of three directorates. One of these, the Directorate for Plans (DDP), he said, "is that element that gathers intelligence and also performs such other functions as required by the President and the National Security Council. You here in the auditorium will be working in the DDP."

An audible sigh of relief and a happy buzz of conversation greeted this announcement. We were to be directing spies around the globe. The news was great. We were to be in the forefront of America's battle against the scourge of the international communist conspiracy. After the group stopped congratulating one another and quieted down, the instructor continued: "Another directorate is the Directorate for Intelligence (DDI). It collates and analyzes intelligence and is responsible for coordinating the dissemination of all finished intelligence. The third directorate is the Directorate for Administration (DDA). This directorate consolidates the management functions of the two other directorates." He then proceeded to explain the organizational breakdown of the three new directorates, but who could pay attention to all the meaningless initials? Time and experience would teach us what we had to know.

The orientation course featured melodramatic, frightening movies on communism. One concerned an FBI penetration operation into the American Communist Party and was titled, appropriately enough, *I Was a Communist for the FBI*. Another with about the same theme was called *Walk East on Beacon Street*, and we again saw that excellent training film, the FBI's "White Shoes." But these were just the preliminaries. The grand finale, the last word on communism, was to be heard in a lecture scheduled for the last day of the course.

As the time approached, we could tell that this was to be something special. A number of important-looking officials jammed into the already crowded room. The course director introduced the guest speaker. "Mr. Smith [all instructors used aliases] has just returned from a European nation where he successfully monitored and helped counter the efforts of the Soviets to use the local Communist Party and its front groups to subvert the government. While he was in Europe, he was involved in several dangerous incidents, and he has been recalled temporarily for his protection. We are most fortunate to have Mr. Smith here today to speak to us about communism."

The eyes, minds, and hearts of the students opened wide to this man who so represented the ideal we all hoped to achieve. Mr. Smith, a conservatively dressed man of medium height, had sharp eyes and a close-cropped head of curly, rusty-colored hair. His every movement and gesture epitomized intensity under control. He looked at the audience and gave the impression that he was sizing them up. Standing behind the podium, he spoke in quiet, modulated tones. He presented the history of communism from the overthrow of the Czar in Russia to Mao's defeat of Chiang Kai-shek's government in China. He summarized events in the Soviet Union: "The ruthless Stalin has used the secret police to purge millions, sending multitudes off to Siberia to die a death of forced labor and starvation. Stalin has conscripted millions more and is preparing his armies for world domination. He has prohibited religion in the Soviet Union and has persecuted those who only want to worship God."

As he talked, his speech gathered momentum and his voice hardened. He moved out from behind the podium and strode back and forth across the stage while his eyes seemed to challenge any in the audience who might doubt. "Not satisfied with conquest of his own countrymen," he continued, "this monster has set forth a master plan for world conquest. Through the International Communist Movement he has created havoc in Iran, Greece, and Turkey. He slammed the Iron Curtain down around the countries of Eastern Europe. He uses *agents provocateurs* to subvert the labor unions and governments of Western Europe!"

Mr. Smith angrily described the functions of the Communist International Department (COMINTERN) and its direct control over the Communist parties of the world. He elaborated on the deceits of Stalin in appearing to dissolve the COMINTERN and replacing it with the so-called Communist Information Bureau (COMINFORM). He said the change was a devious attempt to confuse world opinion. "But the COMINFORM," he said, "continues to control foreign Communist parties just as tightly as before." He pounded his fist into his hand and asked what could be done.

His speech had me sitting on the edge of my chair, and I looked around to see how it was affecting others. Most were sitting bolt upright and intensely following his words. They seemed mesmerized.

"The Soviet Union preys on lonely, shy, antisocial outcasts in this country and recruits them into the American Communist Party. These people have no friends, no links to decent society. The Soviets brainwash and exploit those undesirable humans to the point where they plan to violently overthrow our government."

I thought back to a movie I had seen, possibly as part of the course. It portrayed a shy young man such as Mr. Smith described. After a traditional childhood he had left home and returned a changed man — an obvious victim of Communist brainwashing. He challenged all family, religious, and government authorities and traditions — he was a thoroughly despicable person who deserved to be put away.

"The Soviets attack our flag and our country. Stalin is fighting to destroy all religion, our allies, and our way of life." Mr. Smith paused here and seemed to look each one of us in the eye, and then said, "You here in this room are not going to let that happen."

We all jumped up, spontaneously shouting and cheering our commitment. I was deeply moved and transformed by his stirring speech. I sat down, drained of all emotion, but finally joined a group that slowly adjourned to the adjacent cafeteria. There was none of the usual banter. We quietly discussed how we could defeat this scourge. Thinking about it years later, I realized that the purpose of the course was to fire us up emotionally to fight communism rather than educate us about what communism was and how it operated. As I was to learn later, we and the nation would have been better served if the Agency had made us study the subject seriously rather than simply trying to indoctrinate us.

After we completed the orientation, most of the men received further training to become case officers — American staff officers working at all levels in the Directorate for Plans who served as intelligence gatherers, propaganda writers, or covert operators. The women, on the other hand, went to work as secretaries or intelligence assistants, handling routine paperwork, running file traces, and doing other tasks the case officers did not wish to do. Until recently the Agency followed a strict policy against using women as case officers. The policy was based on tradition, the perceived inability of women to operate in foreign male-oriented societies, and probably a strong dose of pure sexism.

I was among about 50 from the orientation who went on to the basic operations course given in a World War II temporary building near the I-J-K-L complex. The trainees were all young and Caucasian.

The basic operations course taught, among other things, how to pick locks, how to take photographs undetected, and how to open letters and reseal them without leaving traces. A major portion of the course dealt with the principles of clandestine communications with an agent — an agent is the classic spy, a foreign national who agrees to provide information to the CIA case officer. The techniques ran from secret writing to radio codes and included leaving messages or packages in an opening behind a loose brick in a wall (a dead drop), giving them to a person who traveled regularly from one place to another (a live drop), or sending them through the mail to an address that would prevent a direct link between the sender and the recipient (a mail drop) — not too different from the way some firms use post office boxes.

The course presented the concept of targeting individuals, groups, or organizations having access to the information needed by the Agency. We were taught how to spot, assess, recruit, use, and terminate agents. To assess an agent, various investigative methods were employed to learn details of his motivations, especially his exploitable weaknesses. Once identified, his weaknesses were used to recruit him as our spy.

Working with the agent required the techniques of flattery, cajolery, discipline, and pressure. Because of his cooperation with you, blackmail was always the unspoken threat. When an agent was no longer useful, he was subject to termination, an ominous word that merely meant how one fired or retired him without creating a fuss.

After this intensive six-week course there was another narrowing down of the number of trainees. About 30 of us were chosen for further instruction in paramilitary (PM) topics. The approximately 20 others went on to assume their new jobs.

We did not know it at the time, and it was years later before we fully comprehended the various differences in personnel types, but we, the paramilitary officers or PMers, were most definitely not the elite. We were tagged with such pejorative nicknames as knuckledraggers, mesomorphs, and gorillas. The stratification of Directorate for Plans personnel began during World War II when President Franklin Roosevelt asked William J. Donovan, a Wall Street lawyer, to establish a wartime intelligence and special activity organization called the Office of Strategic Services (OSS). To head this new government agency, "Wild Bill" Donovan recruited many of his friends from Ivy League schools, from Wall Street, and from the corporate offices in New York — earning it the nickname of Oh So Social. Many of these people stayed in the intelligence business, and when the CIA was created in 1947 they assumed most of the top positions in it. Years later they were called the Bold Easterners.

Other individuals who joined the Agency in its formative years and gradually moved up through the ranks ultimately became known as the Prudent Professionals, although there was some overlap and movement between them and the Bold Easterners. The Bold Easterners in the 1950s concentrated their interest on the Soviet Union and Europe, whereas in the 1960s much of the Agency's attention swung to operations in Third World countries. Many of these operations involved large-scale programs directed by the Prudent Professionals.

The PMers came at the very bottom rung, and virtually none rose to any position of consequence within the CIA. The low status of the PMers did not mean that they were relegated to unimportant activities — quite the contrary, since PM programs predominated in the Far East from 1953 on. But it was the Prudent Professionals who assumed all the top positions in these programs, not the workmen PMers.

The paramilitary training was held at Camp Peary, the Agency's training base located in Tidewater, Virginia, within a few miles of Williamsburg. Camp Peary had been a Naval training base during World War II but was handed over to the CIA after the war. Even though the sign over the entrance to the base said "Armed Forces Experimental Training Activity," the official version, everyone in the Agency called it the "farm." The camp buildings were nestled in 10,000 acres of pine forests surrounded on three sides by a 12-foot-high chain-link fence topped with barbed wire, with the north border protected by the York River.

Of the approximately 30 students, about half had played college football and some, like myself, had tried out or done brief stints with professional football teams. The Agency, it seemed, liked to recruit football players for its "burn and bang" paramilitary operations because football players liked the active life and were not overly intellectual. Many of the rest of the PMers had either military backgrounds or some special talent needed for paramilitary activities.

Most of us were bright-eyed and bushy-tailed and displayed all the enthusiasm expressed by the term "gung ho!" We were young, well-conditioned, eager, caught up in the mystique — of just what we were not quite sure, but we were ready and willing to learn and give it our best. One student seemed to epitomize all of the characteristics that the Agency desired in our group of PMers. I will call him Jimmy Moe. He was gaudy, noisy, in superb physical condition, and not a man to worry about subtleties. Jimmy was a refugee from Hungary and an ex-Marine noncommissioned officer who had been wounded at Iwo Jima. I had first met Jimmy at the orientation course, where he was always in the company of the only older woman in the class. When we teased him about this, he said: "Give me an older woman any time; they never know when it will be their last." He apparently had few inhibitions when it came to sex and made ribald comments about the joys of varied sexual approaches.

In accordance with the DDP's mission at the time — primarily paramilitary activities in Korea and Communist China and in Eastern Europe — our group was trained in all aspects of working in and with local resistance movements: parachuting, clandestine radio communications, map reading, survival, explosives, escape and evasion, small unit tactics, and the genteel art of killing silently. To get us in the proper military mode, we had to wear military fatigues, march in rank to all classes, eat in the cafeteria, and bunk in barracks. Because of the busy schedule, few of us left the camp to visit our families on the weekends, and all were forbidden, for security reasons, from visiting nearby Williamsburg.

Every morning during the three-month course we were forced to attend physical conditioning workouts that included, among other things, the hellish obstacle course. Our instructor for this segment, whom I shall call Rob Carson, also taught the arcane skill of dirty fighting — how to kill, disable, or disarm an opponent with a knife, a wire, a silenced gun, or a variety of other devices.

One night Rob assigned an exercise where we were to sneak up on dummy sentries and quickly disarm them. Jimmy Moe got into the spirit of the exercise and disemboweled the straw-filled sentry. His violent attack on the inanimate dummy made some of us a little queasy.

The parachute training taught us how to exit a plane, how to steer a chute, and how to land. In this training we used a mock-up door of a C-47 and a 34-foot-high jump tower. We had to exit from the door of the tower harnessed in parachute straps and hooked to a suspension cable. I dreaded this tower, as did many of the other students. The close perspective of the ground and the height of more than four floors made it most difficult to force yourself to jump. I never did get over my fear of the infernal exercise, and several trainees dropped out after refusing to jump. Jimmy Moe found it a joy and clamored for more than his share of turns. His exuberant "Geronimo!" as he leaped as high and hard out of the tower door as possible could be heard at the cafeteria a mile away.

Every free evening our group would gather in the recreation room/bar to drink beer, play pool or ping-pong, or just to sit around and shoot the bull. Jimmy came to these gatherings in his own special uniform. He wore a floppy black Army hat and a dark camouflage suit with a webbed military belt in which he carried two large hunting knives. After a few beers he would get wound up and would practice his exits from the aircraft "door," using chairs in the room. Later he would jump out the recreation room window, shouting "Geronimo!" Jimmy's primary weakness — though in our capacity as PMers it was considered a strength — was his distaste or perhaps even a fear of being boxed in. After a few hours of inside classroom sessions he became agitated and restless and would hurry outside at the first opportunity.

At the culmination of the parachute training we jumped three times from a C-47. Many of the football behemoths in our class found the World War II chute too small for their heavy frames and smashed into, rather than floating down on, the plowed landing strip. We had been warned of the mathematical possibility of something going wrong in the jumps — a cigar roll chute that doesn't open correctly; a landing in a tree; and a Mae West, where a shroud line crosses over the top forming, appropriately enough, two smaller bulges rather than one large canopy. All of these things happened, but fortunately no one was seriously hurt.

Our training also included moving and operating in small units and crossing a simulated Iron Curtain border; learning to assemble, disassemble, and fire a whole assortment of foreign and domestic pistols, rifles, and sub-machine guns; and practice in firing the bigger weapons such as bazookas, mortars, and grenade launchers. Second to the parachute jumps in danger and excitement was training in explosives — the characteristics and use of TNT, C-3 and C-4 plastic, and dynamite. We were taught to use various exotic detonators such as pressure release, push-pull, delay, and slow fuse. We learned how to shape and place explosives to cut bridges and to blow up generators and other installations. Creating a dust explosion using ordinary materials required a little more expertise, but we all seemed to master the technique.

Near the end of our demolition course, a new group of trainees arrived and we old hands decided to initiate them by booby-trapping their barracks. We used the various push-pull triggering devices loaded with powerful military firecrackers. We tied trip wires to door handles and bed springs. It was a lot of innocent fun, except that one demolition "expert" went to the extreme and booby-trapped a john. He concealed a pressure detonator with the firecracker under a toilet seat. The surprised occupant was nearly castrated and the toilet bowl was smashed. The instructors took an exceptionally dim view of the perpetrator's abilities and judgment. They believed this to be a deadly serious business, knowing only too well what we did not yet fully understand: we were preparing to be warriors.

The training culminated in a comprehensive problem utilizing all that we had learned. On that occasion, after escaping from jail and surviving in the mosquito-filled swamps, I found I was too exhausted to go case an enemy security service barracks as required. Fortunately for our group, Jimmy Moe volunteered. While we rested, he moved undetected across several miles, cased the installation, and returned. He was then ready to travel right back with us to "attack" the site. The man had remarkable stamina.

Although a few students considered Jimmy Moe to be a little weird, he did seem to have all of the attributes that were desirable in a PM case officer. He was aggressive, in superb physical shape, he knew how to survive, and he was fierce in his attack on the sentry. His Marine Corps experience proved his courage under fire. He knew weapons and explosives, and he could move undetected across hostile territory. He demanded an outdoor life and could never endure the more prosaic existence of an embassy-based intelligence case officer. However, and probably most important, as required of all DDP officers, he saw situations in black-and-white certainties. He was not worried about nuances. He did what he was told and did not ask questions.

The rest of us failed in various ways to measure up to the high standards set by Jimmy Moe, but most fell into the desired general mold. I personally could take or leave it. I still longed for the job of the debonnaire spy master and most assuredly did not want to spend the rest of my life jumping out of airplanes. As we left Camp Peary, we wished each other well and eagerly looked forward to our first assignment. We were unaware that over the years we would meet again in different, and in many cases, tragic circumstances.

2.
JAPAN AND
THE PHILIPPINES:
INNOCENTS ABROAD

IT was May 1, 1953, and I was on a street corner on the outskirts of Tokyo with my arms outstretched making a noise approximating that of an airplane. I was surrounded by a throng of curious Japanese who stared in silence at this weird *gaijin* who had so obviously flipped. No one seemed to comprehend my one Japanese phrase, "Haneda doko desuka?" (where is Haneda?), which I kept shouting between revving up my motors. Since I could not speak Japanese, I could not explain that I was on my way to Haneda Airport to pick up my wife and daughters and had got lost. Seeing no flicker of comprehension on the faces around me, I jumped back into the Agency station car and took off in the direction of the last plane I had seen in the air. I was worried, first, that Norma and the children would arrive at the airport in this strange land with no one to meet them and, second, that there might be trouble with the Japanese on the street. For this was May Day, and the Agency had predicted that the Japanese Communists might make trouble for Americans. Just a few days earlier the United States military command had issued orders restricting all troops to their bases on May Day.

I followed the high trail of airplanes on a zig-zag course through the narrow back alleys of Tokyo suburbs and the streets through the adjacent industrial complex. Finally I came to a main road with a sign in English and Japanese pointing the direction to the airport. In a short time I arrived at Haneda. Luckily the Pan American Trans Pacific Stratocruiser flight was late.

I sat down on a bench near the gate where my family would be arriving. As I waited, I began to think about my life with Norma, my wife. We had first met in the summer of 1946 at a youth gathering at the Normal Park Presbyterian Church on the South Side of Chicago. Norma was sitting with a group of her friends, her blonde hair combed over her forehead in low bangs. She reminded me of Lana Turner. After the youth meeting broke up, I hitched up my courage, penetrated the cortege of her friends, and asked if she would join me for some ice cream. To my lasting joy, she said yes. This was a special occasion, so I took her to a locally famous ice cream parlor on 63rd Street under the overhead El tracks. It was then that I decided I wanted to marry her. After two years of dating on summer vacations and weekends away from Notre Dame, we were married. One daughter was born in Chicago and another a year later in Dayton, Ohio, where I was line coach for the University of Dayton Flyers.

Thinking back on it at the airport, I realized that although we had been married five years, we had never really established a settled, comfortable family life. I had left Norma and the kids in Chicago to go off to the Green Bay Packers training camp. Then after being cut and working for Montgomery Ward, I had rushed off to Washington in response to that fateful cable. I had spent three months there without my family. I wanted to wait until I was accepted before moving them, and after I received the security clearance it had taken another six weeks to locate affordable and suitable housing — a small, rundown frame house two miles outside of Cherrydale in Arlington, Virginia. Those had been lean days. My GS-5 salary amounted to about $4,000 a year, barely enough to meet expenses. We had harrowing but memorable times attempting to balance a budget ravaged by breakdown spasms of my 1941 Ford coupe.

At the lowest point in our financial planning, we found we had a dime surplus. Norma desperately needed some hairpins and we all wanted some fresh lettuce. The lettuce won out. This was before Christmas 1952. We, of course, did not have enough money to go out to celebrate the holidays but looked forward to a present we had received from Norma's parents. The shape of the package indicated a bottle of wine or whiskey, and an accompanying package obviously contained long, slender items, which we assumed were swizzle sticks. This would be our celebration. Christmas Eve after the kids were in bed, we opened the present — it was a pencil sharpener and some pencils.

Following the orientation and basic operations courses, Norma and I had been separated again during the three-month-long PM training at Camp Peary, but I had managed to spend a month with the family before being transferred to Japan. I had been alone again here for three months before our housing officer located suitable quarters for the family. The numerous separations made me pause. I wondered if a career with the CIA would mean a life of transiency and separation from family, and if so, how it would affect Norma and the kids and me.

One marital problem had immediately sprung up when I joined the Agency — the restrictions of secrecy. As soon as I was hired, I signed the secrecy agreement. It said, among other things: "I do solemnly swear that I will never divulge, publish or reveal either by word, conduct or any other means such classified information, intelligence or knowledge, except in the performance of my official duties and in accordance with the laws of the United States, unless specifically authorized in writing in each case by the Director of Central Intelligence." I honored this agreement to the nth degree and refused to tell Norma any more than was absolutely necessary. It was as if a wedge had been driven between us, and I worried what to do.

I felt that I could not discuss my work with my wife because it was both illegal to do so and, according to authorities, a threat to national security. In addition to not telling what I was doing, I had refused to tell our parents what agency I was really working for. This kind of secrecy disturbed both Norma and me. We were just as upset that we had to lie constantly to our neighbors and friends. The most normal question, after all, was "Where do you work?" We had found it easier back in Cherrydale not to get too friendly with neighbors because it was impossible to sustain the cover that I worked for the [two words deleted]. As a consequence we had slowly restricted our contacts to Agency friends. This was our first experience of the self-imposed isolation that allowed Agency employees to lose touch with the viewpoints and the information shared by the broader American population, whose interests we supposedly represented.

I had found that Norma had an unshakable sense of what is right and good. She intensely disliked lying to our friends and relatives and had made it an article of faith never to deceive the children, a vow she had to break because of my employer. Norma, of course, knew I worked for the Agency, but I kept all details of the training to myself. She felt alone and had no nearby friends to lighten the sense of isolation. I had moved her to an out-of-the-way house in Virginia, refused to discuss my work with her, told her not to tell anyone that I worked for the CIA, and then had taken off for three months training at some mysterious site, leaving her all alone with two young daughters, unreliable transportation, and an extremely tight budget. Worse than that, I had returned from the training and advised her that we were going to Japan, and had taken off again — still without revealing details of my work. All of this had caused long, bitter arguments. Norma felt that she had an equal right to know what was happening in our lives and that my actions indicated I did not trust her. I silently agreed, but could not bring myself to break the secrecy agreement.

After all these problems and separations, I hoped that now our married life could really begin. I had found a beautiful house a few blocks from the Emperor's summer palace in Hayama overlooking Sagami Bay on the Pacific Ocean. Our financial woes were behind us. The Agency paid for all the rent and utilities and had given me an enclosed jeep for my personal use. I had been promoted to a GS-7 and while in Japan my salary was augmented by a 20 percent "differential," an amount paid to compensate for the supposed differences in expenses between living at home and living in Japan. All our medical expenses would be taken care of by the government. We could buy all food, clothes, and essentials at the PX and commissary with their more than reasonable prices (a bottle of good bourbon cost only $1.25). The relief from the pressure of financial worries, the home on the ocean, and the many Agency friends in a rather close society all seemed to guarantee a new, happier life for us. We might even consider trying for the son I wanted to have.

"Pan American Flight One arriving at Gate 14." They were here. My older daughter, four-year-old Peggy, broke away from her mother and was racing toward me with Jean, the three-year-old, close behind. They called out, "Daddy, Daddy." I grabbed them up, hugged them, and ran toward Norma, who appeared overjoyed to see a familiar face. We formed a single unit as I clumsily hugged and kissed Norma while holding the girls in my arms.

After we got the suitcases and loaded the car, we headed toward our new home and life. The girls' eyes lit up when they saw the Japanese garden dotted with tiny pine trees and carefully spaced clumps of bushes. Hanayo and Sammy, the maid and gardener I had hired, came hurrying out to the car. Sammy was all smiles and carried the luggage into the house. Hanayo was shy, but she and the girls quickly decided they liked each other. I took Norma and the girls on a tour of the place, showing them the foyer where the Japanese leave their shoes, the ancient crankup phone, the moveable lattice-work doors covered with rice paper, and the yard as long as a football field. From the balcony I pointed out Mount Fuji, majestic and snow-capped, off in the distance. The girls were excited and intrigued at all of the potential hiding places the house offered, especially the bomb shelter downstairs. Norma could not believe the size of the place and was particularly pleased with the completely tiled Japanese bathroom and the huge kitchen.

While we toured the house, Hanayo prepared a combination Japanese-American dinner, and we all sat down for our first meal together in more than three months. I was positive then that I'd made the right move in joining the Agency. We were two Depression-era kids from the South Side of Chicago. We had struggled and now we were in Japan in a gorgeous house overlooking a spectacular bay. We could put our worries about separations behind us, and thanks to the Agency, we were in clover.

While in Japan I worked for the China operations group, whose responsibilities included overseeing or supporting the following CIA units: a large unit in Seoul established in response to the Korean War; a huge station on Taiwan that conducted a variety of agent, guerrilla, propaganda, and overflight operations against mainland China; a refugee interrogation unit in Hong Kong operated jointly with the British; and a major base on Okinawa that provided logistical support for the Agency's far-flung units.

At first I worked at an isolated training area located at the base of a mountain not too far from Tokyo. Armed sentries denied entry to all but official personnel. Our job was to train foreign nationals in the mechanics of intelligence gathering, but after we trained one small group, the compound was closed in favor of more accessible training sites. As a relatively new and junior employee, I, unfortunately, was assigned to the records office as a file checker, which had all the appeal of a Montgomery Ward section head.

Even though I felt that what I was doing was not of itself of any great import, I believed it contributed to the more important efforts of others. I was but one tiny cog in the immense and noble effort to save the world from the International Communist Conspiracy and to help roll back the Iron Curtain. I did not plan to work in the records office forever and continued to be on the lookout for an opportunity to get directly involved. I wanted the greater prestige and challenge given to the case officer out on the front lines, but for the time being I was content to do the less glamorous, but necessary, file tracing to support the Agency's important global work.

Yet the truth is that I was only generally aware of the nature of CIA operations at the time. The strictures of the "need-to-know" policy — in which each employee was allowed to know only that information necessary to perform his job — made it difficult to ascertain just what the Agency was doing. It was only many years later that I learned that the Agency in the decade of the 1950s, reacting to a perceived threat from monolithic international communism, had conducted hundreds of covert operations around the world. That period saw a concentration both on operations and development of the infrastructure necessary to implement those activities, including funding mechanisms, proprietary companies, airlines, and media organizations. Within the Agency the international organizations division was coordinating an extensive propaganda effort aimed at developing an international anti-communist ideology. According to the U.S. Senate's Church Committee report of 1976, "The Division's activities included operations to assist or to create international organizations for youth, students, teachers, workers, veterans, journalists, and jurists. This kind of activity was an attempt to lay an intellectual foundation for anti-communism around the world. Ultimately, the organizational underpinnings could serve as a political force in assuring the establishment or maintenance of democratic governments."[1]

The influence and power of the Agency increased greatly after the election of President Eisenhower, who had come to power based in part on his pledge to lift the Iron Curtain. Eisenhower appointed Allen Dulles as director of the CIA and John Foster Dulles, his brother, as Secretary of State. The triumvirate of Eisenhower and the Dulles brothers gave the Agency immense power not only to conduct operations but also to formulate foreign policy. Allen Dulles was an activist, totally absorbed in covert operations, who ignored the Agency's intelligence-gathering and coordination functions. "With the Soviet Union and communist parties as the targets the Agency concentrated on developing anti-Communist political strength," wrote the Church Committee. "Financial support to individual candidates, subsidies to publications including newspapers and magazines, involvement in local and national labor unions — all of these interlocking elements constituted the fundamentals of a typical political action program. Elections, of course, were key operations, and the Agency involved itself in electoral politics on a continuing basis."[2]

"Geographically the order of priorities," the report noted, "was Western Europe, the Far East, and Latin America. With the Soviets in Eastern Europe and Communist parties still active in France and Italy, Europe appeared to be the area most vulnerable to Communist encroachments. The CIA Station in West Berlin was the center of CIA operations against Eastern Europe and the German Branch of the European Division was the Agency's largest single country component."[3]

Here, by region, is a brief summary of some of the Agency's operations in the 1950s, most of which I knew nothing about at the time.

* Eastern Europe. The Agency was sponsoring various intelligence-collection missions and resistance movements aimed at the countries of Eastern Europe. It established Radio Free Europe to broadcast to Eastern European countries and Radio Liberty aimed at the Soviet Union. The combined budgets of the two stations amounted to between $30 million and $35 million annually.[4] Beginning in 1950 the Agency funded

the Congress of Cultural Freedom, a private cultural organization which ultimately received more than $1 million.[5] The Agency also was in contact with a resistance movement in the Soviet Ukraine.[6] In the early 1950s it was providing men, gold, and military and communications equipment to the Polish Freedom Movement.[7] This support only ceased when Polish security announced that it controlled the movement. Beginning in 1950, the CIA in a joint operation with the British also organized efforts to overthrow the Enver Hoxha government of Albania.[8]

All of these attempts achieved little and the CIA for a period seemed to slow its efforts to lift the Iron Curtain. In late 1956, however, it reinitiated those operations and laid plans for uprisings in Hungary, Czechoslovakia, and Rumania. Radio Free Europe assured Eastern European audiences of United States backing for their liberation aspirations at the same time that CIA groups, called Red Sox/Red Cap, were being infiltrated into those nations' capitals to make plans with the "freedom fighters" to throw off the "yoke of communism." In fact, neither the external nor the internal support was as promised, and the Hungarian freedom fighters' call to fight communism was answered by Soviet Premier Nikita Khrushchev, who ordered Soviet forces into Budapest on November 4, 1956. Up to 32,000 people were killed, more than 170,000 fled the country, and Janos Kadar, sponsored by the U.S.S.R., became the first secretary of the ruling Hungarian Workers Party.[9]

General Lucian Truscott, the CIA's deputy director for "community affairs," evaluated the failure and ongoing plans to try again in Czechoslovakia. He concluded that if allowed to proceed, the Agency's plans would raise "the prospect of a general war in Europe to an intolerable level."[10]

* **Western Europe.** In this area in the 1950s the "CIA subsidized political parties, individual leaders, labor unions, and other groups. . . . Millions of secret dollars were being poured into both Socialist and anti-communist parties in Portugal, France, West Germany, among others."[11] In Italy, especially, the CIA was beginning covert financing of the Christian Democratic Party "with payments averaging as high as three million dollars a year. . . ."[12]

* **Far East.** Here the Agency was conducting the gamut of

operations. According to the Church Committee, "The out-break of the Korean War [in 1950] significantly altered the nature of OPC's [the Office of Policy Coordination, the pred-ecessor of the Directorate for Plans] paramilitary activities as well as the organization's overall size and capability. Between fiscal year 1950 and fiscal year 1951, OPC's personnel strength jumped from 584 to 1531. Most of that growth took place in paramilitary activities in the Far East. . . . The Korean War established OPC's and CIA's jurisdiction in the Far East and created the basic paramilitary capability that the Agency em-ployed for twenty years. By 1953, the elements of that capa-bility were 'in place' — aircraft, amphibious craft, and an experienced group of personnel. For the next quarter century paramilitary activities remained the major CIA covert activity in the Far East."[13]

In Korea itself, of course, the Agency was training and infiltrating hundreds of South Korean paramilitary troops be-hind enemy lines. But its activities extended far beyond that country. In 1950, the Agency established a large cover struc-ture on Taiwan known as Western Enterprises.[14] It and one of the Agency's airlines, Civil Air Transport, were CIA vehicles for preparing and dropping teams of Chinese Nationalists on mainland China. The Agency sent two different types of teams — commando and resistance. Resistance teams were to parachute into China, contact dissident people there, and gradually build a viable resistance to Mao Tse-tung's govern-ment. Commandos usually were sent in via small boats from the offshore island of Quemoy, later famous as a subject of the Kennedy-Nixon debates of 1960. Their mission was to attack and destroy key installations on the mainland. Word of these operations began to leak out after two Americans, Thomas Downey and Richard Fecteau, were shot down in 1952 on a mission over the mainland.

Though I was not aware of it, the Agency was at this time also supporting an attempt to invade Communist China. In 1949, when the Chinese Communists drove the Nationalists from the mainland, a force of Chinese Nationalists under Gen-eral Li Mi had fled across the Yunnan border into Burma. They established themselves in Burma at sites near the Thai border. With the cooperation of the Thai government the Agency's airline, Civil Air Transport, began massive supply operations to those troops. The 200-man CIA structure in

Thailand known as Sea Supply Company,[15] with its brother, Western Enterprises Company, undertook the logistical effort to build and outfit Li Mi's army.

In 1951, several thousand of General Li Mi's troops invaded Yunnan Province and were quickly defeated and driven out. The Agency, predicting that the peasants in Yunnan would rise up in opposition to Mao's government, readied another large invasion. Li Mi's troops augmented their own strength by recruiting 8,000 men from the indigenous hill tribes in Burma. The CIA shipped in another increment of about 1,000 crack Chinese Nationalist troops from Taiwan, and its airline began regular shuttle flights to bases and camps in Burma, using Thai airstrips for refueling and resupply.[16] In August 1952 this army invaded Yunnan, reaching into the province up to 60 miles. Once again the peasants did not rise up as predicted, and the army was driven out.[17] General Li Mi gave up attempts to defeat China, established a quasi-independent state in Burma, and became involved in running the lucrative opium trade. In this endeavor he had the help of General Phao Siyanon of Thailand.

In Thailand, the Agency, via Sea Supply Company, threw its full support behind the political ambitions of General Phao, making him the strongest man in the country. In exchange he allowed the Agency to develop two Thai paramilitary organizations — the Police Aerial Reconnaissance Unit and the Border Patrol Police.[18]

In the Philippines from 1950 through 1953, U.S. Air Force Colonel Edward Lansdale conducted a series of Agency operations to destroy the communist Huk insurgency. With a strong effort from the Agency, Philippine General Ramon Magsaysay not only successfully destroyed the Huks but also was elected President of the Philippines.[19]

Following Colonel Lansdale's successes in the Philippines, the Agency in 1954 sent him to South Vietnam to help create the Diem regime. The burgeoning effort first to install the Catholic Ngo Dinh Diem in power and then to legitimize and extend his control over the rural Buddhist South Vietnamese was one of the Agency's most successful operations. It was not until years later, through the publication of the *Pentagon Papers*, that details of this operation became known. At about the same time it was installing Diem in the South, the CIA launched sabotage and guerrilla operations against North Vietnam.[20] (For more detail on the CIA's involvement in Vietnam, see Chapter 10.)

In Indonesia in 1958, Agency B-26 bombers supported rebel units in the Celebes fighting to overthrow the government of President Achmed Sukarno,[21] something that was not accomplished on this attempt but was achieved in 1965 by another Agency operation.

In 1959, the Agency began instigating the Tibetans to fight the Chinese. The Agency established a secret base at Camp Dale in Colorado and trained Tibetan guerrillas who were then infiltrated back into Tibet to fight. The Agency-trained guerrillas helped the Dalai Lama to flee.[22]

The Agency's airline, Civil Air Transport, provided air support for many of these operations. Civil Air Transport, which flew mainly in the Far East, was one of the earliest of the various airlines the Agency developed over the years. The CIA at one point attempted to audit its widespread airline holdings. After a three-month investigation it could not say exactly how many planes it owned, but two of its airlines, Air America and Air Asia, along with the Agency's holding company, the Pacific Corporation, employed more than 10,000 people.[23]

* Latin America. The United States has always considered Latin America to be within its particular sphere of influence and has dominated the political life of that area. In the 1950s the Agency was given the primary role of imposing U.S. will over Latin America. Its most famous operation there was in Guatemala, where on June 18, 1954, it led the coup ..at overthrew the government of Jacobo Arbenz. CIA agents trained and supported the forces of Colonel Carlos Castillo-Armas, who assumed power after the defeat of Arbenz. Agency support included the provision of CIA-piloted World War II fighter-bombers, as well as guns and ammunition.[24]

But there were other Agency operations in this region in the 1950s as well, including an unsuccessful Agency attempt in 1953 to overthrow the elected government of President Jose Figueres in Costa Rica.[25] In 1956 the Agency also helped in the establishment of Buró de Represión Actividades Comunistas (BRAC), the police force of Cuban dictator Fulgencio Batista. BRAC became famous for its brutal methods of torture.[26]

* The Middle East. In the 1950s the Agency was conducting a variety of operations to stabilize or destabilize the governments of this region. I had heard through the grapevine that the Agency was instrumental in overthrowing the government of Iranian Premier Mohammed Mossadegh in 1953 and reinstalling Shah Mohammed Reza Pahlavi. This was confirmed later by, among others, former CIA operative Kermit Roosevelt, grandson of President Theodore Roosevelt, in his book *Countercoup: The Struggle for Control of Iran.*[27]

In Syria the CIA planned a coup in 1956 to overthrow the government. By chance, the coup attempt occurred on the same day that Israeli troops invaded Egypt. As a result, it was seen as linked to the Israeli operation and was quickly aborted. In that same period the CIA planned to overthrow two other Middle Eastern governments.[28]

* Africa. In 1957 the Agency began working with Israeli intelligence to penetrate the independent states of Black Africa.[29] Since that time it has spent at least $80 million on such operations.

In the Third World in general in the 1950s the Agency's propaganda operations were multiplying. "Foreign editors and columnists were recruited, newspapers and magazines subsidized, press services supported," wrote former CIA employee Harry Rositzke. "Propagandists ranged from paid 'agents' to friendly collaborators, from liberal and socialist anti-Communists to simple right-wingers. Facts, themes, editorial outlines, model essays were sent out to third world stations to be reworked for local consumption."[30]

While all these various covert operations to overthrow or bolster foreign governments were being carried out, the Agency was also supposed to be gathering intelligence. But intelligence-gathering operations did not match in size or scope the efforts to overthrow governments, and most intelligence gathering from 1952 to 1963 was carried out through liaison arrangements with foreign governments. According to the Church Committee report, CIA director Allen Dulles cultivated relations with foreign intelligence officials, and because of the United States' predominant postwar position, governments in Western Europe, in particular, were very willing to cooperate in information sharing. Liaison provided the Agency with sources and contacts that otherwise would have been denied them. Information on individuals, on political parties, and on labor movements all derived from liaison. The Church Committee concluded that liaison created its share of problems: "The existence of close liaison relationships inhibited developing independent assets. First, it was simply easier to rely on information that had already been gleaned from agents. . . . It was far easier to talk to colleagues who had numerous assets in place than to expend the time required merely to make contact with an individual whose potential would not be realized for years. Second, maintenance of liaison became an end in itself, against which independent collection operations were judged. Rather than serving as a supplement to Agency operations it assumed primary importance in Western Europe. Often, a proposal for an independent operation was rejected because a Station Chief believed that if the operation were exposed, the host government's intelligence service would be offended."[31]

The Agency's primary, if not sole claim to fame in intelligence gathering came in the mid-1950s with the development of the U-2 airplane and overhead photography. Since that time its record in intelligence has at best been dismal. The Church Committee that investigated the Agency in the mid 1970s concluded: "CIA intelligence was not serving the purpose for which the organization had been created — informing and influencing policymaking."[32]

We now know that in the 1950s the CIA was also conducting many covert operations within the United States, in violation of the law. It was creating hundreds of dummy corporations, called proprietaries, that it used to provide cover for its operational agents.[33] It was also continuing programs with academic institutions started during the days of the OSS. It expanded its operations with universities until some 5,000 American academics were doing its bidding by identifying and recruiting American students and identifying 200 to 300 future CIA agents from among the thousands of foreign students who come to the United States each year.[34] The Agency had hundreds of teachers and graduate students on more than 100 campuses who worked for it secretly in recruiting, writing propaganda, and running covert operations.[35]

Thomas W. Braden, former head of the Agency's division

of international organizations, which had extensive facilities in the United States, stated that by 1953 the CIA was operating or influencing international organizations in every field where Communist fronts had seized the initiative and in some where they had not yet begun to operate. He also said that in 1951 or 1952 he gave Walter Reuther of the United Auto Workers $50,000 in CIA funds to support anti-Communist labor unions.[36]

From 1952 until 1967 the CIA funded the National Student Association, giving about $3.3 million to support the organization's operations.[37]

CIA director William Colby confessed that beginning in 1953 the CIA "conducted several programs to survey and open selected mail between the United States and two Communist countries."[38] According to a secret Senate memorandum, the CIA survey focused on mail sent to and received from the Soviet Union and China and was centered in New York and San Francisco.[39]

The Agency was also establishing close links with both book publishing houses and media organizations in the U.S. at this time. It felt that in the world of covert operations, book publishing had a special place. The head of its covert action staff said, "Books differ from all other propaganda media, primarily because one single book can significantly change the reader's attitude and action to an extent unmatched by the impact of any other single medium . . . this is, of course, not true of all books at all times and with all readers — but it is true significantly often enough to make books the most important weapon of strategic (long-range) propaganda."[40]

Altogether from 1947 until the end of 1967, the CIA produced, subsidized, or sponsored well over 1,000 books. Approximately 20 percent of them were written in English. Many of them were published by cultural organizations backed by the CIA.[41]

The Agency was also conducting extensive operations with newspaper, magazine, and television organizations. It maintained liaison relationships with about 50 American journalists or U.S. media organizations. An uncensored portion of the final report of the Church Committee said: "They [the 50] are part of a network of several hundred foreign individuals around the world who provide intelligence for the CIA and at times attempt to influence foreign opinion through the use of covert propaganda. These individuals provide the CIA with direct access to a large number of foreign newspapers and periodicals, scores of press services and news agencies, radio and television stations, commercial book publishers, and other foreign media outlets."[42]

Domestic "fallout" — a story that filters into U.S. media from abroad — was a deliberate result of these operations in newspapers, magazines, TV, and book publishing. At least two proprietary news services that the CIA maintained in Europe had U.S. subscribers. The larger of the two was subscribed to by more than 30 U.S. newspapers.[43]

In a long article entitled "The CIA and the Media," Carl Bernstein wrote that more than 400 American journalists had secretly carried out assignments for the Agency, from gathering intelligence to serving as go-betweens with spies.[44]

This was the kind of work that the CIA was up to throughout the 1950s and that I unquestioningly supported. I would like to believe that if I had been aware of more of these operations at the time, I would have had some doubts about the Agency. But I'm not at all sure that I would have and I'll never really know because I simply wasn't aware of most of what was going on.

We lived in Japan for two years. Although my work was not what I had visualized, the lifestyle was thrilling. Like most young Agency employees, Norma and I were intoxicated with the romance of being overseas. We loved traveling around and exploring the exotic wonders of Japan, learning its customs and traditions. We loved eating new and strange foods. We loved living in comparative luxury, having servants. And we loved drinking on the beach, going to parties, and participating in the camaraderie that developed in the close-knit community of Agency families. We felt part of a big family and part of a grand cause.

On April 24, 1954, Scott was born at the Naval hospital in Yokosuka. On May 5, as was the Japanese custom, I erected a tall bamboo pole and flew from its top a cloth streamer shaped and painted to resemble a carp — a symbol of strength. This was Boys' Day, a national holiday, and I was announcing to the world the arrival of a son in the family of McGehee.

After the birth of Scott, Norma went to work as a secretary in the China operations group's administration office. Prior to being hired she had to submit the horrendously long personal history statement and wait for the security clearance. It had taken several months but finally she was cleared. I advised, "I can talk to you now about my work."

This infuriated her.

"A piece of paper from the CIA doesn't change who I am," she fumed. "The marital bonds and trust should be stronger than that paper."

I knew I was on the losing end of this argument and I silently agreed, but the constant indoctrination about the dangers of loose talk, the need-to-know principle, and the necessity for secrecy had embedded themselves in my consciousness and I could not have done otherwise.

Near the end of the two-year tour in Japan, I had to submit a field reassignment questionnaire. Everyone joked that Headquarters looked at your request and then assigned you a job diametrically opposed to what you wanted — a joke with some truth in it. The China operations group moved to Subic Bay in the Philippines. My boss asked me to extend for a year and move to its new location. This would give us the opportunity to experience another foreign country. Norma and I talked it over and we decided to extend.

Before moving the station, the Agency constructed more than 100 expensive modern homes, a large two-story office building and a big warehouse at Subic Bay. The move was completed about October 1955.

My work in the Philippines was pretty much the same as in Japan except for one incident. My boss went on leave and left me in charge. The chief of station, a tall, impressive Bold Easterner, Desmond FitzGerald, called down one day and demanded that I come to his office immediately. He was steaming mad. He had cabled Headquarters to pin down the whereabouts of an important top secret document. Headquarters replied that it had sent the document to the station more than two months earlier. FitzGerald's secretary had checked with the records office's top secret control officer and had found it in his safe. The control officer, in addition, had a whole stack of other top secret documents stored there. For reasons known only to himself, he had dutifully logged every document in and had locked them in his safe, without distributing them to any of the designated recipients.

This unfortunate incident may have been a blessing in disguise, for it highlighted the irrelevance of this mini-headquarters. For several months most of the key documents had been mislaid, and no one had missed them.

Following this incident, less than a year after the expensive move to Subic Bay, China operations group was deemed superfluous and was shut down. The abandonment of all those expensive buildings seemed to me a shame and a waste of time and money, but it seemed an aberration to me then and it in no way shook my faith in the Agency.

3.
WASHINGTON:
FUN IN THE FILES

IN mid-1956 I checked in with the Far East division administrative office at Headquarters. My next stint within the Agency was to be at home in Washington as the chief of records for the counterintelligence unit of China activities. This news did not exactly thrill me. I would be supervising virtually the same work I had been doing in Japan and the Philippines.

I reported to the records unit offices on the second floor of J building in the temporary I-J-K-L building complex along the reflecting pool mall. The place had depressing gray walls decorated with a few calendars and a single plant and seemed hopelessly overcrowded with people, files, and desks. I soon discovered that the unit consisted of 15 women and myself. Having an "outsider" named chief caused some bitterness among the long-time female employees. They felt, appropriately enough, that they were better qualified, had more experience, and could do a better job. They were right, but the Agency at the time did not normally place women in supervisory positions. After a few months of working together, most of the women became convinced that I knew what I was doing and we at least achieved a *modus vivendi.*

Our group was responsible for processing all of the hundreds of file trace requests that emanated from Agency stations, bases, and offices operating against China around the world. There were two kinds of requests: (1) a file trace, which was simply a check of any record that Headquarters might have on an individual. This might be done if the individual was suspected of working for another intelligence service, or of fabricating intelligence, or for any number of other reasons. (2) A clearance, which was a more thorough review of all information available on an individual whom the Agency wanted to use as an agent. The purpose was to evaluate his personal record and to determine if he was in a position to provide the necessary services.

Although CIA-approved books by William Colby (*Honorable Men*) and John Marks and Victor Marchetti (*The CIA and the Cult of Intelligence*) discussed clearances and traces, the Agency felt my treatment of the subject was too explicit and therefore deleted it as classified information. To give readers an idea of the clearance process, I include this passage from former CIA case officer Philip Agee's book, *Inside the Company*:[1]

> Whether to use or not to use a particular prospective agent is determined, from the CI [counterintelligence] viewpoint, by the 'operational approval' process. It is an integral part of every relationship between the CIA and foreign agents no matter what a given agent's task might be. The operational approval process begins with the initial spotting and assessment of a prospective agent and continues through field and headquarters' file checks and background investigation to the operational approval system established in the CI staff of the DDP.
>
> No person may be used in an operational capacity by a field station without prior approval by the Operational Approval Branch of the Counter-Intelligence Staff of the DDP in headquarters (CI/OA). Requests for approval start from the field stations and are outlined in a document known as the Personal Record Questionnaire (PRQ) which is divided into two parts. The PRQ Part I contains some seven pages of basic biographical data including full name, date and place of birth, names of parents, names of family members, schools attended, employment history, marital history, military service, present and past citizenship, membership in political organizations, hobbies, any special qualifications, and use of drugs or other vices. In itself the PRQ Part I reveals no operational interest or plans. The PRQ Part II, which never carries the prospective agent's true name or other identifying data, is a document of similar length with all the details of operational plans for the agent. It is reconciled with the PRQ Part I by a numbering system and usually bears the cryptonym assigned to the prospective agent. In the PRQ Part II the proposed task for the agent is described, the means through which the information in PRQ Part I was obtained and verified is detailed, the cover used by the person who spotted and assessed the agent is given, and all the operational risks and advantages are discussed.
>
> The officers in CI/OA run a series of name checks in headquarters and, after studying the case, give final approval or disapproval for the proposed use of the prospective agent. Assuming no serious

problems exist, CI/OA issues a Provisional Operational Approval (POA) on the agent, effective for six months, at the end of which an Operational Approval (OA) is issued, based on additional investigations by the station and the CIA staff.

Files are maintained on all agents and they always begin with the number 201 – followed by a number of five to eight digits. The 201 file contains all the documents that pertain to a given agent and usually starts with the PRQ and the request for POA. But the 201 file is divided into two parts which are stored separately for maximum security. One part contains true name documents while the other part contains cryptonym documents and operational information. Compromise of one part will not reveal both the true name and the operational use of the agent.

To protect the identity of Agency employees, pseudonyms were used. Pseudonyms consist of a first name, middle initial, and a last name. Discussions within the Agency took on an unreal character because they were often conducted only in cryptonyms and pseudonyms. For example: "Bertan F. Finley said RSROCK who is working in RSBOATLOAD [a project cryptonym] is acting suspicious. He failed to load the dead drop last week, so we may have to flutter him [LCFLUTTER was the cryptonym for the lie detector test]." This special language was undecipherable to all but the *entre nous*. It added an aura of mystery and reinforced the tendency to clanishness within the clandestine services. [Two sentences deleted.]

Our file-tracing task wasn't easy. The Agency, because it was young and learning, had adopted recordkeeping procedures appropriate for a small organization. The Directorate for Intelligence remained rather small and its recordkeeping unit, Central Reference Service, seemed able to handle its requirements. But the Directorate for Plans had grown rapidly in the early 1950s and its records integration division had been unable to cope. Whereas the most mechanized and best of systems would have trouble establishing a world index of names, the records division used archaic methods and it slowly began to sink under the weight of the mass of work.

It continued to make a record of almost every name, American or foreign, that was mentioned in a document. Each card usually included the permanent file location of the document from which the name had been carded plus a short excerpt of the information in it. These cards then were used as the information base for field file-trace requests. The absurd theory behind this antiquated method was that one obscure item of information might be *the* key to unlocking the great secret. Thus, carders of documents would use no discretion and would make a new record of virtually everything — even when only a first or last name was mentioned. Thousands of "Dwight (last name unknown)" and "Truman (first name unknown)" index cards flooded the system. Several field stations sent in telephone books, and the records division dutifully went about carding them. An entire huge room was stacked high with documents awaiting carding. To try to keep up with the crush, the records division operated in shifts around the clock.

The huge index room, commonly referred to as "the snake pit," was surreal. The small window air conditioners would break down under the strain of the masses of sweating humanity trying to squeeze into the narrow aisles between six-foot-high wooden file cabinets. Earthy aromas greeted those who entered from the relatively fresh air of the corridor. There was a noisy din of shouted instructions, disgruntled conversations, and flirtations. To check a name in the index, you had to use fancy footwork to dance around the opened drawers and mobs of humanity. Inevitably you were shoved, elbowed, kicked, and jostled.

We in the China records unit had our own private hell as romanized Chinese names created a special form of file-tracing torture. The Chinese language had no alphabet. It was composed of about 10,000 commonly used ideographs or symbols representing ideas or words. This posed an extremely difficult problem for the records division and the file tracers, none of whom knew how to read or write Chinese. The most common Chinese surname is Ch'en, but there were more than a dozen ideographs that romanized out as Ch'en. The same with given names such as Cheng. A request for a trace on a Ch'en Cheng presented a near impossible task of sorting through the hundreds or thousands of index cards on that name. How to discriminate between them?

A system of numbering every major Chinese ideograph was devised and was slowly being incorporated into the indexing system. Under this system each ideograph was assigned a four-digit number, which was included on the index card; i.e.,

Ch'en Cheng (7115/2638). In this way the tracer could look only for those Ch'en Chengs writing their names with the 7115 Ch'en ideograph and the 2638 Cheng ideograph — a vast improvement. But the system was new and it required a staff of Chinese to process the numbers.

Perhaps the most difficult of all problems was the records division's habit of lending out its record copies of documents. Someone conducting a trace on Ch'en Cheng would attempt to gather all documents mentioning that name. If there were 1,000 references to documents, then the tracer theoretically would attempt to gather every one of those documents. But as frequently was the case, other people outside of the records division had some of them. To do a thorough job, the name tracer would have to go to the office of each person and ask to see the document. The main corridor in the I-L complex was almost a half-mile long, and it was not infrequently that one traveled from one end of the building to the other and back again. In many cases the person who had borrowed the document had been transferred, and the document was lost forever.

The rules for processing the operational clearances, in light of the various deficiencies in the records systems, made it impossible to do a thorough job. We in the records unit had to compromise the rules severely or China activities would have come to a standstill.

When I assumed command of the unit, it had a horrendous backlog of clearance and name-trace requests. By refining some of the processes, gradually I was able to whittle away at the large stack of requested actions. Some unprocessed requests were several years old, and I sent frequent dispatches to see if the station was still interested. The replies fed my growing concern that the Agency was not as efficient as it ought to be: in many cases, it turned out, the station had hired the agent without waiting for clearance.

My first doubts about the quality of information kept in the CIA's highly touted files stemmed from an incident during this period involving an agent in Saigon who claimed to have a series of intelligence nets with radio operators in mainland China. The agent, LFBOOKLET, said his people were not pro-Nationalist but were definitely anti-Communist. Claiming that he had been an important politician and his men were all personally loyal to him, he offered to share his intelligence with the Agency in exchange for financial support. China at the time was a denied area, and the Agency had no sources on the mainland.

After questioning him for a few weeks, the Agency case officer was convinced of the validity of his story and recruited him to work with the CIA. The agent began reporting on events on the mainland and activated more and more of his intelligence nets. The reports started pouring in, and the operations expanded over the next two years. The case officer increased LFBOOKLET's funding to millions of dollars a year. But slowly doubts about the agent began to surface. An allied intelligence agency alerted us to a newspaper clipping service located in Saigon; this turned out to be LFBOOKLET's home address. One of the radio intercept facilities tried to monitor LFBOOKLET's radio contacts and heard nothing. When confronted with this information, LFBOOKLET said he had to alter the frequency of the transmitters because the Chinese Communists had begun to employ radio direction-finder detecting systems. To resolve its doubts, the Agency asked LFBOOKLET to move to Subic Bay, where CIA radio operators could "help" maintain contact with his teams. His constant refusals to move even for a few weeks and a careful counterespionage review of his case led to the conclusion that he had been fabricating the information all along. When confronted with evidence of his duplicity, he confessed, at least in part. He had operated a clipping bureau. He would gather mainland newspapers that found their way into Saigon and clip items concerning minor events in scattered locations in China. He would rewrite details of those incidents, blowing them up into great significance, and pass the report to us as if it had come directly from his team in the area. Since each item had a germ of truth behind it, his reports seemed plausible.

After the operation was exposed as a fabrication, I was given the job of figuring out some way to remove from the record system all of LFBOOKLET's three years of intelligence reports and the thousands of index cards based on them. Unfortunately no one had a record of the identification numbers assigned to LFBOOKLET's reports. I could devise no other solution than a month's shutdown of the work of the records unit for full concentration on digging out those cards and reports. This was deemed unworkable, and we decided to be on the alert for his reports and pull them out as we encountered them. We would pass such reports to the records division with instructions to remove from the files all index cards that had been based on the report. This process may still be going on today.

The mess in the records division was growing out of control. A priority name trace from another government agency would take a minimum of three months to complete. The documents in the carding room piled higher and higher. Early attempts to computerize the records with the then unsophisticated state of the art seemed merely to exacerbate the problem. It was obvious that something would have to be done or the entire system would collapse. Allen Dulles appointed a former Rhodes scholar I shall call Charles Thompson, who had worked in both the Directorate for Plans and the Directorate for Intelligence, as head of a task force to delve into the problem and find solutions.

Thompson was the ideal man for the job. A bespectacled Irishman with the gift of gab, he was brilliant, pragmatic, and thoroughly versed in the needs of the operating and intelligence sides of the Agency. He was a dynamo and soon after being appointed could be found getting his own hands dirty in the file and index rooms.

Thompson held a series of meetings to ask workers about their problems and to hear their recommendations. I served as the Far East division's representative at these sessions. After cataloging the problems, Thompson suggested a complete revision of records division procedures. He recommended greatly restricting the criteria for carding new names into the index and hiring competent carders who would be given some leeway in determining what to card. If a document mentioned Joseph Stalin 10 times, it would not be necessary to make 10 cards on Joseph Stalin; only one card would be prepared and then only if the writer added a special section to his correspondence asking that Stalin be carded. He suggested that no more first-name-unknown or last-name-unknown names be indexed and that the present collections of those be destroyed. He recommended a cleaning out of the files to begin with a review of all intelligence reporting. The reviewers would mark for destruction all documents deemed of no value. Once a document was designated for destruction, it would be sent to the index card room, where all cards based on that document would be removed and destroyed. When a file trace was completed on a particular individual, a detailed form would be filled out so that no one would have to repeat the process for a later request.

He suggested that a huge photocopy machine be bought and put in the file room and that individual permanent file copies of documents not be lent out; instead such documents should be copied and given to the person making the request.

Many of Charles Thompson's proposals were put into effect. The piles of documents slowly began to recede, the card files thinned out, and the troublesome searches for loaned documents became infrequent. My unit was designated to review all documents on China and mark for destruction those deemed of little value. Joy was rampant. Can you imagine turning 15 people loose to destroy documents that had tormented them for years? You only go around once in life, and we went with gusto. I set up some informal guidelines for our office on what should and should not be destroyed, but these guidelines somehow were more ignored than honored. China activities won Charles Thompson's prize for the greatest reduction in file holdings.

On October 4, 1957, the Soviet Union orbited the world's first satellite, *Sputnik 1*, and sent the "free world" into a tailspin. Here was the potential for the ultimate spy in the sky, the takeoff point for even greater and more potentially dangerous weaponry. The press responded with visions of doomsday and calls for an all-out effort to catch up to the Soviets.

Allen, my friend who had worked with me in Japan and now at Headquarters, was distraught. This news so upset him that his usual self-assured, forceful, let's-get-the-job-done attitude seemed to have vanished. We went for a long walk around the Lincoln Memorial reflecting pool.

"How can we fight those commie bastards?" Allen asked dejectedly. "If they decide to do something, they just tell people where to go and what to do. No one can object. Now all their top students are forced to concentrate on math and science. How can we hope to fight that?"

"Look what we did in World War II," I replied. "Our fleet was destroyed at Pearl Harbor, the war in Europe seemed almost over and the Germans were winning everywhere, but once people were aroused to fight, we became the world's greatest arsenal overnight. We can do the same thing this time. We can launch our own satellite."

"But the threat is different this time," said Allen gloomily. "How many Americans recognize the danger? A tiny sphere circling the globe doesn't alarm people like an all-out war."

"Well, I still think our democracy can respond to the challenge," I said, but Allen wasn't convinced. He seemed to have lapsed into apathy.

"International communism is a different kind of threat," he grumbled. "It's like a cancer; it grows slowly until it destroys you. They can direct anyone to do anything. They can order their people to move, to study certain topics, to concentrate on weapons development. We have our freedom of choice, our effort is voluntary. It seems like there is no way for us to keep up."

Allen wasn't alone in his pessimism. The Agency seemed permeated by it. We all feared that our way of life, our freedom, our religions were directly exposed to the cancer. But this pessimism ultimately turned to rededication. Our national leaders moved to launch our own satellite. After a few misfires and a lot more teeth gnashing, despite Nikita Khrushchev's disparaging remarks about our orbiting "grapefruit," we knew we were on the road to success. We in the Agency felt that the battle for the freedom of the world was now, to a large extent, in our hands.

Both Allen and I hoped to play a large role in that fight. We felt our talents were under-utilized in our present paper-shuffling jobs and wanted to get directly involved in operations against the communist menace. After numerous appeals, one day in the summer of 1958, we were called into the office of our crusty boss. He gruffly announced that we were getting our chance — we had been chosen to go to the career training course for case officers.

In a daze I went back to my desk. I reached down and opened the bottom drawer of my safe that for several years had held the accumulated backlog of dreaded clearance and trace requests. I couldn't believe my eyes. The drawer was nearly empty. My days of dull paperwork were over. Finally I was to become a case officer — the cream of the Agency's manpower. Finally I would be out on the front lines gathering intelligence and conducting covert operations against the communists.

Following three months training back at the "farm," Allen and I both got the same assignment: Taipei, Taiwan.

4.
A COMPANY MAN
IN CHINA

NORMA, the children, and I landed at Taipei's airport in early February 1959. We were greeted by a cold drenching rain and by Tom, a bubbly extrovert who had worked with Allen and me in China activities back at Headquarters. Tom drove us to the house that we had been assigned on the outskirts of Taipei and then announced that we were expected to attend a party my new boss was throwing that night for Chinese intelligence liaison. A car and driver and a baby-sitter would arrive at about seven to pick us up. Norma objected vehemently to leaving the children with a stranger, in a strange house, in a strange land. However, this appeared to be not so much an invitation as a command.

After Tom left, we took a quick tour of the house and surrounding area. The neighborhood — rice paddies and pounded-out tin shacks — seemed to offer little potential for the children. There were obviously few Americans living in the area and the isolation from other children would not be good for them. The house was no better. Water was seeping in around the edges, most of the appliances were broken, and a high concrete fence that surrounded the small lot blocked the light from the windows. At this point, our eight-year-old, Jean, asked, "Daddy, is that cow ours?" We all looked out the window and there in the small front yard was a huge water buffalo. The children found this quite exciting, but Norma didn't. I grabbed a broom and a bit hesitantly went out and shooed the beast away.

That night a baby-sitter arrived with the chauffeur-driven car. Although extremely uneasy about the children, we dutifully went off to the liaison party. My new co-workers, both American and Chinese, seemed pleasant. My boss, whom I shall call Al Barton, a former Naval officer and a dyed-in-the-wool cold warrior, took it upon himself to tell Norma about the new assignment.

"Ralph will be required to work long, hard hours," he said. "He'll have to be gone weekends and on occasion he may be gone for periods of several days or weeks. His work is extremely important, but it must remain secret. You must not ask him where he goes or what he does. You must just understand and accept it. There's some danger associated with his work, but we all recognized this when we joined the company."

Al's timing was poor. Norma was unhappy enough about the move. For three years we had lived on Cherry Street in Vienna, Virginia, where we had many close friends, young couples like us with small children. We had partied together and visited back and forth. The children had played together, gone to school together, and become good friends. For the children and Norma it had been an idyllic time, and they were reluctant to leave. But we had talked over the decision and as happened so many times, Norma had put aside her doubts to accommodate my plans and visions of career advancement. Now she was being told that she'd come all this way to a leaky house in a rice paddy, and she wouldn't even be allowed to know where her husband was. She said nothing to Al, but when we got home, she hit the ceiling.

"What in hell does he mean I won't know where you'll be? You could be fooling around or dead for that matter."

"It's the rules, Norma."

"Yes, but you're the only one who follows them. Everybody learns everything at cocktail parties."

I didn't know what to say.

"This damn Agency is hell on families," she sputtered. "First it separates us, then it doesn't let me know what you'll do or where you'll be. We can't even talk honestly to each other."

We had been through it a hundred times. I said nothing and figured she'd calm down once she was adjusted. But I decided right then that we had to find a better place to live.

Soon we moved to the housing compound on Yan Ming mountain just outside of Taipei. We found a good maid and baby-sitter, and our lifestyle began to resemble that of America's sybaritic rich. We fell in with a socially active crowd. The kids entered the Taipei American School, which was well-run by its competent, primarily American, teaching staff. There were many playmates in the compound, and it also had playgrounds, tennis courts, traffic-free roads, and occasional free movies at the club.

Shortly after we arrived in Taipei, Norma found out that she was pregnant. We had not anticipated this, but she had plenty of company. There was a baby boom in the compound. In September 1959 Norma delivered a cute, healthy, red-haired son, whom we named Dan. Tom's wife delivered Tom, Jr. in October, and a whole succession of family additions among our circle followed.

I felt a real thrill beginning my job as a case officer in Taipei. Mostly I worked in liaison with the various Chinese Nationalist intelligence services. My assignment was to send agents to the mainland to gather intelligence about developments in Communist China. Others in our office worked with the Chinese Nationalists to train and drop teams of Chinese on the mainland to develop resistance movements and gather intelligence.

As the junior man in the office I was given the least exciting, non-demanding assignments. Even so, working with foreign nationals against the Soviet/Chinese monolith in the atmosphere of those days was exciting. On several occasions I went to Chinmen (Quemoy) Island to debrief mainland Chinese fishermen who had strayed too close to the island's shores and had been captured by the Chinese Nationalist troops there. To get out to the island, we flew on Chinese Nationalist Air Force C-47s. To avoid Communist radar, the pilots would fly out just above the water, rise up quickly as they approached the island to get above its high peaks, and land immediately. At that time the Chinese Communists had announced that they would shell Chinmen on alternate days, which they did. I spent my first night on the island in a tin-roofed shack while the shells fell outside. At first this seemed terribly dangerous. But later I came to realize that the

Nationalists and the Communists seemed to have a gentlemen's agreement. Both sides shelled at specific hours and aimed their shells at barren areas. Neither side wished to risk the escalation of shooting at the numerous out-in-the-open targets.

When I made these trips out to the island, I never got any significant information from the detainees, but they did provide background information on developments on the mainland. And after the debriefings, the Chinese Nationalist generals always took the opportunity to impress their American friends by inviting us to dine with them. The food was great and the atmosphere pleasant. The one thing I couldn't bear was the toasting between courses. The Chinese toasted with the fierce Gao Liang liquor, which smelled and tasted like turpentine. The various toasts ended with either *sui bian* (drink as much as you please) or *gan bei* (bottoms up). My first drink was a *gan bei*, and I was unprepared for that strong, heavy fluid. It went down the wrong pipe and to all of the diners' embarrassment, especially mine, I couldn't stop coughing for some minutes.

Two recently arrived American case officers worked in the same office with me. One was Jimmy Moe, whom I had known as a paramilitary trainee. Jimmy seemed uptight in the office routine, and you had the feeling that he was going to burst if he did not get out. Shortly after Jimmy moved to Taipei, he was transferred to work with the Thais and the hill tribesmen in the beginning of the secret war in Laos. (The tribe called itself the Hmong. The Agency, however, usually used the derogatory Chinese term, Meo.) Jimmy was thrilled at the prospect and quickly packed up and moved to his new job.

About half-way through my tour, I was assigned to manage an operation that seemed to have considerable potential. One of the Chinese Nationalist intelligence services offered to share its best agent with us. They said they would give him all of their training and requirements, after which we could do the same. The agent then would go to the mainland and try to satisfy all of the requirements of both services. The Chinese said that this agent had gone on trips before to the mainland and had returned with good intelligence. Since we had yet to place one solid reporting agent on the mainland, we eagerly agreed to their proposal.

The agent — I will call him L/1 — was a Chinese James Bond. There seemed nothing he could not do. Our training officers taught him our system of secret writing, radio communication, photography, observation and reporting, and numerous other subjects. Our intelligence reporting staff briefed him on major intelligence requirements. I gave him his travel documents and briefed him on the cover story. No matter what the topic or instructions, all the training officers said L/1 was the best agent they had ever trained. He grasped broad concepts as easily as he mastered demanding technical points. We all were a little awed by L/1, but a few were put off by his condescending manner.

Our plan was to send L/1 to the mainland, where he would contact and recruit a friend to serve as our spy. He was also to set up a clandestine radio in the friend's house. We gave him a detailed daily time schedule for radio contact, at which time our people would monitor his radio's frequency. After he recruited his friend (L/2), he was to travel around China for several months while occasionally sending out radio reports and encoded letters.

After two months of training and briefing, we launched him into China.

L/1 lived up to all of his potential, except for radio contact. He began sending back a series of encoded letters, which decoded perfectly, and described his travails along the way. After nearly four months he reappeared in Taiwan. This was the first successful operation of this type that the station had ever had, and we were all elated. I planned to get the best mileage out of the operation and set forth a debriefing schedule for every day, both morning and afternoon. As it turned out, the debriefing went on for a full month. I had to rely on an interpreter, but that seemed only a minor problem since L/1's answers to my questions were crisp, short, and straight to the point.

During the debriefing L/1 gave us details of L/2's house and life in a commune in China. Food and clothing were rationed, he said, apportioned according to one's status and function. Everyone was required to participate in political meetings that continued sometimes until late in the evening. In the morning everyone was required to get up early and participate in group exercises. The government's radio station would broadcast exercise instructions and music to exercise by.

There was one thing about L/1's story that disturbed me — the lack of radio contact while he was in China. L/1 claimed that he could not make contact because our schedule called for early-morning communication when, according to him, the electricity in the town was turned off. Yet the government's exercise program came on early in the morning and was received by L/2's commercial radio. How was one radio able to operate but not another? I began to wonder if L/1's claim about no morning electricity might be contrived. But I did not want to confront him with the discrepancy until I had closed all avenues of possible retreat. I wanted desperately for him to allay my suspicions, but I just as avidly wanted to know the truth.

One aspect of the operation complicated my attempts to resolve the problem. The intelligence service of the Chinese Nationalists might have substituted their crystals in our radio, thereby allowing L/1 to report only to them. I had to be careful not to expose any possible duplicity on the part of the liaison service, since the ongoing relationship was probably more important than determining the truth about this operation. Throughout the last two weeks of the debriefing, I casually asked L/1 about L/2's radio — where he had purchased it, what its brand name was, what stations it could receive, and what kind of batteries he had to buy for it. L/1 responded that it did not have batteries and that it operated off the house current. That was the wrong answer.

On the last day of the debriefing I asked why, if L/2's radio operated off the house current in the early morning, was it impossible for him to make use of that same electricity for our radio? L/1's look archly acknowledged that I had got the best of him. He jumped up, went into the next room, and brought out several gifts for me. He handed me a bottle of true mainland Gao Liang, a pack of mainland cigarettes, and a few trinkets that had originated in China. The debriefing was over.

I could never prove that L/1 lied to conceal duplicity on the part of the Chinese Nationalist intelligence service or that he was working for the Chinese Communists. But these questions hung over that operation until it was terminated.

We were never quite sure when the Chinese Nationalist intelligence services were playing games with us, and I am sure they felt the same way about the CIA. I had found out shortly after I arrived in Taipei that LFBOOKLET, the agent fabricator who had led us on such a merry chase with his Saigon clipping service, loading our files with pro-Chiang Kai-shek and anti-Mao Tse-tung misinformation, was actually an officer of Chiang's intelligence service.

On June 18, 1960, President Dwight Eisenhower visited Taipei. The Chinese Nationalists were ecstatic and Generalissimo Chiang Kai-shek and his men arranged a grand reception, featuring major speeches by both Chiang and the President in the Plaza in downtown Taipei. Tom and I were anxious to see President Eisenhower and went down to the Plaza. As the hour grew near for the Generalissimo and the President to appear, the Plaza became jammed with more than 200,000 Chinese, and possibly a few Taiwanese. The excitement mounted, and the orderly crowd changed into a pressing, pushing, shoving mass. Both Tom and I stood over six feet tall, but we worried about suffocating. I can't imagine how the shorter Chinese were feeling. The speech by Chiang reiterated his annual "back-to-the-mainland" cry, while President Eisenhower vowed American support for the Generalissimo's government.

The crowd grew more out of control, and both Chiang and Eisenhower fled from the podium — out the back way — to avoid that swirling crush of humanity. An electric enthusiasm motivated the crowd, but I feared that it could quickly turn to violence. Tom and I moved to the edge of the crowd and hurried back to the safety of our office compound.

While President Eisenhower was in Taipei, the Chinese Communists launched an unprecedented, vicious artillery barrage on Chinmen Island, their way of expressing disapproval at the visit. The great turnout at the Plaza and the unnecessary attack on the island reinforced the view within the station of the correctness of our policy toward the two Chinas. The demonstration led us to believe that Chiang, in fact, held the allegiance of the people, while Mao's bombardment revealed the true brutal nature of the international Communist movement.

I did not know then how the Generalissimo's government had come to power. Only later did I learn that in 1949, as the mainland fell, the Chinese Nationalist forces and camp followers had been evacuated to Taiwan by the American Navy. Once on the island, they had used their American-supplied weapons to dominate the more numerous Taiwanese — one Chinese to every seven or eight Taiwanese. In fact, the Generalissimo in the early days was able to maintain his authority only with extensive repressive measures. All of this at the time seemed to escape my attention and the attention of my colleagues at the station.

Our life was almost totally divorced from that of the more unfortunate Taiwanese and Chinese. Living in a compound, we spent all of our time with Agency friends. The only local contact we had, other than liaison officers I worked with, came on shopping trips, traveling to and from work, or going to restaurants. If we had not been so removed, we might have noticed the true situation on Taiwan and reported back some decent intelligence about it.

Despite my boss's early warnings, the duties on Taiwan seemed more directed at having a good time than at productive work. When we were not throwing a party for our counterpart Chinese officials, they were having us to sumptuous multi-course banquets. In addition, the station personnel were inclined to party, and every week required attendance at one affair or another. We realized that we had isolated ourselves from the Taiwanese people, but the constant partying and the good company kept us from worrying much about the problem.

Ray Cline was the chief of station. He had few pretenses and was gracious to the lowest- as well as the highest-ranking of his employees. He had an unusual way of accepting an Agency wife into the station family. When he felt a woman had earned a place in the loyal fellowship, he would deliver a pinch to the fanny. This was such a tradition that many women felt left out until he delivered his own version of official acceptance. It was all in rather good fun and no one seemed to object. Early in his tour Ray struck up a close friendship with the Generalissimo's son, Chiang Ching-kuo. Chiang and his wife could frequently be seen in our club bar playing the slot machines.

To welcome new arrivals and to say goodbye to departing people, the station held monthly hail and farewell parties. One

March night in 1961 we held a special hail and farewell costume party. Our clique of seven or eight couples, who had
been together for more than a year, decided to do it up right.
We held several meetings to decide the theme and type of costumes. Someone came up with the brilliant idea of an Indian
tribe. Someone else said that a local tailor would surely be
able to make the costumes for about $20 each — about the
monthly salary of some Taiwanese workers. After a few drinks
at one of our planning sessions, we decided to be the Sit Tribe.
The women picked names such as Chicken Sit, Bird Sit, Running Deer Sit, while the men chose more macho names, such
as mine — Big Chief Bull Sit.

After fittings at the tailor, our costumes seemed ready,
except for the chief's headdress — another excuse for a party.
This special meeting was to dye feathers and sew them on a
headband. The headdress was a spectacular thing with vividly
colored feathers. It was also heavy and awkward, but anything
for the cause.

The hail and farewell party resembled a bacchanalian
orgy with free food, free drinks, free entertainment, and some
clandestine fooling around. Our tribe won an award for the
best costume group, and all were called to the stage to receive
the award from Ray Cline, who in his good-willed manner
accepted the challenge to introduce each member of the Sit
Tribe by his or her tribal name — an interesting task after a
few drinks, and he almost made it without a slip, but not
quite. Ray also gave an award for the best female costume to
the statuesque, beautiful wife of one of the case officers; her
costume was a revealing bathing suit. After Ray gave her the
award, she put her arms around him, turned his back to the
audience and bestowed a most obvious pinch, to the delight
of the crowd.

Driving home from the party in a caravan of cars, dressed
up in our costumes, sipping champagne out of fancy crystal
glassware, we passed by the hovels of the Taiwanese people.
I looked inside one tin shanty and saw several people in virtual
rags huddling over a charcoal fire. My eyes met those of a
young man. He stared uncomprehendingly out at me, while
I looked through him. We seemed people from two different
worlds — one of affluence, comfort, dedicated to having fun;
the other of grimy poverty, where it was a struggle to stay

alive. Over the years I have thought of that moment and wondered how we in the CIA could ever have expected to understand what was happening in a foreign country when we existed in such a rarefied world, cut off from those we ostensibly were there to help.

5.
LIFE AT LANGLEY

IN August 1961 I returned to a Headquarters rife with despair and upheaval. The Agency's poor performance at the Bay of Pigs, plans for a government-wide reduction in force (RIF), and the anticipated move from the Lincoln Memorial mall to the new building at Langley, Virginia, added to the turmoil.

Following the Bay of Pigs disaster in April 1961, Allen Dulles, the CIA director, sent out an all-station cable that tried to put the best face on the tragedy. The cable implied that had events taken their planned course, we would have been victorious in that invasion of Cuba. Be that as it may, there were many who questioned the operation. I had little knowledge of what happened other than what I read and saw on television, but it did seem that the Agency had relied too much on an anticipated uprising by the Cuban people.

The layoffs in the Agency were code-named the 701 program. It seemed that the RIF program was aimed more at the CIA than other agencies of government, possibly as a result of the Bay of Pigs misfire, and President John Kennedy's anger at it. This was a tension-filled, dismal time. I was assigned back to China activities, where I shared one small office with five other case officers. None of us had much to do, but we all made a real effort to appear busy. We all dreaded being called into the office of our superiors. All around people were receiving their notices. The halls seemed filled with the strained, anxious looks of the soon-to-be unemployed.

The move to Langley began shortly before the New Year 1962. The thrill of acquiring new, more spacious offices — usually no more than two people to a room — was dampened by the continuing 701 program. About one of every five was fired. The tension became too much for some. On several occasions one of my former office mates came to the office howling drunk and worked his way onto the 701 list. When the Agency announced the end of the program, we lucky ones felt immense relief and also began to consider ourselves members of an elite. We had to be good because we hadn't been fired.

The new building had been planned by Allen Dulles, but as a result of the Bay of Pigs he was replaced and never got to enjoy it. The 219-acre site, located above the Potomac River about nine miles from Washington, resembled a college campus. As Dulles had intended, the employees soon took to lunch-time strolling around its tree-lined walks, jogging out onto nearby roads, or just relaxing in the sun on the numerous park benches. The building itself was seven stories high and was made of concrete and Georgian marble. On the huge main entrance on one side, a biblical verse was etched: "and ye shall know the truth and the truth shall make you free. John VIII-XXXII." On the opposite wall were a bas-relief bust of Allen Dulles and memorial stars, each honoring a Central Intelligence Agency employee whose life was lost in the service of his country.

To get inside the building, you had to pass a security system consisting primarily of badges with identifying photographs. Once past the guards, you entered onto the wide first-floor corridors. This first floor housed many of the Agency's service functions — the travel office, the medical staff, the credit union, the library, the insurance claims office, the various cafeterias and records management facilities. One corridor wall was reserved for portraits of former directors of the Agency and another for displays by various Agency clubs — the photo club, the art club, and others. Four banks of elevators hurried the employees to the upstairs office corridors, which were painted off-white with dark green-grayish vinyl floors. Later, to relieve the monotony, the office doors were painted in solid bright colors.

China activities occupied a major portion of C corridor on the third floor. My office was Room 57, or in government-ese, 3 C 57.

Those of us remaining after the ravages of the 701 program responded to the increased work space, the campus-like grounds, and the relaxed atmosphere. Our spirits soon revived.

It was only years later that I was to learn of the many covert operations that the CIA was conducting around the globe at that time. As in the previous ten years, covert operations dominated the Agency in the decade of the 1960s. It was employing all of the techniques of covert action, including disinformation, to accomplish policy goals. A dramatic surge in paramilitary activities in support of counterinsurgency programs was occurring in Laos and Vietnam.[1]

In the 1960s Cold War attitudes continued to shape foreign policy. In the early part of the decade, according to the Church Committee, an expansive foreign policy, exemplified by the invasion of Cuba at the Bay of Pigs, reflected American confidence and determination. The following confrontation with the Soviet Union over the installation of missiles and the rapidly escalating paramilitary activities in Southeast Asia drew the Agency into these major developments.[2]

The DDP functioned as a highly compartmentalized organization with a small cadre responsible for and knowledgable of selected operations. This ethos helped foster the development of such operations as assassination plots against foreign leaders.[3]

The 1960s saw the emergence of revolutionary movements in Southeast Asia and Africa. United States policymakers called for the development of counterinsurgency programs to fight this challenge without precipitating a major Soviet-American military confrontation. To implement its responsibilities in this field, the Agency developed a network of worldwide paramilitary capabilities, and these assets consumed major portions of the Agency's budget.[4]

The period between 1964 and 1967 was the most active era for covert operations: political action, propaganda, international organizations, and paramilitary.[5]

With the development of an extensive weave of farflung paramilitary infrastructures, the Agency implemented covert operations in Laos and Cuba and expanded the ongoing effort in Vietnam. The failure at the Bay of Pigs was followed by a series of other operations directed at Cuba. Those operations became so aggressive and extensive, it led one Agency official to state: "We were at war with Cuba."[6]

As in the decade of the 1950s this 10-year period saw the implementation of hundreds of covert operations each year with primary attention given to operations in Asia, Latin America, a growing endeavor in Africa, a continuing program in the Middle East, a somewhat reduced effort in Europe, and a burgeoning illegal internal U.S. operational program.

    * **Southeast Asia.** The Agency's large-scale involvement in Southeast Asia continued in Laos and Vietnam. "In Laos," wrote the Church Committee, "the Agency implemented air supply and paramilitary training programs, which gradually developed into full-scale management of a ground war."[7] The CIA recruited and trained a private army of at least 30,000 Hmong and other Laotian tribesmen. This group was known as L'Armee Clandestine. Pilots hired by the CIA flew supply and bombing missions in CIA-owned planes in support of the secret army. Expenditures by the U.S. to assist this army amounted to at least $300 million a year. Forty or 50 CIA officers ran this operation, aided by 17,000 Thai mercenaries.[8]

In Vietnam, the Agency conducted the gamut of operations — political, paramilitary, psychological. (For more on those programs, see Chapter 10.)

In Indonesia in 1965 a group of young military officers attempted a coup against the U.S.-backed military establishment and murdered six of seven top military officers. The Agency seized this opportunity to overthrow Sukarno and to destroy the Communist Party of Indonesia (PKI), which had three million members. As I wrote in *The Nation*, "Estimates of the number of deaths that occurred as a result of this CIA [one word deleted] operation run from one-half million to more than one million people.

"Initially, the Indonesian Army left the P.K.I. alone, since it had not been involved in the coup attempt. [eight sentences deleted] Subsequently, however, Indonesian military leaders [seven words deleted] began a bloody extermination campaign. In mid-November 1965, General Suharto formally authorized the 'cleaning out' of the Indonesian Communist Party and established special teams to supervise the mass killings. Media fabrications played a key role in stirring up popular resentment against the P.K.I. Photographs of the bodies of the dead generals — badly decomposed — were featured in all the newspapers and on television. Stories accompanying the pictures falsely claimed that the generals had been castrated and their eyes gouged out by Communist women. This cynically manufactured campaign was designed to foment public anger against the Communists and set the stage for a massacre. . . . To conceal its role in the massacre of those innocent people the C.I.A., in 1968, concocted a false account of what happened (later published by the Agency as a book, *Indonesia — 1965: The Coup that Backfired*). . . . At the same time that the Agency wrote the book, it also composed a secret study of what really happened. [One sentence deleted.] The Agency was extremely proud of its successful [one word deleted] and recommended it as a model for future operations [one-half sentence deleted]."[9]

In Thailand in the 1960s the Agency continued its involvement with the Police Aerial Reconnaissance Unit and the Border Patrol Police. Those counterinsurgency forces then supplied much of the manpower for the secret war in Laos. The CIA also developed a series of internal security and counterinsurgency programs jointly with Thai security forces.[10]

In Cambodia the CIA played a role in the coup that toppled the government of Prince Norodom Sihanouk in 1970, which paved the way for the U.S. military invasion of that country in the spring of 1970.[11]

* **Latin America.** Many Agency operations in Latin America in the 1960s centered around Cuba and removing Fidel Castro's government. Prior to the invasion of Cuba by CIA-trained Cuban exiles in April 1961, the CIA attempted to assassinate Castro. The Agency enlisted the help of Mafia figures to arrange his murder. The first attempt to kill Castro was made in early 1961. Five more assassination teams were sent against the Cuban leader in the next two years.[12]

A CIA-trained force of Cuban exiles made an unsuccessful invasion of Cuba at the Bay of Pigs in mid-April 1961. Four Americans flying CIA planes and nearly 300 Cuban exiles died during the invasion. More than 1,200 survivors were captured by Castro's forces.[13]

The Guatemalan President, Miguel Ydigoras Fuentes, successor to Castillo-Armas, had permitted the CIA to use his country for its training camp for Cuban exiles. In November

1960 a rebellion broke out in Guatemala. The CIA secretly came to the aid of Fuentes and sent in B-26 bombers against the rebels. The insurgency was crushed and Fuentes remained in power.[14]

Beginning in 1961 the Agency conducted operations to bring down the regime of President José Velasco Ibarra of Ecuador after he refused to sever diplomatic relations with Cuba. Ibarra was overthrown in November 1961. His successor, Carlos Julio Arosemena, soon fell out of favor with the United States and once again the CIA used destabilizing tactics to overthrow his government in July 1963.[15]

In 1964 the CIA, with the cooperation of the Agency for International Development and the State Department, secretly funneled up to $20 million into Chile to aid Eduardo Frei in his successful bid to defeat Salvador Allende for the Presidency.[16] Failing to block Allende's election to the Presidency in 1970, the CIA directed a destabilization campaign of economic and political warfare which led to the 1973 military coup that toppled Allende.[17]

In British Guiana, according to a report by the Center for National Security Studies, the "CIA funded strikes and riots that crippled Guiana in 1962 and 1963, and led to overthrow of [Cheddi] Jagan's governing People's Progressive Party. CIA funneled its secret payments that placed Forbes Burnham in power through the AFL-CIO and AFSCME."[18]

In Brazil, the CIA funded unsuccessful candidates in opposition to President João Goulart, who had moved to expropriate International Telephone and Telegraph subsidiaries and maintain relations with Cuba. The CIA then orchestrated, continued the report, "anti-government operations by labor, military, and middle-class groups, including courses in 'labor affairs' in Washington, D.C." The resultant coup in 1964 established a military dictatorship in power.[19]

During the mid-1960s the Agency secretly aided the government of Peru in its fight against rebel guerrilla forces. The Agency flew in arms and other equipment. Local Peruvian troops were trained by personnel of the special operations division of the CIA as well as by Green Beret instructors loaned by the U.S. Army.[20]

In Bolivia, the CIA gave assistance to government soldiers in 1967 in their successful effort to track down and capture

Ernesto "Che" Guevara, the Cuban revolutionary leader. Guevara was captured on October 8, 1967 by CIA-advised Bolivian rangers. He was murdered shortly thereafter.[21]

In Uruguay, the CIA manipulated politics throughout the 1960s, pressuring the government to accept an AID police training mission which provided cover for CIA case officers. Their job: to secretly finance and train local police and intelligence services.[22]

* **Africa.** "In the early 1960s the decolonization of Africa sparked an increase in the scale of CIA clandestine activities on that continent," wrote the Church Committee. "CIA actions paralleled growing interest on the part of the State Department and the Kennedy Administration in the 'third world countries.' . . . Prior to 1960, Africa had been included in the European or Middle Eastern Division. In that year it became a separate division. Stations sprang up all over the continent. Between 1959 and 1963 the number of CIA stations in Africa increased by 55.5%."[23]

In Angola in 1960 the CIA recruited Holden Roberto, the leader of one of the Angolan groups. In 1975 the CIA supported two factions in the civil war in Angola against the Popular Movement for the Liberation of Angola (MPLA), spending millions of dollars on ammunition, air support, and mercenaries.[24]

In the early 1960s the CIA became involved in the political struggle in the Congo. In 1960 the CIA planned to assassinate Patrice Lumumba, the Congolese leader, and in fact worked with the African dissidents who murdered him in 1961.[25] The Agency paid cash to selected Congolese politicians and gave arms to the supporters of Joseph Mobutu and Cyril Adoula. Eventually the CIA sent mercenaries and paramilitary experts to aid the new government. In 1964, CIA B-26 airplanes were being flown in the Congo on a regular basis by Cuban-exile pilots who were under CIA contract. Those pilots and planes carried out bombing missions against areas held by rebel forces.[26]

In South Africa the CIA worked closely with BOSS, the South African secret police. By 1975 the Agency was secretly collaborating with the South African government in the Angolan civil war.[27]

* **United States.** Illegal CIA operations in the United

States in the 1960s continued to utilize the funding, corporate, and press mechanisms established during the preceding decade. But this era saw the beginning of the exposure of some of its internal U.S. operations. One of the earliest revelations was a 1967 *Ramparts* magazine article, which exposed CIA funding of private voluntary organizations that had begun in the 1950s. "The revelations resulted in President Johnson's appointment of a three-person committee to examine the CIA's covert funding of American educational and private voluntary organizations operating abroad," wrote the Church Committee. "Chaired by the Under Secretary of State, Nicholas Katzenbach, the Committee included DCI Richard Helms and Secretary of Health, Education and Welfare, John Gardner. . . . The Katzenbach Committee recommended that no federal agency provide covert financial assistance to American educational and voluntary institutions. . . . Although the CIA complied with the strict terms of the Katzenbach guidelines, funding and contact arrangements were realigned so that overseas activities could continue with little reduction."[28]

In this decade the CIA was initiating many internal U.S. operations while continuing those started in the prior decade. Following the Bay of Pigs invasion of 1961, Cuban exiles were directed and paid by CIA agents to compile secret files on and watch over other Cubans and Americans "who associated with individuals under surveillance." By the late 1960s such activities were being supported by the CIA in several key American cities, including Los Angeles, New York, and San Juan. It was estimated that at the height of these activities, roughly 150 informants were on the payroll of a Cuban "counterintelligence" office located in Florda.[29]

E. Howard Hunt, a former CIA agent, stated that in 1964 during his tenure with the CIA's domestic operations division he was ordered to arrange for the pick-up, on a daily basis, of "any and all information" that might be available at Senator Barry Goldwater's presidential campaign headquarters. Hunt said that the documents obtained about Goldwater were delivered to Chester L. Cooper, a White House aide who had worked for the CIA.[30]

In 1966, 1969, and 1971, the CIA conducted three separate domestic break-ins into the premises occupied by CIA employees or ex-employees. All three entries were made, according to the CIA, because it believed that security concerns warranted such actions.[31]

Following the revelation in 1967 that the CIA had subsidized the National Student Association (NSA), it was disclosed that the CIA had funded other labor, business, church, university, and cultural organizations through a variety of foundation conduits. It was estimated that at least $12.4 million had been secretly spent in this manner by the CIA.[32]

On August 15, 1967, Richard Helms set up a unit (Operation CHAOS) within the counterintelligence office of the Agency "to look into the possibility of foreign links to American dissident elements." This unit "periodically thereafter" drew up reports "on the foreign aspects of the antiwar, youth and similar movements, and their possible links to American counterparts."[33]

Documents released in early 1979 by the CIA as the result of a lawsuit indicate that the Agency's Operation CHAOS, contrary to earlier accounts contained in reports of government committees, infiltrated political groups in the United States in order to collect purely domestic information. The documents also reveal a number of aspects of CHAOS and related programs not reported by the Church Committee, including: "that the Agency investigated domestic political groups as much as five years before the initiation of CHAOS, that Operation CHAOS collected information on prominent Americans including Robert Kennedy, Martin Luther King, Bella Abzug, and Ronald Dellums, that CHAOS information was preserved and continued to be used after the termination of CHAOS in 1974, that the program was for several years assigned *highest operational priority, ranking with intelligence collection on the Soviet Union and China. . . .*"[34] (Emphasis added.)

According to William Colby, the CIA's office of security "inserted 10 agents into dissident organizations operating in the Washington, D.C., area" in 1967 in order to collect "information relating to plans for demonstrations, pickets, protests, or break-ins that might endanger CIA personnel, facilities, and information."[35]

The propensity to operate illegally within the United States continued into the 1970s. In 1970 CIA director Richard Helms joined with others in recommending to President Nixon "an integrated approach to the coverage of domestic unrest," which came to be known as the Huston Plan.[36] After the Huston Plan was rescinded, the CIA "recruited or inserted about a dozen individuals into American dissident circles" in order to secure "access to foreign circles." It was believed that in this manner these individuals would "establish their credentials for operations abroad." In the course of their work some of these individuals "submitted reports on the activities of the American dissidents with whom they were in contact." This information was kept in CIA files and reported to the FBI.[37]

In 1971 and 1972 the CIA employed physical surveillance against "five Americans who were not CIA employees," *The Washington Post* reported. This was done because the CIA had "clear indications" that the five were receiving classified information "without authorization." It was hoped that the surveillance would "identify the sources of the leaks." A secret Senate memorandum indicated that three of the five subjects were columnist Jack Anderson, *Washington Post* reporter Michael Getler, and author Victor Marchetti.[38]

In 1971 and 1972 the Agency secretly provided training to about 12 county and city police forces in the United States on the detection of wire taps, the organization of intelligence files, and the handling of explosives. The training program, involving less than 50 policemen, was reported to have included representatives from the police forces of New York City, Washington, D.C., Boston, Chicago, Fairfax County, Virginia, and Montgomery County, Maryland.[39]

Nine months after returning to Headquarters I was asked if I wanted to go back overseas — this time to Thailand. I had heard many good things about that country and its people and immediately answered that I wanted to be considered. The next day I was called for an interview with the deputy chief of station in Thailand, whom I shall call Dave Abbott, who was then at Headquarters on a recruiting trip. I was escorted into his office and sat down on a small, hard chair. Abbott was poring over a personnel file, mine I supposed; he did not look up or acknowledge my presence. So I sat there and studied him. He was a man of medium build with straight sandy hair, thick horn-rimmed glasses, and a peaches-and-cream complexion that belied his 40 years. He continued to read for some time, then suddenly looked up, stared straight at me, and with no amenities said, "I hear you want to go to Thailand."

Somewhat taken aback by his approach, I responded, "Yes, but I would like to know something about the job before deciding."

Abbott, with his unwavering stare and without a trace of emotion, outlined the job possibilities. He said the station was reviewing its liaison operations with a nation-wide security service, and he was looking for people to fill specific positions. He noted my excellent record in Taipei, where I had earned a reputation for working in liaison with the Chinese Nationalist intelligence services. "In view of your background," he said, "you might qualify for an assignment to the North."

The reason so many new officers were being recruited for Thailand had to do with events in neighboring Laos. During the reconstituted Geneva Conference on Laos in 1961-1962, which followed a cease-fire there, the United States was upset that a neutralist government might be established in Laos. At the urging of the CIA, the Agency-backed rightist General Phoumi Nosavan broke the cease-fire by sending his troops to Nam Tha, just 15 miles from the China border in an area traditionally under the authority of the Communist Pathet Lao forces. But the Pathet Lao forced Phoumi's troops to withdraw and evacuate across the Mekong River into Thailand. The United States accused the Pathet Lao of violating the cease-fire, and the National Security Council used this pretext to create a crisis that existed only in Washington.[40] To counter the Pathet Lao's so-called threat to Thailand, the U.S. sent 5,000 troops to Thailand. As part of the buildup, the CIA began to bolster its staff, whose job it was to advise Thai security and counterinsurgency forces. My assignment to Thailand was part of that buildup. In May 1962 Secretary of Defense Robert McNamara announced the creation of the U.S. Military Assistance Command Thailand to assist the government, and U.S. troops were in Thailand to stay.

That night after the meeting with Dave Abbott, I talked over the prospects of a tour with Norma and the children. I pulled out a copy of the Thailand post report, a document prepared by the government outlining living conditions for those anticipating overseas tours. I also offered several travel books containing pictures of Buddhist temples and the colorful *klongs* (canals) heavy with boat traffic. Despite my enthusiasm and the books, there was considerable unhappiness and grumbling.

Several days later I was told that I was accepted. Norma and I agreed that I should go ahead first to Thailand to arrange housing before she and the children followed. Our neighbors seemed to believe my rather outlandish cover story of quitting what appeared to be a good, secure government job for one of indefinite duration in an exotic location overseas.

6.
NORTH THAILAND:
SAVING THE HILL TRIBES

"DAD, what do you do?" my 13-year-old daughter Peggy asked about six months after we had settled into our home in North Thailand. She had been observing my strange comings and goings, my home office with its safe, map, and cameras, and my frequent hushed conversations with a variety of visitors. She wanted to know what it was all about.

I braced myself. I knew that simple question was inevitable, one that every child asks sooner or later, but I had dreaded it. In earlier years the children were either too young to notice or my activities were less overt, so I had gotten away with a joking, "Oh, I'm just a paper pusher." As Peggy persisted this time, though, I knew this answer would no longer do.

Norma had felt all along that we should be truthful with the children, that our family trust came before my oath of secrecy to the Agency. This very clear set of priorities had been reinforced in her mind a hundredfold by her personal experience when she arrived in Thailand. I had flown ahead to North Thailand to make the necessary arrangements for the family to join me. Once I found a house, I wrote to Norma to fly to Bangkok, where I would meet her. But the housing deal fell through, and the next day I had written to Norma not to come yet. She never received the second letter. She had gone ahead, sending me her flight number and arrival date, but that letter had been held at the Thailand station, and I never received it.

After a grueling, sleepless flight of 16 hours with four cranky children, she had arrived to find no one there to meet her. Since we were traveling on unofficial passports and no one had notified the Thai authorities, she had trouble getting past customs and had to talk her way into a two-week visa. Speaking not a word of Thai, she took a taxi to a good hotel, but in one day the expense exhausted the cash she had in her purse.

The next day she went to the American Embassy and asked if they could put her in touch with me. After a lot of hassling in which everyone claimed never to have heard of me, she made contact with an official who explained that I was in the North. He didn't understand how I had not known of my family's arrival, but he promised that I would be contacted immediately. In the meantime Norma explained that she was out of money and had five mouths to feed. She asked if an advance could be made. He made a call, but the finance officer said that she could not be authorized funds because my assignment was in the North.

There is no anger or determination like my wife's when something threatens her brood. The official offered her money from his own pocket to tide her over until I could be contacted, but she refused. She said she was so mad that she would sit on the street corner right in front of the American Embassy and beg with her four children if she had to. Fortunately, I had by chance come to Bangkok on Agency business that day and everything straightened out before it came to that. But to make matters worse, the next day I had to send her and the children to the North on the train while I remained behind a few days on business. When I finally joined her, Norma's greeting was not the warmest I have ever received. "If you plan to ship us off somewhere else," she raged, as close to divorce as we'd ever been, "it had better be right back to the States." She went on to describe three miserable days in a hotel with no shower and nothing for the children to do, with mosquitos swarming all over, lizards crawling the walls and ceilings, and huge rats scurrying on the floors.

This experience — both the Agency's utter disregard for the well-being of her and the children and my own cockeyed priorities of putting Agency business above my family — had left Norma enraged and totally disillusioned with the Agency. While she knew that I still had complete faith in the Agency and could not be persuaded to leave it, she was now at least insisting that I not lie to the children any longer. The Agency had done enough to her and the children, she told me repeatedly; she would not allow its ridiculous secrecy rules to sow distrust in our family.

Now Peggy's innocent question had brought the matter to a head. Because of all the indoctrination I had received and my gung-ho attitude, something inside me still resisted. I felt I should keep my activities secret — even from my own daughter.

"Daddy, it's embarrassing," Peggy was saying, staring up at me. "All my friends know what their fathers do. I'm the only one who doesn't."

I could feel Norma's eyes on me. What was I going to do? If I told Peggy, I would be breaking my oath. But of course people broke that oath all the time. Everyone knew that secret information was bandied about at Agency cocktail parties as if it were a weather report. Sometimes it seemed I was the only one who played it strictly by the rules. I wondered: would it make any difference to the Agency's mission if my children knew that I worked for it? Would it hurt the United States? I looked up at Norma, and we silently acknowledged that the time had come.

I breathed deeply and sat both of my daughters down (the boys were still too young to understand). With the same sense of compelling seriousness that I had used in regard to crossing streets, not going with strangers, and not taking anything that belongs to others, I said, "I work for the Central Intelligence Agency, which protects our country from anyone who might want to do it harm. I could not tell you before, because you were too young and would not be able to keep it a secret from your friends. But you must do just that. You must promise you will not talk to anyone but your mother and me about where I work."

Neither daughter seemed particularly excited about the news. They looked at me and said, "Oh." This was not at all the response I had expected, but I thought that they probably, like myself 10 years earlier, had not the least notion of what the CIA was and did. Years later when preparing to write this book, I asked each of them what they had thought when I told them about my work. Jean said she had been quite impressed and had thought the job must be difficult and exciting because of all my flying around. Her friends who had observed this activity had pumped her, and she felt frustrated that she could not confide in them.

Peg said she had felt the same frustration at not being able to tell her friends. She also was curious about what specifically I did for the CIA on the various flying trips around North Thailand. I said that I would tell her after I retired — a promise, until now, that I never kept, for by the time I retired I was disillusioned and angry and did not want to lay this negative burden on my children.

I told our elder son, Scott, several years afterwards. Later he admitted that he had been humiliated in a classroom exercise where each child was asked to talk about his father's job. Scott had to say he did not know. After I told him, he said he had more respect for my lifestyle. But that did not alter the fact that he still could not admit he knew what his father did, or confide in his friends.

Norma told our younger son, Dan, in Bangkok when he was 11 years old. He said later that he had not been too surprised since we so carefully avoided the subject of my work. His reaction at the time, though, was to ask, "Oh, does he carry a gun?"

The Border Patrol Police [BPP] . . . were responsible for security along Thailand's international frontiers. . . . They were well-armed, mobile, counter-insurgency fighters specializing in intelligence-gathering along Thailand's borders and in conducting cross-border combat and reconnaissance operations. . . . The United States, through its . . . CIA advisors, continued to exercise almost complete control, both in training and operations – the PARU [Police Aerial Reconnaissance Unit] and BPP were "their" units. . . .[1]

– Thomas Lobe

Beginning in the early sixties, the BPP developed special programs among the hill tribes in the north and quickly became the only [Thai government] service to enjoy any kind of rapport with the tribal communities. It established and manned two hundred schools as well as dispensaries and development centers with garden plots and the like. This Remote Area Security Program, as it was called, . . . [was supplemented by] the recruitment of tribal volunteers into a police auxiliary service called Border Security Volunteer Teams. There is evidence in the *Pentagon Papers* . . . that U.S. support for the BPP was conducted by CIA.[2]

– Douglas S. Blaufarb

While in North Thailand I converted a small servant's quarters in my home into an office. I lined the wooden walls with a large-scale map of North Thailand, and on the wall closest to where I sat I hung a large poster. The poster depicted a ravenous, fanged Mao Tse-tung and Ho Chi Minh with burning eyes, outstretched arms, and clawed fingers, leaning over a map of Southeast Asia. Blood from a swirl of massed humanity flowed from the North down over the countries of Southeast Asia. The poster illustrated in graphic, startling form the domino theory, so much a part of what I believed. It was evocative, disturbing, and for me and other Agency officers represented the *raison d'être* for the work of the CIA in Thailand. We were there to protect the Thai people from the Communist monsters of the North. We believed if the Communists won, there would be a bloodbath, liberty and religion would be destroyed, and nation after nation would fall before the swelling red tidal wave.

My small part in fighting the menace was to gather intelligence concerning Communist subversion and at the same time to teach the Thai counterinsurgency force how to develop its own intelligence capability. I held several courses for the officers, using as my interpreter Captain Song (not his real name), who had associated with Americans for a long time and spoke a form of idiomatic English. He was a good friend and constant associate, frequently visiting us at home and bringing some of his fellow officers with him.

Since Captain Song headed the operations of the counterinsurgency unit, we worked together daily. A maverick who got along beautifully with his co-equals and his subordinates, he took an immediate dislike to anyone with direct authority over him. He had a trace of royal blood in his veins, which undoubtedly had helped him attain the rank of captain. Every day he and I would review the incoming intelligence from the counterinsurgency unit's scattered posts. There wasn't a lot of hard intelligence, since not much was going on.

Most of our reports covered the activities of the various ethnic groups in and around the Thai border area that were plotting their independence from Burma — the Karens, the Shan State Independence Army, the Red Lahu, and others. We also kept an eye on any possible Communist incursions among the numerous hill-tribe people who populated the highland areas around the border — the Hmong, the Yao, the Lisu, the Haw.

Many of the hill tribes had lived in China but had migrated south. Most lived in mountain villages at an altitude above 3,000 feet. They practiced a slash-and-burn style of agriculture and as a result had to move frequently to look for new fields. They raised rice, poultry, and livestock, but the major cash crop was opium from the poppy.

In addition to gathering information, I or another Agency officer would accompany the Thai commander of the counter-insurgency unit on his jeep trips to remote outposts. During the rainy season some areas were inaccessible, and we would schedule one of the station's planes to take the commander on his trip. One time the station sent up a C-47 with instructions to use it. The station's contract with the Agency airline, Air America,[3] called for a minimum number of hours of use each month. At that particular moment, in a most unusual situation, absolutely no one seemed to have any requirements for a plane. I offered the use of it to the local officers of the Joint United States Military Advisory Group, who had done many favors for us. They were delighted, and we took off for Chieng Khong, a small airstrip on the Lao-Thai border. The pilots were new to the area and had difficulty locating Chieng Khong. We flew much too long and suddenly we spotted a large airfield. We immediately turned around and headed for home. After we got back, we recharted our time, speed, and direction and determined we had been flying over China — an incident none of us reported to our superiors.

The other Agency officer and I coordinated our activities with the American consul, Larry Pickering, who was a thoughtful and disciplined diplomat. He frequently invited us to official functions, and I briefed him weekly on any intelligence. I was somewhat in awe of Pickering's status until one occasion when I began to understand the influence of the State Department compared to that of the Central Intelligence Agency. This occurred at a ceremony marking the beginning of the construction of a university.

On that day the Thai Prime Minister, Sarit Thanarat, came north with a large entourage of Buddhist priests, senior foreign diplomats including the U.S. ambassador, high-level Thai officials, and some members of the royal family. The

CIA chief of station, whom I shall call Rod Johnson, also came but was not a member of the official party. I picked him up at the airport and took him to the ceremony, where we sat in the open stands at the side of the processional route, far from the official area, which was covered and roped-off. The sun was bright, and it was as steaming hot as only Thailand can get. As the ceremony concluded, the dignitaries in the enclosed area formed a line behind the Prime Minister for the recessional. As the group slowly moved our way, the Prime Minister spotted Rod in the stands. As he drew near, he held up his hand for everyone to stop. He signaled Rod down to him. While the assembled laymen, clergy, and royalty sweltered in the sun, Sarit told Rod that he would like him to join him at a party at his Doi Su Thep mountain retreat. Sarit complained that the American ambassador had heard of his plans and had asked to come along. The Prime Minister did not especially like the ambassador and wondered if Rod could in any way prevent him from attending the party. Rod said no. As the conversation ended, the slowly melting official groups staggered out to their waiting cars.

Pickering had scheduled a briefing for the ambassador at the consulate following the ceremony, and I was one of those there to brief him. An hour or so after the incident at the ceremony an angry, red-faced ambassador stormed into the consulate. He did not want to be briefed. He went into an adjoining room and furiously wrote out a message. Apparently at the party Sarit had waited for about half an hour and then asked the ambassador to leave because he wanted to have a private conversation with his good and close friend, Rod Johnson, the chief of station.

This incident demonstrated the relationship that many chiefs of station have with heads of state — primarily, I suppose, because of the Agency's ability to back a chosen individual as the leader of his country. In this case Rod Johnson not only had the powerful CIA behind him but also was a model for the role. He was a gregarious, six-foot-four-inch, red-headed, back-slapping extrovert who avoided all confrontations. He had a genius for developing close relations with whoever became a country's leader. After Sarit died, there was a period of strained relations between the CIA and the new government of Thanom Kittikachorn and Praphat

Charusathien. Praphat officially was the number two man in the government, but in fact he held the real power. Rod Johnson quickly overcame the tension and developed such a close relationship with Praphat that the Thai foreign minister complained that he could seldom get in to see Praphat because Praphat was always with Johnson.

Johnson liked to tell the story of his trip to see Praphat early one Sunday morning under orders from Headquarters in Langley. He arrived unexpectedly and Praphat came out to greet him in his undershorts. After settling business and after a few drinks, things loosened up a bit, and playful blows between Johnson and Praphat developed into a full-scale wrestling match. The battle between the six-foot-four-inch Caucasian and the short, fat Thai (who so closely resembled in appetite, conduct, and appearance the word many Thais used to describe him — pig) began to favor Johnson. Praphat got angry, and the chief of station, deciding diplomacy was more important than victory, allowed Praphat to pin him.

Rob Carson was also assigned to the North. His responsibility was to oversee the equipment and physical plant of the counterinsurgency force. Rob, who was about 50 and in great shape, had been the instructor for the survival/dirty fighting/physical education courses at the "farm" during my paramilitary training.

Both Rob and I started studying the Thai language at the same time and after a few months I — no whiz at language study — was able to order food in a restaurant and exchange pleasantries with Thais. Rob, on the other hand, spoke hesitantly. It was painful in a restaurant when he tried to order in Thai. Others would just name the dish, but not Rob. Every time he would go slowly and carefully through the ritual, enunciating each word, *"pom dtong khang"* (I want), while the Thais looked on in impatient exasperation.

But this aside, Rob was quite pleasant and we worked smoothly together. In the small community, if we had not liked each other, it would have been very difficult.

One day after I had been in the North for about six months, I received a message from the deputy chief of station,

Dave Abbott, to report to the station. Before seeing Dave, I first checked in with my parent office. Everyone seemed to be furious, and I quickly realized that the reason was Dave Abbott. Demanding and critical, Dave was genuinely disliked; each person in the office had his own stock of Dave Abbott stories to tell.

Sam, one of my friends in the office, took me down to the cafeteria for lunch. He said most of the officers in my parent office — two of whom were my direct supervisors — had formerly been with the Agency's training division. Abbott had it in for trainers. He had really gone after my boss John, and John had had a heart attack. The American doctor wanted to send a dispatch to Headquarters pointing out Dave's inability to handle people and specifically what he had done as the deputy chief of station. Both Dave and the chief, Rod Johnson, pleaded with the doctor that such a dispatch would ruin Dave's career. The dispatch was never sent.

"Dave and Rod are a typically matched Agency chief and deputy chief of station," said Sam. "They form a great team. Where one is weak, the other is strong. Dave pays attention to detail and is the shouting top-sergeant type who sees everything is done on time. Johnson is the so-called good guy. He butters up the Thai leaders, he greets everyone, 'How are you, you old rascal?' and never has a harsh word for anyone — at least not to their faces."

Sam warned me that Dave would probably follow a strict ritual at our upcoming meeting. "He'll make you wait in the secretary's office up to half an hour before having you escorted in," said Sam. "Then he'll pretend he is reading and make you sweat while you stand there waiting for him to acknowledge your presence. Then he'll look up and say, 'Well, what do you want?'" According to Sam, Abbott did this with all subordinates to keep them on the defensive.

After lunch I was called to Dave's office. Much to my surprise, I was immediately escorted in, and he was standing there waiting to greet me. Dave gave me a big hello, came around from behind his desk, and motioned me to take a chair while he did the same. He asked how things were going in the North. I told him I had a problem with my old jeep that kept breaking down and was costing a small fortune to keep running. "I'll take care of it immediately," he said. "You'll have a new one in a few weeks, if I can get the training idiots around here to do their job."

Dave then got down to the purpose of the meeting. "You know these people who head your office here were all forced on the station by the Agency's training division," he confided. "They were all teachers who never had any real operational experience. They really prove the maxim that those who teach cannot do. I have to really follow what's going on here and with you people upcountry or they'll get everything screwed up."

He then asked, "What's happening in there today?"

This really took me by surprise, but I tried to recover and outlined the various administrative things I knew were being done in my parent office. I did not mention the state of angry confusion that seemed to permeate the place.

"Look, Ralph," he said, "I have to know exactly what is going on in there, what they are saying, what they are doing. I want you to become my eyes and ears."

He was tearing down my superiors in my presence and was asking me to spy on them for him! I was angry, embarrassed, and most of all confused. What could I say? How could I respond? I tried to act as if I really did not understand what he was asking, and we parried words for a while before he curtly dismissed me.

I later observed that others who accepted his "recruitment" attempt instantly became important men in the station and had many hurried calls to the front office. But after their tours in Thailand ended, they were marked men. No one wanted a fink in his office. As for me, for the time being I'd kept my reputation, but, as I was to find out later, Dave Abbott never forgot or forgave a man who turned him down.

Early one November morning in 1963, a friend of Norma's came by to tell us the sad news she had just heard over the short-wave radio: President Kennedy had been shot and killed. We were stunned. The prince of idealism who had challenged us all "to ask not what your country can do for you, but what you can do for your country" was dead.

The Thai people had admired the young President and his

beautiful wife. Pictures of them had appeared in the press, and there were favorable comparisons made between the Kennedys and the young King and Queen of Thailand. That day I could not go to work and stayed with my family. We were all confused, angry, and distressed. To occupy my mind, I decided to fix the flat tire on Scott's bicycle. I went to the local hardware store to buy a pump. I took it off the shelf and asked the clerk, *"Gyi baht krup?"* (How much?). He said, *"Baht deeo"* (five cents). I looked at him in disbelief, but his sad eyes insisted. It dawned on me that with this subtle gesture he was expressing his sympathy. I appreciated his heartfelt attempt to assuage my grief.

After I had been in Thailand for more than a year, I was assigned to "observe" a program for the hill-tribe people being conducted by the Thai counterinsurgency organization. The purpose of the program was to help build close relations with the hill tribes and to lessen their vulnerability to Communist subversion. The program included training young tribal members as medics and issuing them basic medicines; training other young men in more advanced agricultural methods and assisting them to develop a cash crop other than opium; and improving the breeding stock of their pigs and chickens by providing breeding boars and cocks. An initial phase of the program required us to convince the hill-tribers to help construct small mountainside airstrips to facilitate transportation to their isolated villages. Of course, coincidentally, this also would allow a military force more rapid access to the area.

Rob Carson was the chief observer for this project. I was not a part of it and continued my intelligence-gathering duties. But I was asked to accompany a counterinsurgency team on a walk up to the villages. It occurred to me at the time that we were sacrificing intelligence-collection efforts to the demands of policy. This was my first indication that, to the CIA, policy might be more important than intelligence.

I prepared for the trip by outfitting myself with boots, fatigues, and a backpack. I decided to test the equipment by walking up the nearby Doi Su Thep mountain with Scott. As we trudged up its many miles, including the 100-plus steps up to the temple at the top, my feet felt increasingly uncomfortable, but I doggedly walked on. When we arrived home, my feet were a bloody mess. With the coming trip to the mountains only a couple of weeks away, I steeled myself to taking that long hike in rubber thongs since my feet were just too blistered for shoes of any kind.

On the appointed day I flew to a small Thai village on the Lao border, where I joined a 10-man team of the counterinsurgency group, accompanied by a pony train. Most of the Thais loaded their backpacks on the ponies, but I, macho man, indicated I would carry my pack myself.

Up the mountain we went, I in my shower thongs with the 50-pound pack. It was at the peak of the monsoon season, and we came to a stream that was rushing wildly, swollen from the downpours. We strung a rope across the stream, and all helped to get the ponies and equipment across. I then tried to cross, holding on to the rope. The chest-high roaring water hit the heavy pack and swept me under. As I was tumbling over and over, I instinctively reached out and grabbed a low-lying tree branch and pulled myself over to the opposite shore. I had had enough of my burden, and as soon as I had wrung out my soaked clothes and taken a reserve pair of thongs from my pack, I loaded it on one of the ponies.

We climbed up and up. It seemed we would never reach our destination. Crossing another shallow, slow-running stream, my feet were attacked by leeches. Never having encountered them before, I quickly grabbed them and pulled them off. I should not have done that. The normal procedure is to put a lit cigarette to their backs, and they will release and fall off. When I grabbed them, they simply clung tighter and bit me, injecting a serum that decoagulated my blood. As I pulled them off, I ripped small holes in my skin which proceeded to bleed for hours. They bled so much that my rubber thongs became slippery, making it impossible to keep them on, so I walked the rest of the way barefooted.

We continued to struggle upward through heavy jungle, passing various types of wildlife, including a large translucent snake with bright red eyes which stared at us from a ledge within striking distance of the trail. By late afternoon I assumed we were approaching the village. We stopped, and the team leader said we should camp for the night. But we had scheduled an airdrop of food and equipment for the next morning, and I did not want to have to radio back and admit we could not reach our destination. In my inadequate Thai I argued with the team leader, a master sergeant who was not at all happy to have an American with him on the trip. After an angry discussion we started up again. We had been walking along a trail that continually wound around and rose slowly upward, but we now came to a steep straight shot. I figured that now we must be approaching the village. Wrong again. We had to do more climbing now than walking, slowly and painfully dragging ourselves up this precipice. Just about dusk we arrived at the village. We were a worn-out, haggard group. All the team members blamed me for their condition. After making arrangements for the morning parachute reception, I was given a spot on the floor in one of the hill-tribe houses. I broke open my sleeping bag and crawled in.

The next morning the Air America plane arrived on schedule and parachuted its load all over the adjacent forest, so we had to cut down a couple of huge trees to recover the equipment. We then had an egg, pepper, and bamboo shoot breakfast. I don't know where the cook learned his trade, but as the weeks progressed his meals grew from bad to intolerable. He gathered bamboo shoots as we walked along the trail, and he added them and the fiercely hot small green peppers to everything. On the three-week trip I lost 20 pounds down to 175, a weight I had not seen since late grammar school.

Having rested and eaten, I began to walk around the Yao village. This was my first opportunity to study a semi-primitive society. About two dozen bamboo houses with roofs of thatch were scattered on level spots at various intervals on the mountain. Livestock and chickens ran loose around the village, and the pigs seemed more wild than domesticated. The human and livestock traffic had worn paths between the houses. An elevated system of bamboo water pipes ensured a steady supply of water. The adjoining fields were alive with the reddish hues of the opium poppy, the main crop of this and most other hill villages. We ignored the poppy fields as we were here to make friends, not to cause problems. (There may have been other reasons for ignoring the poppies: some said that the counter-insurgency force got a rakeoff from the opium traffic.)

The villagers resembled the Chinese, although they

seemed to be somewhat smaller. The men dressed in an assortment of Western and native clothes, the basic outfit being
black pajamas. The women wore jacket-like blouses made of
heavy red worsted yarn, loose-fitting dark trousers with fancy
ornamental embroidery, and unusually colorful and decorative
turbans around their hair. On festive occasions they added
heavy silver neck loops and earrings, and sewed silver coins
and buttons to the front and sides of the blouses.

At noontime, after a bamboo-shoot, pepper and Spam
lunch, I went off to nap and recover from the long trip. I had
been assigned a space on a raised bamboo platform inside the
main house, a long rectangular structure with bamboo curtains
to provide privacy. I had just lain down when a heavy, sweet
smell permeated the air — the Yao men had lit their opium
pipes prior to their mid-day nap.

That evening the village headman, a gentle, intelligent
man who in his mid-forties was old by hill-tribe standards,
threw a banquet for us. We all sat on the floor around low,
square, bamboo-pole tables. The team leader took the opportunity to explain the program to the village headman and to
introduce each individual team member. Since my demand
that we continue the journey the day before, the team leader
and I were not speaking, and I was the last to be (barely) introduced. The headman agreed to all facets of the program and
said he would send some young men to Mae Rim, the headquarters of the counterinsurgency forces, for the training. He
also said that in the morning we could pick out an appropriate
site for the airstrip, and construction — using the tools dropped
in the morning air delivery — could begin as soon as feasible.

The meal was served Chinese-style with individual bowls
of rice and community bowls of meat and vegetables in the
center for all to dip out of with their chopsticks. Just as I was
about to dip into one attractive-looking dish, the Thai at my
side nudged me and said in a low whisper that it was a dish of
worms. My chopsticks made a quick turn into a more recog-
nizable dish of pepper and bamboo shoots.

Over the next few days we located a potential airstrip
site and began to clear and level it. The team medic treated a
young child and gave the mother a supply of antibiotics. The
mother, assuming that if one pill helped then the entire bottle
would help more, gave her child the entire contents in one

dose. We sat up all night, hoping and praying that the child would not die. Fortunately, by morning, the child began to recover.

We remained in the village for four days and made all the arrangements for the airstrip and other facets of the program. We then moved on to the next village on the stop. Three weeks later we walked out of the mountains many miles away from our starting spot. Our team had the best record of any subsequent teams. We had built, or had arranged for the building of, airstrips in several villages. We had recruited the required number of potential trainees. We had made friends with the villagers and had accomplished everything required of us. I felt proud of a job well done, but was happy to get back to my more prosaic intelligence job.

I wanted to stay for another year in that beautiful area, but other Agency men were clamoring for a tour in the North. Dave Abbott, who had never forgiven me for refusing his recruitment attempt, quashed any efforts of the commander of the counterinsurgency force to have me remain.

On the day of my departure the entire counterinsurgency force turned out for a formal military review. I hated to leave. I really liked the Thai people and especially the men I had worked with. At the time I did not realize that my work in Thailand had been part of a plan by the President's national security advisers to develop and deploy CIA paramilitary capabilities around the world. I still naively believed the CIA's main purpose was to gather intelligence. I left the North with sadness, but with enormous pride in myself and in the CIA for having done an important job well.

That pride turned to bitterness and anger when I eventually learned of the fate of the hill-tribe villages my team had visited and tried to help. A few years later, because of growing communist influence in the Lao border area, the villages were shelled, bombed, and napalmed by the Thais. Our efforts had apparently laid the groundwork for the tragic destruction of the hill tribes.

7.
HEADQUARTERS:
DUPING CONGRESS

IN mid-1964, after moving back into the house we had bought three years earlier in Herndon, Virginia, I returned to work at the Headquarters building in Langley. I was assigned to the Thai desk, where I was responsible for keeping track of the programs that I had worked on directly in Thailand. This was a paper-pushing job, and I soon longed to get back out into the field, a yearning shared by the majority of CIA case officers.

As part of my desk duties I evaluated our field intelligence reports, most of which covered the activities of the Communist Party of Thailand. Though I had been in North Thailand and reported on the party, I knew virtually nothing about it. I maintained a file of past CIA intelligence reports on the Thai Communists, and to evaluate the new reports I would review the more recent past reporting. If the new report was not too different, I would give it a good grade, adding some innocuous comment such as: "This report reinforces earlier indications on developments in the Communist Party of Thailand. We would wish for additional details on the size of the movement, particularly in the key Northeast area."

Early on, the desk chief had warned me that if I wanted another tour in Thailand I should not be too critical of the station's reporting. He said the chiefs of station have long memories, and they do not like to receive criticism of station operations. So the operator who wanted to get ahead gave most reports at least a good rating. He said I should consider doing the same, "unless you feel strongly otherwise." This was said more as a threat than anything else.

Once a week the Far East division chief, William E. Colby,

later to become CIA director, would sit down with all of the desk chiefs and review the reports and the various grades assigned by the desk officers to the reports. They would make a few comments, but for the most part they merely accepted the rating the individual desk officer had given a report. The comments coming from these meetings were more often platitudes than substantive criticisms. I realized I was just a junior case officer, and if this was how the game was played it certainly was okay with me. Also we lower-level officials lacked the "big picture" or "atmospherics." If we had this special overview, as we were so often told, we would realize the correctness of this procedure. After the division chiefs' meeting, we desk officers prepared a dispatch forwarding to the station all of the comments on all of the reports. At the station the rating sheets were assessed with gravity. Each word was considered for any hidden meaning. For the rating sheets went out as Headquarters comments — not mine or any other desk officer's — and as such they carried the weight of knowledgeable authority.

One day, with other case officers from the Thai and Lao desks, I was called to a meeting in Colby's office. I was extremely pleased and flattered to be called in by the division chief. The purpose of the meeting was to lay the groundwork for a briefing Colby was going to present to a congressional committee concerning our efforts and plans in Laos. Colby stressed to us that congressional briefings were of the utmost importance. I and the others were to devote the entire next three weeks to preparing for his talk.

Colby was an unprepossessing, mild-mannered man you would never notice in a crowd. He had straight brown, gray-flecked hair and heavy glasses. When he talked to you, he devoted his entire attention to you and his eyes always seemed to express his understanding. His manner and attitude evoked confidence and trust. This was obviously one of the reasons he rose in the Agency. In the years hence I have watched him when I knew he was lying, and not the least flicker of emotion ever crosses his face. He comes across as completely honest and believable — a remarkable talent.

Colby emphasized the importance of selecting just the right words and charts to convey the desired impression to Congress. He regarded word usage as an art form, and he was a master at it. He explained that the Agency had been working with the Hmong hill tribes in Laos for several years. (In fact, that was where my old paramilitary training friend Jimmy Moe had been sent.) We needed to increase the number of armed Hmong teams that we were directing in a fight against Communist Pathet Lao forces.

To sell the idea to Congress, Colby's briefing had to convey just the right impression — that the situation in Laos was extremely serious, but with a greater effort it was salvageable. The map depicting the contending forces had to be prepared to present just the proper balance between the Communist forces and those of the Lao government and our Hmong units. The chart had to show an extensive threat, but one that was ultimately controllable. Factual data had little part in the briefing material. One unfortunate fellow on an early version of the map used the color red to indicate the government/ Hmong forces. This was completely unacceptable. Colby ordered that red could be used only for Communist forces.

At the time in Laos the CIA had a number of armed and trained Hmong organized into a couple of dozen platoon-sized teams. But the CIA now wanted financial support for more than 100 teams. The problem was, how do you indicate to Congress that you have more than 100 teams when you actually have only one-fourth that number? The answer was simple: the couple of dozen teams were divided, on paper only, into platoons of only a few individuals each, and instantly there were the necessary number of teams. Of course the briefing did not explain the instant creation of the 100 teams nor their anemic manpower. Also overlooked was the fact that many of the Hmong were untrained teenagers. Whether it was true or not, the briefing material had to indicate an existent force that was primed and ready to go and needed only one thing: congressional authorization for the necessary funding. The thinking at Langley was that if Congress approved the program, the group could be brought quickly up to strength. So why not fudge a few details? On paper the struggling, ragtag group of Hmong fighters began to resemble a small army.

After the first meeting we subordinates held a long series of discussions to determine just the right name to call the new army. The name chosen was to have little to do with the function of the team; it was important solely for the response it would evoke from Congress. "Hunter-Killer Teams" was rejected because it portrayed the image of an aggressive force involved in assassinations. "Home Defense Teams" or "Self-Defense Units" or similar names were rejected as too passive. The name finally adopted for the briefing was "Mobile Strike Forces" — a marvelous combination of defense-offense flexibility and superb word usage. After deciding on the name and after numerous revisions of the chart, Colby briefed Congress. He won approval to go ahead with the program. The Agency then undertook efforts to make the illusion a reality.

This was my first exposure to how the Agency shapes policy. It was, of course, a perfect example of policy being decided from the top in advance and then intelligence being selected or created to support it afterwards — precisely the opposite of the way it should be done. Not only was it all backwards, but it was a complete hoax contrived to deceive Congress, which naturally swallowed it hook, line, and sinker.

At the time I was not disturbed by any of this. Not the faintest doubt crossed my mind. After all, we were in a death struggle with the communist hordes, and if we failed to beat them in Laos, the dominoes would fall possibly all the way to our shores. A little fudging of the facts here and there to reinforce the proper impression seemed a small price to pay for protecting our liberties. For years I didn't realize the disastrous consequences of these practices.

This was only one of many examples of the CIA's deceptions of Congress. Another is described by Frank Snepp, an Agency analyst in Vietnam, in his book, *Decent Interval*.[1] He says a major portion of his time was devoted to briefing touring congressmen. His briefings were carefully orchestrated to convey the exact impression desired by the chief of station, one having little foundation in fact.

The Agency did worry about congressional investigating committees and took emergency measures to forestall effective action by such committees. Agency officials who did not perform well at these investigations paid dearly. In one case a rising star in the Directorate for Operations (previously called the Directorate for Plans) was called to testify before a committee concerning Agency operations in Laos. He went beyond Agency-approved boundaries for testimony and "opted" for early retirement before the week was up.

Vietnam was looming ever more important on the foreign policy scene, and I shared with my fellow workers the strong conviction that it was necessary to smash the Vietnamese Communists to halt the spread of that cancerous growth. I believed that all we had to do to win the war was to devote enough time and effort to the task, and then North Vietnam would cease its efforts to subvert South Vietnam.

In mid-1965, it was announced that President Lyndon Johnson was going to make a major speech concerning Vietnam. On July 28, 1965, a group of fellow officers and I went out to a delicatessen in McLean — a hangout for the Agency — to watch the fateful speech on television. We ate our hot pastrami sandwiches and drank our cold beer while we watched and listened. As the President spoke, I virtually prayed that he would send additional forces to fight the invading North Vietnamese. He announced that the United States military strength in Vietnam would be increased from 75,000 men to 125,000 almost immediately. However, he said, it was not necessary now to order reserve units to active duty. The purpose of his announcement was twofold: to disclose the military measures being taken, and to emphasize the desire of the United States for negotiations to end the conflict.

"We do not want an expanded struggle with consequences that no one can perceive," Johnson drawled, "nor will we bluster or bully or flaunt our power. But we will not surrender and we will not retreat."

Gravely, the President explained that the United States was involved in the Vietnam conflict because "we have learned at a terrible and brutal cost that retreat does not bring safety and weakness does not bring peace." The United States learned from Hitler, he said, "that success only feeds the appetite of aggression."

He continued: "We cannot dishonor our word or abandon our commitment or leave those who believed us and who trusted us to the terror and repression and murder that would follow."[2]

There it was — we were going to fight and win. All of us

at the table exchanged congratulations with each other and with others at nearby tables. We would show those commie bastards that they couldn't play with Uncle Sam.

I just could not sit at a desk while important things were happening all around. This was especially true with regard to Thailand, for on December 3, 1964, a clandestine radio station, the Voice of the People of Thailand, had announced that the Thailand Independence Movement was beginning a revolution. The radio station and the movement were China-based organizations, and the implications of the announcement were not lost on the Thais or the Agency. The broadcast signaled the beginning of covert guerrilla activities, and in the next six months incidents between government and insurgent forces multiplied, especially in the critical Northeast area adjacent to Laos.

I asked my desk chief, who was going out to Thailand on a short trip, to plead my case with the chief of station and especially with the deputy chief, Dave Abbott. I noted my fluency in the Thai language, my ability to get along with Thai officials, my knowledge of the station programs, and my generally good record while in the North. I hoped my request would put Abbott in a difficult position, for the increased guerrilla activity meant increased Agency manpower requirements for Thailand. Dave would have a hard time refusing me when faced with a critical shortage of people.

When the desk chief returned, he said I was to be assigned to Thailand just as soon as possible. What great news! I went home to tell my family. Their excitement at my revelation seemed more than controllable.

8.
IN SEARCH OF REDS

IN September 1965 I began work in Bangkok. At the time Thailand was supposedly a constitutional monarchy, but in fact was more a military dictatorship. The real power was in the hands of two military officers — Prime Minister Thanom Kittikachorn and the *de facto* leader of the government, Deputy Prime Minister Praphat Charusathien, who also headed the military establishment. King Bhumibol and Queen Sirikhit were powerful emotional symbols, but they seldom contradicted the military. There was an on-and-off parliament, but it acted more as a rubber stamp than an independent branch of government.

The CIA station, led by the effervescent Rod Johnson, was involved in numerous anti-communist liaison operations with various departments of the Thai government. [Eight words deleted.] The Agency will not permit me to say what these were, but Douglas Blaufarb's book, *The Counterinsurgency Era*, says:

> In Thailand, information on the identities, size, movements, armaments, and operational patterns of insurgents was collected by . . . BPP [the Border Patrol Police], Provincial Police, and Special Branch. (The latter is the senior police intelligence service but concentrates largely on the Bangkok area. It does have a small section working in the affected areas). . . . [The various organizations] produced a large amount of low-level information which was useful when professionally handled and promptly exploited. This was the task of the . . . centers . . . set up under the CSOC mechanism. . . . the Communist Suppression Operations Command . . . [had the responsibility] to plan and conduct suppression activity nationwide. . . . The central concept was the establishment of a framework for a coordinated effort by civilian, police, and military services linking

> Bangkok to regional Headquarters and then to combat areas. The
> system, called CPM, established suppression centers . . . in all the
> [communist] affected provinces and regions. Several regional intel-
> ligence offices (Joint Security Centers or JSCs) were also established
> to combine the inputs of the various intelligence services working
> in the affected areas.
>
> Existing sources say nothing about the U.S. agency working to
> develop and improve these intelligence efforts, but the very fact
> suggests that the task was performed by the CIA.[1]

Shortly after I arrived in Thailand, I received a command
to appear before the deputy chief of station, Dave Abbott.
I arrived at the appointed time and then began the entire series
of Dave Abbott put-downs. I had to wait in the reception area
for more than a half hour. Then I stood in his office for an
interminable time while he assiduously read a file before he
finally deigned to recognize my presence. His babyish complexion, his owlish eyes staring behind heavy glasses, his pear-
like physique all were disarming — yet I was wary. After looking at me for a long time, he said, "Well, you just couldn't stay
away!"

I had hoped to begin this new tour with a clean slate, but
Dave obviously hadn't forgiven me for refusing to become his
office spy when I was in North Thailand. His angry gaze delivered an explicit message; I pretended not to notice. "Yes, I
know I can do a good job," I responded. "I speak some Thai
and my work on the Thai desk will help me appreciate the
problems of Headquarters. I know you won't be disappointed
in me."

Inwardly I felt confident, like a professional athlete at
the peak of his ability. My analytical talents had developed. I
got along with the Thais, and I was eager to participate in our
great anti-communist crusade. I considered Dave an aberration
from the norm of Agency leadership. He was a fearful figure,
but deserved pity rather than hate. His anger and deceits probably masked his insecurities and lack of self-confidence; I
thought that my work would speak for itself and therefore
I had little to fear from Dave's intrigues.

"I have assigned you to work with Jason [not his real
name]," said Dave. "I told Jason if you give him any problems
to let me know and I will transfer you."

Clearly Dave was the boss. My future, and specifically

this assignment, depended on him. With a wave of his hand he curtly dismissed me.

I was not unhappy with the assignment, except that Jason was considered one of Dave's top informants in the station. To me Jason seemed pleasant, if somewhat reserved, but quite defensive about his position. At the time he was the chief liaison officer with a small Thai counterinsurgency force, and I was to be his assistant in this organization. The word liaison may not adequately describe the Agency's relationship with this organization, for the CIA had planned for, created, trained, equipped, and helped breathe legal life into this service. The organization had a Bangkok headquarters with offices scattered throughout the outlying provinces. Its functions paralleled to some degree the duties of our FBI but with particular responsibility for gathering information on communism. As so frequently happened with Agency-created services, however, it also had become a secret police for the government.

I worked with Jason in a private office at the headquarters of what I will call the "FBI." Jason's area of responsibility included headquarters and the key Northeast area where the Communist Party had made the strongest inroads, while I was given the responsibility for the less critical South and North Thailand. Our Thai staff translated the most relevant reports on Communist activity coming into the "FBI" headquarters from field offices and from most other government agencies, including the military intelligence services. Jason and I read them and maintained geographic files of all reported Communist-inspired incidents. If in my daily work I came across a report of significance, I put it into Agency format, dressed up its language, and submitted it to the station's reports office for possible dissemination to the American intelligence community. In a sense we justified our support to the "FBI" by the number of reports it produced, so it was essential that I do this aspect of my job well.

I remained in this assignment for more than six months, and I began to develop a critical sense about the quality of reporting of the various Thai intelligence services and especially their ability, or rather inability, to recruit agents from the Communist Party of Thailand. These services for the most part had to rely on numerous second- or third-hand access agents, usually friends or relatives of party members. Such agents generally produced low-level information of doubtful reliability. An analyst collating all of that type of information could make of it just about anything he wanted to. If it was to the benefit of his service — or his career — to paint the picture of a serious Communist threat, then he would make it a serious threat. Conversely, if it was more advantageous to paint the picture in more rosy perspective, then that also could be done.

I also fell victim to this fundamentally unreliable intelligence. I wanted to be in the center of the action, to be called to station meetings, to submit and get credit for a large number of reports, and to earn promotions. As part of this ambition, I prepared one collated report on the strength of the Communist Party in Southern Thailand. Based on poorly sourced, subjective information, my report stressed the existence of various entrenched, military-like Communist camps in mountain redoubts in the South. In reaction to my analysis, the Thai military conducted a sweep in the South and found exactly nothing. This taught me several lessons: my information was as good or as poor as my sources; I needed to be skeptical of intelligence from agencies with a vested interest in the issues; and I had to be especially aware of my own preconceptions and ambitions, for it had benefited me to show how serious the situation was in the South since that was "my" area and I had a special interest in that piece of the action.

I decided that in the future I had to be certain before ever again sounding an alarm. I began to appreciate the weaknesses in the evaluation system. Reflecting back to my duties on the Thai desk at Headquarters, in my ignorance I had evaluated reports on the strength of the Thai Communist Party that probably had been as flawed as my own assessment of the situation in the South, and I had found them to be reasonable and accurate. But had they been?

On one occasion the Thai police and military arrested and interrogated more than 200 people in Pattalung Province in mid-South Thailand for presumed involvement with the Communist Party. When a stack of 200 interrogations reached Bangkok, another station officer and I were assigned to try to make some sense of them. The reports reflected the work of untrained interrogators, and any pearls of information were lost in the mountain of verbiage.

For several weeks we worked long, hard hours to isolate

those pearls and to put together one complete picture. As we read and reread the massive reports, we could remember that somewhere in another report we had read a confirming item, but without rereading all of the reports we could not locate the item. We did not card the information, nor did we set up geographic and subject files. We were trying in essence to work with that mass of data without processing it. We were winging it, and the results were terrible — the inchoate mess remained just that. But again I learned a lesson that later I had the opportunity to apply on a massive scale: you could not analyze large amounts of information without careful and adequate preparation.

About this time I came across an example of the use of intelligence to promote the ambitions of one individual. One of the station's most important penetration operations into the Thai Communist Party was run by a case officer I shall call Sam, who had been in Thailand for several years. Sam had the primary responsibility for collecting and recording information on the Thai Communist Party and followed a strict need-to-know policy for anyone seeking information from his files. No one was permitted access to his inner sanctum, a vaulted room within our secure area. Sam's sophisticated deception operation against the Thai Communist Party was done via his principal agent. A former official of the Thai Communist Party, the principal agent supposedly had created a splinter group dedicated to peaceful revolution. Through the splinter group the CIA hoped to divide the Communists and restrain their violence.

The Agency awarded Sam the Medal of Intelligence for his successful deception. However, after Sam left the station, his carefully guarded files were opened for general use, and the new case officer who had replaced Sam began working with the principal agent. The new case officer found that Sam had been more effective deceiving the station than the Communists. His operation was more fantasy than fact. The new case officer dropped the operation and the principal agent.

But the story does not end there. A few years passed, and the CIA again assigned Sam to Thailand. He proposed that the Agency rehire his old principal agent. At the time I worked in the international communism branch at Headquarters. The chief of the Thai desk asked me to evaluate Sam's proposal.

I did so with a vengeance. I recounted the history of the operation and said the agent had no access and probably was a fabricator. (The Thai Communist Party espoused armed revolution as dictated by Asian Communist methodology, and at that time only a fool would openly opt for peaceful revolution, as he would immediately find his motivation questioned.) I predicted disaster if we rehired the principal agent, but he was rehired and authored a series of fabricated intelligence reports. When our enthusiasm for him finally waned, the principal agent took another tack. He wrote a book about CIA activities in Thailand, claiming to reveal, among other things, an agent of the CIA.[2] With this operational disaster one might expect the case officer finally to get his due. Sam, in competition with numerous other officers, was given an assignment to a prime overseas post. He later was named chief of personnel for the East Asia division, where he presumably looked for others with his own unique capabilities.

This, as I was to discover later, was not atypical of Agency personnel policies. But at the time I still felt cases like Sam's and Dave Abbott's were aberrations. To see them otherwise would have required me to rethink my own motivations and justifications. And I wasn't ready to do that. After all, I was happy. I believed in the Agency and our policies in Southeast Asia, which I regarded as somewhere between the Peace Corps and missionary work. I was proud of my family. My four children — two teenage daughters, one ten-year-old and one five-year-old son — after overcoming their initial reluctance to leave their Herndon friends, had adjusted happily to the traditional high school atmosphere at the American-run international school. My wife was enjoying her job as secretary for the Agency. I had no inkling that before this tour ended, everything for me would turn upside down — not because of professional failure, but because of unparalleled success.

Six months into my tour Dave assigned me temporarily to mid-South Thailand where I was to help establish an organization to collate information on the Thai Communist Party. I had been in a provincial capital in the mid-South for two months when one night I suddenly felt an excruciating pain under my right rib cage. The pain was accompanied by diarrhea and weakness. I suspected that my problem was something I had eaten at a restaurant and that the pain would disappear as quickly as it had come. But as the hours passed, I got sicker and weaker.

The next day I was scheduled to go with the governor of the province to sign a construction contract. I had been working on this signing for two months, and I did not want to miss it. That morning I was just able to drag myself up and get dressed and go to the meeting. Afterwards my counterpart Thai officers checked me into the local hospital. They then notified my superiors in Bangkok that I was seriously ill.

The hospital, a small one-story wooden building, lacked most facilities. I was taken to a room that had a bed and a combination Thai toilet and water barrel shower. The bed had a hard, kapok-filled mattress and a musty, holey mosquito net that kept out the only breeze in that sweltering heat while letting in selected hordes of mosquitos. The doctor was pleasant and seemed to know his business, but spoke no English. My interpreter's abilities did not extend into the technical field of medicine, and all I got from him was that my body was under attack by tiny internal bugs. Further than this his English would not go. By this time it did not matter to me, as I was drifting in and out of consciousness and just wanted to be left alone.

After three or four days in a fog, I vaguely perceived that I was to be shipped to Bangkok on the U.S. military's C-54, which made a milk-run stop every Friday. Even in my dazed condition it seemed odd to me that the station, with its own fleet of planes, would allow me to languish in this out-of-the-way place. But my mind could not focus enough to take the necessary initiative to arrange transportation to Bangkok.

Norma was in a panic when she saw me, for my condition had grown quite serious. The American doctor for the official American community met the plane, but his main concern seemed to be the inconvenience of having an ambulance at the airport to pick me up, something the doctor in the South had insisted upon.

When the party arrived at the Seventh Day Adventist Hospital in Bangkok, I was assigned to a room that had neither a toilet nor an air conditioner, a virtual must in the oppressive

Bangkok heat. A Thai-style public toilet was located several doors away, and it was a constant and frequent challenge to use that facility. The diarrhea had not abated, and I had to wait in line with other patients and visitors. Once inside, I found it nearly impossible to squat Thai-style over the hole in the floor, but by careful placement I could brace my back, which kept me from collapsing.

My official doctor and the hospital doctors, all American Seventh Day Adventists, began to squabble over the cause of my condition. Our "Doc" was not sure what I had, while the staff doctors all diagnosed it as an amoebic attack on the liver — which sounded similar to what the doctor in the South had been saying. As the doctors bickered, my condition grew steadily worse. I was so weak that the nurses, when trying to take my temperature, had to prod me to keep me from lapsing off into unconsciousness. After a week of sparring between the doctors, Norma received an urgent message from Doc, who told her my condition was deteriorating and that he was going to perform exploratory surgery right away. Norma arrived at the hospital after the nurses had completed shaving the entire front of me and painting me with a red antiseptic. She looked ready to faint when she entered the room.

As the time scheduled for the operation came and went, we began to question the nurses, who gave noncommittal answers. Some days later a staff doctor told me what had happened. He said the entire staff of doctors had been convinced that I was suffering from an amoebic attack on my liver. Doc, a surgeon, did not agree. He had scheduled the surgery, which, according to the staff doctors, would have killed me. The staff doctors issued an ultimatum: if Doc persisted in his plans to operate, he had to take me to another hospital. Further, if I stayed there, the staff doctors would begin immediate treatment for my condition. Doc finally relented. A staff doctor stuck a long, tube-like needle into my swollen liver and slowly drew out a mass of pus and dead cells. The treatment to kill the amoeba worked, and I started on the several-month-long road to recovery. To this day I suffer from a damaged liver and curse Doc for his incompetence and stubbornness.

While recovering at home, I began to dwell on the way the Agency had bungled my situation. The station's management had allowed me to deteriorate in a small isolated town while its Air America planes flew VIPs around at whim. The doctor for the official American community had totally misdiagnosed my illness. If it hadn't been for the staff doctors at the hospital, I surely would have died. I wondered how much real concern the Agency had for a lifelong employee. As my condition improved, though, my faith in the CIA correspondingly revived. I convinced myself that I had been the victim of special circumstances beyond Agency control and blamed myself in part for not taking a more active role in getting to Bangkok.

Several months after my recovery, I was called to the office of the CIA station executive officer. He and a new deputy chief of station — Dave Abbott had finally left — had assumed the duties of running the day-to-day activities of the station, leaving Rod Johnson, the chief, full time to court the Thais.

The executive officer greeted me with a big smile and a hello and asked me to sit down. After asking about my health, he said, "Ralph, I have been watching your programs lately, and I am most impressed. Rod and I have chosen you to assume a major new responsibility. As you know, AID [the Agency for International Development] has traditionally worked with the 50,000-man national police, but they are incapable of establishing an intelligence-collection program for them. We want you to initiate an intelligence program for the police."

I was dumbfounded. Was this a big put-down, or was it a major new responsibility? I was well aware of the traditional hostility between the CIA and AID, particularly when one tried to horn in on the other's territory. "How does AID feel about this?" I asked.

"The ambassador has given us specific authority to take on this assignment," he said, "and Rey Hill [the local AID chief] concurs. We also reached an agreement with the commander of the police."

A gnawing doubt remained, for in some CIA programs of this type there was a tendency to provide money, jeeps, weapons, equipment, and training to the foreign liaison service. It would take a large staff of American officers to handle such a requirement. "What about support for the police?" I asked.

Approaching the crux of the matter, the executive officer explained, "Oh, you won't have to worry about that. We don't want to get into another logistical operation. We intend for you to piggyback on AID's largesse. If you need any special help, we can come up with a few bucks."

Here was my "Mission Impossible": convert a bunch of unschooled patrolmen into sophisticated intelligence gatherers and do it without money or the authority that comes with it. I could not have asked for a more difficult or challenging assignment.

The first step on Mission Impossible was to locate Colonel Chat Chai (not his real name), the head of the police intelligence office. I called his office and was told that he was on a trip to Pattalung Province, investigating the latest communist incident. The executive officer, who was pushing me to get started, provided a station plane to take me to Pattalung.

The plane landed at the small grass airstrip just outside the town of Pattalung. I piled into a *samlor* — a three-wheel vehicle resembling a bike in front with a two-seat chair behind — and we took off. My bulk and the low hills were just about all the driver could cope with, but we soon entered Pattalung, which was as neat as a pin and unusually quiet. It reminded me of a small, sleepy southern U.S. town. The lawns were trimmed and bordered with large whitewashed stones. Except for a jeep or two there were no vehicles other than *samlors*. I wondered how a communist insurgency could take root in such a serene setting.

We pulled up at the open-fronted police station, and I went in to ask the desk sergeant about Colonel Chat Chai. He said the colonel had left that morning for Had Yai, a city further south. The sergeant gave me directions for taking a bus to Had Yai and pointed out the location of the bus station, a wide spot in the road.

After a long wait the bus appeared, or rather chugged, snorted, rocked, and rolled into sight. And what a sight! Its roof was loaded with pigs and chickens in bamboo cages, bundles of the locally famous rambutan fruit, large sacks of rice, and an assortment of bags and ratty suitcases that mushroomed out over the top of the bus, which seemed to defy the law of gravity by not tipping over under the weight of that top-heavy load. With some trepidation I boarded and squeezed my way back onto one of the hard wooden benches at the rear. My six-foot-plus frame could not fit in the space between the benches, so I found an aisle seat where my legs could hang out. Farmers, both men and women, jammed the bus. The women, some of them chewing the unattractive red betel nut, wore traditional farm garb — waist-high, wrap-around sarongs and long-sleeved blouses. Most had removed the conical straw hats that in the fields protected them from the hot sun. The men wore clothing that was stained from their labors. The all-purpose *pakama*, a large rectangular cotton piece of material, usually with a large checkered design, was in general use. It was folded diaper fashion to serve as shorts; it was wound around the head as a turban, and it was used to carry lunches.

After several attempts the driver got the motor started. The bus lurched, coughed, lurched, coughed, wheezed, and took off. Within the next half hour the driver stopped three times. It appeared the driver served also as a courier, as he stopped and passed on messages, or sometimes picked up passengers on the road. These passengers were usually accompanied by agricultural produce or animals, and each stop entailed the long ritual of unloading, loading, and balancing the load. With the overhead load getting bulkier, noisier and more aromatic, my sense of adventure waned. After many hours of start-and-stop driving, we arrived at Had Yai. I booked a hotel room, went out and bought two quart-sized bottles of Thai Singha beer — with a potency close to that of wine — returned to the room, consumed the beer, and dropped off into a thankful mist of sleep.

The next day I found Colonel Chat Chai. He was short even by Thai standards, was in his early forties, and had a round, almost swollen face. As I soon discovered, he had a full complement of personality quirks. He was cantankerous, irascible, and outspoken, but he was also competent, hardworking, and honest. His directness undoubtedly was a liability in Thai society, which seemed to run on extreme politeness, face-saving, indirectness, dropped hints, and circumlocutory evasions. In talks with most Thai officials you had to plumb for the hidden meaning behind the polite words. Not so with Colonel Chat Chai. He said what he thought straight out.

However, to lessen the impact of his directness, he giggled after virtually every statement.

We went to an outdoor reception area of a local hotel to conduct our talk in privacy. I outlined our proposal for him and told him that his commander had agreed to the plan. Colonel Chat Chai obviously had not yet received word from his superiors and greeted my statements with giggles and questioning looks. I suggested as a first step for our joint program that he tell me about the police intelligence structure, its facilities and procedures. This really threw him. Here was a stranger, a foreigner yet, asking a professional intelligence man to reveal his organization's most closely held secrets.

"Why should I tell you this, hea, hea, hea?" he asked. "No one has told me about the plan."

I appreciated his situation, so I explained how the Agency worked with other Thai services. He asked many questions and my informed responses seemed to convince him that I was who I claimed to be and that I knew a lot about the other Thai intelligence organizations. He gradually began to loosen up, particularly after I said that I was not interested in the names of intelligence agents but instead needed general information such as his office procedures, staffing, training, and file holdings.

Slowly and with increasing detail he began to outline the functions of the police intelligence office. It consisted of another colonel and several enlisted men, and primarily recorded and filed reports on communism. The enlisted men received no intelligence training and knew little about Communist organizational procedures. His office had no real charter to gather intelligence aggressively.

I asked how soon he would be returning to Bangkok, where I could visit his office and we could continue our discussions.

"I must first finish my work here," he said. "Then I must get a travel chit for the train to Bangkok, hea, hea, hea. I should arrive in Bangkok in a week or so, hea, hea, hea."

I knew the executive officer would consider such a delay intolerable, so I offered to pay for a plane ticket if he would fly back with me the next day. At this point Colonel Chat Chai began to appreciate the benefits of working with the Agency. "You can buy my ticket, hea, hea, hea?"

I did not want to leave him with the impression that what I was proposing was illegal or could in any way be considered a personal gift or bribe, so I said, "It is most important that we get started immediately. I assure you that I have authority to buy your ticket and that I will make a full accounting to the appropriate authorities."

Later a tour of the police headquarters intelligence facilities convinced me that I could not expect to turn the police into a traditional intelligence agency even if it were desirable to do so. A memorandum I wrote outlined the deficiencies of the police's intelligence-collection program and suggested development of a pilot effort to test various approaches using the police as intelligence gatherers. At the same time I began to read available literature on other intelligence-counterinsurgency programs. I came across one small reference that caught my eye — a "mailbox" operation that had some success in the British fight against the communist insurgency in Malaya. The Malayan mailbox operation was the essence of simplicity. A heavy steel, locked box with a slot for letters was anchored in a problem village. The people in the village were encouraged to drop into the box anonymous written tips identifying communists. The box was emptied daily, and through this simple mechanism the British learned a great deal about communist activity in isolated hamlets.

The operation gave the villagers a chance to inform on communists without being subjected to reprisals. It gave the government forces access to previously unavailable information. The operation did have its drawbacks — it was difficult to confirm the information, and success depended on a villager working up the necessary courage and motivation to inform. However, it had potential, and this germ of an idea I was later to develop into a full-scale, effective intelligence-counterinsurgency operation.

As a first step, Colonel Chat Chai and I traveled throughout the Northeast talking to provincial governors, police and military commanders, American advisers, and officials at the district level (comparable to an American county). At each stop we looked into file holdings and methods of reporting information, and received briefings on the status of the communist movement.

When we returned to Bangkok, I put together a tentative

proposal that we conduct an intensified intelligence-collection operation in one district. In that small, defined area we could in a relatively short time test various theories and methods. We could get a better idea of general communist activity and plan more effective ways to collect information. If any one method proved successful, we would use it in an expanded effort later.

I noted in the proposal that vagueness, incompleteness, and incident reporting seemed typical of current intelligence. Officials often had a visceral feeling about the nature of communist activity, but they could not adequately explain why the local people cooperated actively or passively in communist killings, ambushes, or other incidents. The shifting frequency and locales of such incidents, which had begun about 1963, conveyed the impression that something was going on, but no one seemed to know exactly what.

Agency reporting at the time claimed that the armed communist movement was confined primarily to the mountainous provinces of Northeast Thailand. There were, according to the Agency, only a few armed communists in South and North Thailand, and no more than 2,500 to 4,000 in all of Thailand. The armed guerrilla bands, so it was claimed, hid out in the rugged highland areas of the Phu Phan mountain range, and they would occasionally come down to the lowlands in search of rice, money, and recruits. CIA reporting insisted that the communists had no popular support and that they had to use terrorist tactics to force the peasants to cooperate with them.

My proposal made the rounds of Thai and American authorities in Bangkok. After receiving the necessary approvals, Colonel Chat Chai and I took the proposal to a Northeast province where we hoped to begin our work. The Thai governor of the province enthusiastically approved the idea and assigned some of his best people to work with us. During our first visit we had identified one district as a site for the pilot project. The district had a nascent but growing insurgency. The *nai amphur* of the district (somewhat comparable to a sheriff) was a problem. His reputation reached all the way back to Bangkok — a reputation he earned killing suspected communists "trying to escape." The refugee Vietnamese community particularly feared this quick-triggered man.

The deputy *nai amphur*, Lieutenant Somboon (not his real name), was *sui generis*. In my entire career I had never met a man who possessed such a remarkable intuitive feel for the esoteric art of intelligence gathering. He could penetrate the heart of the matter and write extensive, well-organized reports. At 30 years old, he was a handsome, tireless man, whom people liked and confided in. He was a graduate in political science from Thailand's major university, Chulalongkorn, and spoke good English, but used several jarring phrases. I could never bring myself to embarrass him by correcting the occasional "I don't sure" and its opposite "Do you sure?" that punctuated his conversation. This cosmopolitan Thai official had probably been assigned to the isolated Northeast to serve as a counterfoil to the *nai amphur* and as the governor's eyes and ears in the troubled district.

Somboon was over-qualified for his job as deputy *nai amphur* and was eager to move upward. When Colonel Chat Chai and I had toured the province earlier, he had made himself available and seemed eager to cooperate. Both the colonel and I had been impressed with him and had chosen his district for the trial project to make use of his special abilities.

We ran a trial project attempting the gamut of intelligence-gathering techniques. The traditional approach of recruiting agents did not work. It consumed too much time, resulted in reports of doubtful accuracy, and proved to be no way to try to understand a burgeoning communist insurgency. The expanded "mailbox" operation with Lieutenant Somboon as the team leader achieved good results but also revealed some weaknesses. After several days of discussion among Lieutenant Somboon, Colonel Chat Chai and me, we developed the *modus operandi* for the next team operation, called a district survey. Over the next year we and the team ran four such surveys with dramatic results.

The surveys were designed around an expanded concept of the "mailbox" operation: go into the villages and get the information directly from the affected villagers, but do this in as organized and active a way as possible. To begin the operation, Colonel Chat Chai gleaned the most valuable information on the selected district from Thai organizations at all levels — the provincial police, the *nai amphur*'s office, the special police, the Joint Security Centers, the provincial Civilian,

Police, Military (CPM), the military base called CPM-1, and the Communist Suppression Operations Command in Bangkok. I gathered all information on that district from the various station file systems. The information was carded by name, and reports were filed by village. Using all these files, I made a study to determine the area of concentration of the recent communist activity, and Colonel Chat Chai and I prepared, in consultation with local officials, a schedule for work in the district. I then wrote a situation report for every village to be visited and attached a list of persons reportedly involved in either pro-government or pro-communist activity.

While this was going on, the governor gathered a team of 25 of the best people in his province — provincial police officers, enlisted men, a few military officers, deputy *nai amphurs*, several administrators, and a high-ranking educator. Team members had career status in existing government organizations; the Agency did not create, finance, or sponsor a new bureaucratic structure. They continued to be paid by and remained a part of their parent organizations. This was rare in the history of Agency support to liaison structures. We collected intelligence on the cheap. The best officials in the province worked for us, yet we did not give away vehicles, radios, salaries, or uniforms.

For two weeks we trained the 25-man team in questioning and interrogation, the basics of communism (such as we knew them), and public relations. Public relations training stressed the necessity of maintaining the good will of the people. During a survey a problem developed in this area. A team member raped a girl he was supposed to question. Lieutenant Somboon sent the man packing. The team took up a collection that amounted to a year's income for a rural family and presented it and a formal apology to the girl and her family.

We also provided training in report writing to meet the needs of the survey. Each report of more than basic data consisted of a summary paragraph and pre-selected subject paragraphs on Communist activity; i.e., front groups, weapons and ammunition, propaganda and indoctrination, recruitment, security, guerrilla groups and leaders, campsite locations, training, and conclusions and recommendations.

Before further describing the surveys, I should note that

there was an Orwellian big-brother-is-watching concept inherent in the process we developed. Though it distresses me now, at the time it did not. I regarded communists as ruthless killers out to coerce people to join them and kill those who did not. I regarded the survey as a perfectly legitimate way to halt the spread of the cancerous communist growth while simultaneously winning the people back to the Thai government. After all, other counterinsurgency methods in use at the time included boiling suspects in oil, a practice in which one commander was known to engage; shooting suspects, as the *nai amphur* had done; other forms of torture; as well as our own free-fire zones in Vietnam. Compared to these, I figured our operation was benign.

Our first complete survey began with the governor's 25-man team, Colonel Chat Chai, another colonel of the police intelligence service, myself and four translator-interpreters traveling in several jeeps, land rovers, and an open-backed truck to the district seat. The "downtown" of this village at the intersection of two dusty paths consisted of a few two-story buildings with open-front stores downstairs and quarters for the proprietors above. At high noon the only traffic in town was a yoke of oxen hauling a load of rice and several stooped farm women carrying buckets of water on poles across their shoulders.

The village's small, wooden-framed, thatch-roofed houses were open to allow maximum air flow in the stifling heat. They sat on stilts, and water buffaloes, pigs, and chickens took refuge in the shade underneath.

On the first day Lieutenant Somboon, Colonel Chat Chai, and I visited the village headman at his home to explain our purpose and to get his cooperation. The headman, dressed in loose-fitting, pajama-like trousers and a Western shirt, was impressed by the high-ranking visitors. He was extremely polite, although he had some trouble comprehending what was happening and particularly why an American was involved. While we sat on a straw mat on the wooden floor discussing our work, a servant brought us weak tea. The headman agreed to call a meeting of the townspeople that night at the *sala glang*, the central meeting area.

When the villagers had gathered that night, Lieutenant Somboon announced, "We have come here to help you people free yourselves from the nuisance of the jungle soldiers [the name given to the Communists]. The jungle soldiers come into your village, take your rice and money, and preach about the evils of our government. They say that the government oppresses you with taxes, but they don't explain what your government does with that money. Last year in this village the government collected only a few thousand *baht*, and yet this sum is less than the annual salary of the teacher the government provides to educate your children, but what do the jungle soldiers do for you?"

Lieutenant Somboon's speech was designed to counter the specific propaganda themes that the Communists used in this village, as determined during our research. "I and my group of government officials have come here to learn the problems of you villagers," explained Lieutenant Somboon, "especially problems caused by the jungle soldiers. To help us in this task, we want to talk to each person to learn what is happening and how best we can help you. We will talk privately to each of you so that the jungle soldiers cannot know what is being said. Everything you tell us we will keep in strictest confidence. Tomorrow we will begin visiting each home. Thank you for your cooperation and for coming here this evening."

The next day the team fanned out through the village with each member questioning one person. They would set up just about anywhere — on tree stumps, in a clearing, sitting on high mounds near the houses, but always ensuring that the interviews were conducted out of hearing range of other people.

If the person being questioned was an ordinary villager, the team member would ask if the subject had heard of Communist front groups such as the Farmers' Liberation Association (FLA), jungle soldiers, or others. The person was asked about any unusual events that had occurred in the village. The interviewer wrote down any significant information in a notebook he carried with him and later prepared a written report.

When questioning a suspected or known Communist, the session was more of a confrontation. We had learned during the trial project that the Communists organized three-man cells of what they called the Farmers' Liberation Association. Once the team got the first confession from a member of the

FLA, this was the break it needed. A confessed member of the three-man FLA cell had to name the other members of the cell, the person who had recruited him, and down the line. With this information the team members would interrogate the other named cell members. The interrogators would be able to tell the other cell members the most specific details about their Communist associations — their Communist aliases, the man who had recruited them, the names of the other two people in their cell. The subject was advised that he must cooperate to qualify for government mercy. If he did, he would be forgiven.

With a confession from a member of the FLA, the interviewer would prepare a report of all names, aliases, and other information and pass the report on to Lieutenant Somboon. He in turn would read the reports to look for leads and contradictions and then pass them on to the translators, who put them into English for me. I also looked for leads and contradictions that could help break down the resistance of some of the subjects. For instance, one person claimed that he and his friend Chalong had gone fishing one night, but Chalong had said that he had stayed home. The team members used this disparity and finally wrung confessions from the two friends. In fact, both had gone together to a Communist indoctrination session at a nearby guerrilla camp.

The team approached various confessed members of the FLA to serve as agents for the government. Our purpose in doing this was twofold. First, we needed agents in the organization, and second, we anticipated that some of them would inform their Communist superiors about the recruitment. We did not try to recruit others because we hoped that when they talked with their Communist superiors about their interviews and did not mention a recruitment attempt, they would come under suspicion. By this tactic we hoped to sow dissension in the heretofore solid ranks of the Communists.

In this first village one of the leading Communists refused to admit his role. Never one to be thwarted, Lieutenant Somboon told the man if he did not confess by a certain time his father would be shot. Two-way radio walkie-talkies were set up between Somboon and the "executioners." When the time passed with no confession, Somboon ordered the "execution" to be carried out. Over the radio the suspect could hear the orders to shoot, the shots, and a loud moaning. A man shouted over the radio that the father was only wounded, but quick medical attention could save his life. Somboon said, "No, let him die." Finally the suspect relented and admitted that he was a leading member of the village's Farmers' Liberation Association. Somboon yelled over the radio to rush the injured man to the doctor. After the suspect made a full confession, Somboon explained the ruse was necessary for the man's own good.

Shortly thereafter, the wife of a leading Communist refused to admit her husband's membership in the FLA. She said her husband was out of town looking for work. Somboon accused her of lying and said he was going to have her child killed if she did not cooperate. Somboon later told me that he believed she herself was a hard-line Communist because she never budged or showed a flicker of emotion.

In that same village a young man in his late teens, after being confronted with evidence of his membership in the FLA, finally confessed. He broke down and cried that he was terribly ashamed, that he was a good Buddhist, but the Communists had tricked him. He did not know what his parents would think. He apparently could not live with the guilt. That night he hanged himself.

I was not particularly disturbed by those violations of human rights, as I felt we were fighting the hated communists and that the ends justified the means.

During the questioning phase of the operation the two Thai police colonels, the four translators, and I moved into the local police commander's rural Thai house. The two colonels and the male translator bunked in a large dormitory-like room. The three female translators had the main bedroom, while I slept in an enclosed lean-to adjacent to the open eating area. My "room" was just big enough for a cot and my suitcase. There were no fans, but gaps between the wooden slats let in any slight breeze. Our bathing facilities consisted of a tin-enclosed area containing a large, water-filled, earthen urn. To shower, you had to dip into the urn with a small pan and pour that water over yourself.

The management team — the two colonels, the translators, and I — set up an office in a large, wooden, barn-like structure that served as the village's central meeting place. We worked there on wooden folding chairs and benches seven days a week for three months. The constant eating, working, and living together created predictable tensions. Two of the males paired off with two of the females, creating another set of problems. To add to these strains, Colonel Chat Chai occasionally brought his typewriter back to the house, where he would type until dawn, each strike of a key sending shock waves up my spine.

To escape the pressure, including the constant strain of trying to cope with the idiomatic Thai being spoken, each evening I would take a long walk. These strolls down the dusty paths helped me to relax and gave me a chance to appreciate the beauty of rural Thailand. Occasionally my route took me by the small river where the Thais bathed and did their laundry, evoking in me yearnings for a more peaceful way of life.

The work in the village had an unexpected result, exploding the insurgency as a needle explodes a balloon. For once the secrecy and security behind which the Communists had organized were destroyed, the movement in that village died, at least for the time being. In that village the leader of one of the 40-man cell structures of the Farmers' Liberation Association was confronted with knowledge of his guilt. Subjected to three days of questioning and discussions of the government's "good work," he became convinced that the Communists had duped him. He then helped the team get confessions from his subordinates in the FLA and joined the government's Volunteer Defense Corps.

The U.S. government at the time was sponsoring in Northeast Thailand two programs it had adopted from similar efforts in Vietnam — Census Aspiration Cadre and People's Action Teams. The census cadres were trained in census taking and supposedly could determine the political leanings of villagers by saying they were there to listen to problems and grievances against the government. Census cadres sent frequent reports to their headquarters naming villagers as either pro-government or pro-communist. This American-supported program in both Vietnam and Thailand proved to be at best worthless and at worst a way for Communists to get on an American payroll and feed us a mass of contrived information. For example, Lieutenant Somboon discovered that the census cadre in the first village we surveyed was a long-standing member of the Communist Party of Thailand and the leader of an extensive FLA structure. The man was arrested and jailed.

People's Action Teams were small groups of locally recruited villagers who were trained and armed to assist the village and protect it from the Communists. At this early stage the teams did seem to restrict the movement of the Communists. For instance, in this village and several others later on, the farmers who confessed to being members of the FLA refused to remain in their homes because they claimed the Communists would kill anyone who had cooperated with our survey team. Although the interviews had been conducted out of hearing range, other villagers had observed the farmers demonstrating the weapons firing positions taught by the Communists. As a result, Lieutenant Somboon was informed that 70 people had left the village when our survey team departed. I arranged to have a People's Action Team unit stationed in the village, and the people returned. Later we received reports that all active cooperation with the Communists in that village had ceased.

Our survey team had come to this district just after a unit from the CPM-1 base had conducted a month-long military sweep, looking for armed bands of insurgents. The military patrols had raced through the rice paddies in half-track personnel carriers and tanks, tearing up the fields, and angry, untrained military interrogators with no knowledge of the area had beaten the local farmers. The little information they got had not been collated or analyzed. It had been a typical beat-'em-down-with-hardware type of operation which had succeeded in nothing but earning the enmity of the villagers and swelling the number of volunteers into the Communist ranks. In comparison, our survey team obtained confessions from more than 500 village-based FLA members. We also learned the location of various guerrilla campsites, and one time — although this was not part of our mission — the team tried to oust the guerrillas from their camp. The team was not well-armed, and guerrillas out-fought them, killing one member of the team.

Upon completion of the three-month survey operation in 10 villages, I had all the interview statements translated and copies filed by village and subject paragraphs. All cell members and guerrillas were entered on 3x5 index cards that gave a brief synopsis of the information and the date and file location of the complete interview form. In one case we had more than 20 multiple-entry cards on a political organizing cadre. Security forces using this information, including his group's recognition signals, ambushed the group and killed the cadre.

Using all the index cards and files, I wrote a final report. I prepared name lists of cell members, including their aliases, by village. In this district the list contained the names of more than 500 persons. Those 500 cell members did not appear anywhere in Agency reporting at that time. The CIA estimated there were 2,500 to 4,000 Communists in all of Thailand. But our surveys showed the Communists probably had that many adherents in Sakorn Nakorn Province alone.

We disseminated the final report to American and Thai intelligence organizations. Praise came back immediately. The Agency's Directorate for Intelligence gave the report the highest rating in all six of its grading categories. The State Department rated it the same. The Far East division noted its unique contribution. The Bangkok counterinsurgency command rated police collection efforts tops in intelligence for that month and for every month in which a survey report was produced. Thai Deputy Prime Minister Praphat Charusathien issued a unit award to the team. General Saiyut Kerdpol, the day-to-day commander of the Communist Suppression Operations Command, issued official praise and traveled to the province to learn about the surveys.

Bo Daeng, the governor of the province, was ecstatic. Even though he was a native of the province and had lived there all his life, he said he had no idea what the communists were doing until he read our reports. The American consul in Udorn, Al Francis (who later served as Ambassador Graham Martin's top aide in Vietnam), began spending days at my office avidly reading the reports. Lastly, my own assessment. I had worked in intelligence for 15 years. In all that time I had dealt in vague, partial, shifting, incomplete, fragmentary intelligence that was part of an unknown total picture. The survey reports, I felt, changed all that. They were complete, accurate, detailed, and of excellent quality.

After the survey operation the chief of station, Rod Johnson, called me to Bangkok for a meeting. When I entered his office, he had with him several other of the top station officers, including my branch chief. "Hello, Ralph," said Johnson. This was the first time he had ever used my correct name. For years he had called me Bob. "You old rascal, you. You really did a job up there. How in the hell is everything going?"

He continued, "I want you to know just how pleased everyone is with the results you've accomplished. Yesterday Saiyut [General Saiyut Kerdpol, the operating head of the Communist Suppression Operations Command] told me he had been up there to see you. He said you and Colonel Chat Chai have really turned things around and that Governor Bo Daeng is extremely pleased with your work."

Rod went on in this vein for some time, and the other officials chimed in with their praise. He then said, "You've done such a good job that I plan to assign you PCS [permanent change of station] to that province. If you accept, you'll be the new officer-in-charge of other CIA officers stationed in the province." [One 27-word sentence deleted.]

He need not have bothered with the snow job. I had never in my career seen such dramatic results as we had achieved. The chief would have had a hard time talking me out of continuing the program. I accepted his offer at once.

I worried that the permanent transfer to the Northeast would disrupt my family life, as Norma and the children would have to stay in Bangkok near the international school. I felt, however, the momentum, the career potential, the job satisfaction, the destruction of the hated communist movement, and the benefits to my country all outweighed the problem of family separation.

As it turned out, my older daughter and older son were able to spend several months with me in the province during the school vacation. By that time I had rented an American-style house and had a maid-cook. I felt they would benefit from having the opportunity to see a different aspect of life in a foreign country as well as a chance to see their father at work.

When I returned to the Northeast, we immediately began a second survey with about 50 percent new team members replacing the others, who had to return to their established jobs. The governor had appointed Lieutenant Somboon as his aide, and in that capacity he was to lead this and three more district surveys over the next year. The second survey culminated in a massive phone book-sized final report. This time the management team stayed away from the villages. The first village of the first survey had taught us that it was extremely bad public relations for an American to be seen associated with the operation. The Communists constantly harped on the theme that the Praphat-Thanom clique were running dogs of the American imperialists. My presence with the team lent credence to that story and from that point on, the two colonels, the translators, and I moved to the district seat or stayed in the provincial capital while couriers brought the interrogation reports to us and carried back my follow-up suggestions to Lieutenant Somboon.

Unfortunately, not all American-sponsored programs took this unobtrusive approach, and the impression left on the Thai peasants was not always good. For example, one day a case officer for the People's Action Teams and the Census Aspiration Teams took the monthly payroll directly to the *nai amphur*, who was then to disburse the funds to the individual team members. The bad roads and the lack of security caused by Communist incidents forced the case officer to travel via a station helicopter. The *nai amphur* was holding a combined meeting and festival attended by hundreds of villagers. Our men in the helicopter landed and in front of all those people handed the *nai amphur* stacks of the bright red Thai *baht* — money. The Communists could not have asked for more graphic proof of what they had been saying.

In mid-summer 1967 I received a cable from the acting chief of station. He noted that my tour was scheduled to end in October 1967 but that he and Thai counterinsurgency officials wanted me to sign up for a new two-year tour to head the survey program on a nationwide scale. The new tour would have to be approved by Headquarters, the cable said, but that would be absolutely no problem.

His request was a great thrill. It was just what I had hoped and prayed for. I immediately sat down and composed a cable accepting the offer.

A few weeks later, in about August 1967, William Colby, then chief of the Far East division, came to the province for a day of briefings. I picked him up at the airport. Dressed in khaki, Colby was his usual calm, concerned self. We drove to the CPM-1 base, where he received a short briefing. We then went to another location for a briefing by American and Thai personnel associated with the People's Action Team and Census Aspiration programs. Since I felt so strongly about our work, I reserved the rest of Colby's day for briefings on the district surveys.

I first led him on a tour of the office and showed him the several file cabinets full of reports and interrogation statements. I explained the procedures of the survey and then outlined my general conclusions, including my doubts about previous Agency reporting which said that the Communists did not have the support of the local people and that they forced people to support them with threats and terrorism.

"Such a picture is inaccurate," I told Colby, who just sat there and didn't bat an eye. "We have found that the Communists concentrate the majority, almost the entirety, of their time winning the cooperation of the peasants. Take this village," I said, pointing to the map. "The MMU [Masses Mobilization Unit] of the Thai Communist Party sent two members into the village. They said they were looking for work. For three months they just hung around helping people and making friends. Quietly, however, they were assessing the class structure of the villagers and finding out who had grievances against the government. After three months they reported to their parent MMU unit that the village was ripe for revolution and received approval to proceed to the next phase.

"These two then began to criticize the government, saying the Praphat-Thanom clique were nothing but running dogs of the Americans who support the rich people and landowners against the poor peasants who are the vast majority of the Thai people. The two MMU cadre identified as their first recruit a poor young man who was married and had a child and was angry at the government. He was recruited into the Farmers' Liberation Association."

Colby was listening, but still said nothing. I told him about numerous documents we had found that outlined the goals and beliefs of the FLA. These called for the Thai Communist Party to expel the imperialists, to overthrow the fascist dictatorship, to achieve national independence through armed struggle. Their plan was first to build base areas in the rural parts of the country (some 80 percent of the population were farmers), then to encircle and capture the cities step by step.

Colby still did not respond at all.

"Once they had the first recruit in the village," I continued, "they went after two more and then formed the three into the first cell of the FLA. These three were led out to concealed sites where members of the MMU attached to local guerrilla units indoctrinated them and slowly began to introduce them to a simplified version of the Marxist class struggle. They told the three recruits that the Communists represented the poor people and would lead them in overthrowing the oppressors and setting up a real people's government. Each of the three was then asked to recruit three more people, and the effort spread like a cancer until virtually every man, woman, and child was recruited into some sort of organized revolutionary structure. The local guerrilla units also carried out minor terrorist incidents that were announced in the indoctrination sessions to show the ability of the Communists to fight the government."

At this point I explained that the Thai government's reaction to the terrorism — sending in brutal armed units to beat innocent people — only created an atmosphere of hate that the Communists were able to exploit. The big difference between our district surveys and past government counterinsurgency programs, I explained, was that instead of using brute force we had used our intelligence to penetrate the Communists' crucial shield of secrecy and had thereby effectively crushed their movement. Our work and follow-up actions by the governor's staff seemed to have completely reversed Communist organizational successes. Everything was going fine, the intelligence was flowing in, the insurgency was being destroyed, and the future was looking good.

But I went on to say that what was happening in that village was happening in all 30 villages we had surveyed and was no doubt happening in every village in Thailand where the Communists were organizing. The pattern, which I was not yet aware of and therefore could not tell Colby, was that once a village was fully organized, the most active FLA members became candidates for membership in the Communist Party and a village militia was established along with a provisional government that replaced the authority of the national government. From the militia a few people were drawn off to become full-time guerrillas. The movement would then be expanded to include a regional force and finally a full-time regular army unit. When a number of villages in one area were organized and linked up, they would form what the Communists called a base area — a region where most all villages were united into one complete, active, dedicated revolutionary structure.

Although I did not then know that the early stages of this plan were being followed, it seemed clear to me from our surveys that Communist organizing was well under way in Thailand and undoubtedly in South Vietnam as well. The most alarming part of it, I told Colby, was that previous Agency intelligence had failed to report any of this widespread Communist activity. It had instead reported that there were only a few thousand Communist guerrillas in the mountains who commanded no support from the people.

Colby seemed puzzled by my presentation. I had never seen him at a loss for words before. He looked at the ground, he looked everywhere. Finally he looked at me and said quietly, "We always seem to be losing."

I expected congratulations and for him to rush out and push for immediate expansion of the survey operations into other provinces. What I didn't expect was this non-response. I was shocked. I had presented my best case, and he could say nothing other than, "We always seem to be losing." What in the hell did he mean by that? Thinking about it later, I realized that Colby was probably weighing the broader ramifications of my survey information.

An entourage of jeeps and land rovers escorted Colby back to the airport. He rode with me, but I was too puzzled and concerned by his response to participate in any conversation. Another American, a junior officer, babbled on as we drove.

Two months later, in October 1967, the chief of station summoned me. He was alone when I entered his office and not at all his usual back-slapping self. He read me a dispatch that the station had received from Headquarters giving my next assignment as branch chief of liaison operations in Taiwan, the same branch I had worked for on a prior tour. This assignment

was a real plum. It would put me into the management channel, ensuring rapid promotions and even better future assignments. Taiwan was the Playboy Club of the Far East division,
and if I wanted to go that route, it was open. Taiwan also had
a good American school, good housing, excellent extra pay.
Everything about the job was great — except that I did not
want it.

I told Rod Johnson about the recent work of the surveys,
the cable I had received from the acting chief while Rod had
been in Headquarters, and my positive response. I pulled out
the Directorate for Intelligence rating sheet, told him that the
State Department had rated the survey reports the same, and
said, "We are beating the bastards. We break through their
secrecy and they can't survive without it."

Rod slowly turned the rating sheet over in his hand. He
did not need to read it. He knew what it said. He looked up
at me and asked, "How soon can you get out of here?"

I was momentarily too stunned to reply. I finally began
to calculate what had to be done to wind up my affairs and
replied, "I'm just finishing another survey report, which will
take a few more weeks to write. The team has just gone into
another district and will be there three months, so someone
will have to manage that aspect."

Rod said that after this survey was completed there
would be no one to handle them, so the program would be
ended. "Finish up as soon as possible," he said, "but I want
you out of here in three weeks. Goodbye."

I traveled back to the province in a fog of angry disbelief,
trying to figure out what was happening. How could the
Agency let such a program die? It produced the highest-rated
intelligence, and I thought it destroyed the insurgency. It did
all of this at virtually no cost. What in the hell was going on?
Could it be that Colby and the chief did not want the surveys
to confirm something they already knew?

The American consul stationed in Udorn, who frequently had come to my office to read the survey reports, learned
of the decision to reassign me and to cancel the surveys. He
reacted angrily and traveled to Bangkok several times to try to
change Johnson's mind. The governor of the province said this
was intolerable and sent several cables to Johnson asking that
I be allowed to remain. In fact, when my replacement showed

up, the governor refused to meet him. General Saiyut Kerdpol also made entreaties to Johnson — all to no avail.

During those last confused weeks I continued to try to figure out what had happened. I paced back and forth, going over and over in my mind the events leading up to my dismissal. Had I offended someone? If so, I was not aware of it. But if I had, why not dismiss me and continue the surveys? Had Colby not understood all we had achieved? This seemed impossible. During the entire preceding year we had received glowing reports from Colby's Far East division, so he must have known.

I agonized day and night while enduring a series of very sad farewell parties thrown by the governor, the commander of the CPM-1, other Americans, and the Thai office staff. The office staff and I had developed an extremely good working relationship and they all believed in the work. Their tears at my departure burned me to the quick. Try as I might, I just could not understand what had happened. It was only years later that the truth slowly began to dawn on me: while the survey revelations demonstrated the strategy and composition of an Asian rural revolution and produced a method to contain it in Thailand, the opposite was true in Vietnam — the surveys would have shown there that the communists could not be defeated.

9.
HEADQUARTERS:
GHOSTS IN THE HALLS

WHEN I arrived back at Headquarters from Thailand in late 1967 to begin processing for my new assignment as branch chief on Taiwan, I found out that the assignment had been cancelled. [One 22-word sentence deleted.] I realized that I had been set up by Rod Johnson and Dave Abbott. The dispatch offering me the job of branch chief on Taiwan was a ruse to get me out of Thailand. When it didn't work, Johnson had just told me to go. This deception was an added shock to my already confused state of mind, and I set out to "walk the halls" to look for another assignment. I was apathetic, and in light of all that had happened I was having a difficult time justifying my previously idealistic view of the Agency.

One day the head of China activities offered me a desk job of no real import. I didn't give a damn about the job. My prior tours with China activities indicated that everything there was more shadow than substance. But I was too demoralized to refuse.

The essential personality characteristic necessary to survive the daily minutiae of China activities was patience. Things happened at a snail's pace. You had to slowly digest, regurgitate, and re-digest unimportant information, while pretending to be enthralled by the process. You had to defend vehemently your position on trivia. You had to play the game.

With another case officer I shared an office that had a view of the American flag waving outside. I spent a lot of my time with my feet propped up on the desk looking out the window, ruminating about the Agency, the country, the flag, and what it all meant. I had plenty of time to kill, and so did a lot of others in the same boat. Frequent office bull sessions

117

reminded me of my sophomore days at Notre Dame. Sometimes a few of us would continue the discussions on a coffee break in the cafeteria. This was good for killing about an hour. Lunch entailed a trip to the cafeteria or to nearby McLean, culminating with a long stroll around the Headquarters building that used up at least another hour and a half.

The corridors in China activities gave you the feeling that time had stopped. Ghosts of case officers past roamed the halls, carrying pieces of paper that gave purpose to their eerie missions. The noon hour found the corridors totally empty except for a lone secretary or a true believer.

But every day did bring a few cables and dispatches from China units scattered around the world. Most such documents noted the efforts of the case officers to spot and assess people with access to Chinese officials serving overseas.[1] China activities had begun to realize the near impossibility of recruiting a Chinese official to be our spy. To keep busy and to show progress, the Agency had now developed programs to recruit contacts of these officials.

At one point I was given the task of trying to plan how to recruit a member of the Chinese diplomatic installation. Here I was, thousands of miles away, sitting in my chair, gazing lazily out the window at the flag, planning the best way to contact and assess the target individual. I half-heartedly played the game and set forth my new plan in a dispatch to the field station. This plan born in my not-very-fertile imagination was full of flaws. However, the deputy desk chief carefully considered it for a week or so and then the desk chief did the same. Then I was called in. They were not quite sure the plan would work as outlined, so we held a series of discussions, modified the plan, and sent it forward in great solemnity for consideration by the deputy chief and chief of China activities. After appropriate consideration and delay, they held a series of discussions with my desk chief. He brought the dispatch back to me for incorporation of their ideas. I sent the reworked dispatch back through the same channels and the chief of China activities thankfully, after further thought, decided that the time was not right to attempt the recruitment.

Some people, however, regarded operations against China as a great struggle to oppose the Communist madman Mao Tsetung. We were the guys in the white hats chasing — to recruit as our agents — the guys in the black hats, the Chinese Communists. We tried to recruit them on planes, in toilets, in diplomatic talks, anywhere. But the bad guys never seemed to appreciate that they were the bad and we were the good. We lost, they won. Several hundred case officers scattered throughout the world backed up by a timeless Headquarters bureaucracy pondered and schemed how to recruit that one Chinese official.

If you stayed long enough in China activities, you experienced a sense of *déjà vu*. The same things happened year after year. A top official of China activities would develop a brilliant new plan on how to recruit a Chinese Communist. This plan invigorated everyone, and dispatches were sent to all field installations ordering implementation of the idea. The field case officers, caught up in the excitement, urgently acted to put the plan into effect. After a year or so and with no discernible results, another bureaucrat would develop another brilliant plan. Ultimately the cycle repeated itself, and the new plan was merely a rerun of one that had failed several years earlier.

My evaluation of the performance record of the China activities people is even more negative than that given by a former chief of station, Peer de Silva, in his book, *Sub Rosa*. He writes:

> I find it hard to write about our intelligence work based in Hong Kong against mainland China because there was very little successful intelligence work done, in fact. Much was attempted and much failed. We had two main intelligence targets: the uranium gaseous-diffusion plant under construction at Lanchow and the plutonium plant at Pao Tou, both in north-central China. We wanted to learn the state of construction of these two important scientific enterprises, to determine when they went into full production and the amount of purity of their nuclear products. We accomplished neither, nor had my predecessors, and, as I understand it, neither did my successors. The advent of photographic satellites later in the 1960's, however, changed that bleak picture markedly, but that all took place after my tour in Hong Kong.
>
> It was small solace later to learn that this high-expectation, low-yield experience was not mine alone. Mainland China was simply a difficult target for intelligence penetration on the ground with human agents. We had some minor successes but "minor" was the word.[2]

Some bureaucrats had built their careers around China activities and had a vested interest in continuing operations against China. There was an unrecognized danger in that game, for these people had to sustain the impression of China as an implacable foe of the United States. From at least the early 1970s the Chinese Communists supported a strong NATO and a unified Europe as a counter to what they called Soviet Socialist Imperialism. China's position on NATO and Nixon's trip to Peking caused problems in China operations. How could they continue to portray China as the main enemy when it had adopted our policy and hosted our President? The answer was simple: they ignored events and continued the game. Several examples illustrate the point.

In the mid-1970s when I was working for the international communism branch, China desk asked me to brief the new chief of a European security service on the Marxist-Leninist movement's splinter Communist parties in Europe and their relationship to the Chinese. It instructed me to portray the Chinese Communists as foes because it wanted his service to help us in operations against the Chinese. I was only one of a series of briefers. The chief of the service seemed bored and did not ask a single question. When my turn came, having little fear since I planned to retire at the first opportunity, I gave him my honest assessment of China's foreign policy. He came to life and asked numerous questions and requested that I be made available for a second session. That was the last time China desk permitted me to brief its guests.

At about the same time, the CIA acquired a document of approximately 40 pages covering a briefing by top Chinese officials to a trusted and highly regarded ally. The briefing covered China's long-range policy toward two continents with separate sections on short-range actions in individual countries. Yet when it reached me, I noticed that comments on the internal routing sheet indicated the reports section of China desk had no interest in disseminating the document. Dumbfounded that the information had been rejected, I routed it back to China desk, suggesting it might want to reconsider. Several weeks later the document found its way back to me with a notation from the China desk that it had no plans to disseminate the information. A document that set forth China's intentions — the most difficult and highly desired information on an important country's policy — but we did not want it? Why? Because it showed that China planned to act in a responsible way and that its goals to a large extent paralleled our own. Our operational warriors realized that if they disseminated the report, it might stimulate some government leaders to question the CIA's insistence that China deserved to be on the top of its operational target list.

Case officers developed a very personal interest in keeping China as one of the primary enemies of the United States. Promotions, foreign travel, and assignments abroad all depended on maintaining that concept. Once, in the middle of one of Washington's hottest summers, we learned that a Chinese Communist planned to attend a conference at a cool, expensive overseas summer resort. The chief of one desk of China activities decided to try to contact the official to assess his recruitment potential. She went on an extended temporary duty assignment to that resort area, where she spent her time relaxing by the hotel's pool, dining in its best restaurants, and appearing at other swish spots where the Chinese official might surface and be prompted to speak to her. After several unsuccessful weeks of this hardship duty, she returned to the torrid Washington weather.

I had still not given up on my deepest concerns. I tried to explain the district surveys to the Far East division. William E. Nelson had replaced Colby as division chief, and I thought Nelson may not have had the opportunity to learn about the surveys. I prepared a memorandum covering the survey procedures and routed it to the plans people of the division. They returned it with the comment that I had no jurisdiction in matters concerning Thailand.

I then contacted the suggestion and achievement awards committee, which I had learned of when I had checked back into Headquarters in late 1967. The check-in sheet noted that employees who had developed any unique ideas or procedures for improving performance that might have Agency-wide application should submit them for consideration by the committee. Any suggestion adopted for general use might earn the employee a monetary or honorary award. The check-in sheet also said that a special panel had been established to consider suggestions dealing with covert operations. I spoke with the chief of the committee, and he recommended that I prepare a formal suggestion under the provisions of the special panel.

I did so, describing the survey process and noting the evaluation it had received from United States and Thai government agencies. The panel routed the suggestion to the Far East division to evaluate. The division rejected the proposal. Finding it impossible to believe that the division would knowingly reject a program that at little expense both stopped the insurgency and provided excellent intelligence, I rewrote the suggestion. I located copies of the intelligence reports produced by the survey and attached those old reports to the expanded suggestion and submitted it again to the special panel.

Several weeks went by before the chief of the Thai desk, whom I shall call Bart, asked me to come down and see him. Bart and I had served together in Thailand, and I considered him to be the ideal CIA officer. He was down-to-earth, one of the boys, yet he had progressed rapidly up the Agency's chain of command. He worked hard, played hard, and kept his perspective when in a position of authority. (I later learned that when the Agency planned to lower the boom on an employee, it traditionally gave that unpleasant duty to an official most respected by that employee.)

Bart was alone and asked me to sit down. We exchanged a little small talk, but it was evident that he was quite upset. He said, "You know that your suggestion has caused considerable problems here in the division."

This was news to me. My purpose was to help the division, the Agency, and the United States, not to cause problems.

"Mr. Nelson is most upset," Bart continued. "He said you have not gone through the proper channels and have conducted an end run around the division."

Jesus Christ, I thought, what now? Here was the best counterinsurgency program to come down the pike, I try to make the division aware of it, and this is what happens.

Looking sheepish and uncomfortable, Bart said, "Mr. Nelson wants me to tell you that you have jeopardized all future promotions by your actions."

He then sat there waiting for some reaction. I stared at him in disbelief. A hundred thoughts flashed through my mind. I finally mumbled something like, "I thought I was helping the division. You know what the surveys accomplished."

He said something, but my mind was far away. I stood up, looked at him, and tried to think of something to say. I couldn't, so I turned and walked out.

This was the beginning of my real awakening. I could no longer believe that the Agency was serious in trying to understand the communist movement in Thailand. By all standards of measurement taught in its schools, my survey reports had been excellent. Every principle of good report writing — multiple confirmation, collation, analysis — was utilized in the reports. The reports clearly proved that the Agency had seriously misunderstood the nature of the communist threat in Thailand. (In retrospect, some high-level Agency officials, I am sure, had no such misunderstandings.) Yet here was the division chief rejecting the operation and the information it produced. He not only rejected it, but because of it he was going to destroy my career. What had I done wrong? I recognized that some employees used the suggestions channel as a way to circumvent their immediate bosses, but certainly that was not my intention. I worked in China activities and the only channel open to me was the suggestion and achievement awards committee.

I spent the next months running these thoughts through my mind, trying to make some sense of all that had happened. At the same time, Vietnam was growing even more critical. I knew that many Thai Communists had studied organizational principles in North Vietnam, but I noted that none of the reporting I was seeing coming out of Vietnam was mentioning the mass-based organized civilian structure that undoubtedly existed and was supporting the guerrillas. I read every book about Vietnam in the Agency's library and many that were not in that collection. Some books discussed the mass-based movement but put the number of mobilized civilians at ridiculously low levels. I strongly suspected that Agency reporting, using the same old methods, was as mistaken in Vietnam as it had been in Thailand. I felt that survey operations similar to those I had developed in Thailand were needed in Vietnam. I still did not completely realize that those in the highest echelons of the Agency already knew that any information the surveys might gather would show that we could never win the war. In any case I could not continue to sit in China activities and watch Vietnam go down the tube. After all, I was still fiercely anti-communist. I just felt we'd been fighting the enemy the wrong way.

One night I asked Norma if she would have any overriding objections if I went to Vietnam. She and the children could not come, since this was a family separation tour. Long before I broached the subject, she had recognized all the signs and knew what was coming. She also knew that I would never rest until I got there, so she agreed.

I immediately contacted the chief of the Vietnam desk and told him I wanted to volunteer. He said great, but he would have to clear it with the China activities people. The Agency at the time found it necessary to draft people for tours in Vietnam as not many wanted to serve there, so I guessed that I would have little problem getting the assignment.

At about this point I was contacted by the office of training. It had just begun a course in counterinsurgency operations and had received a copy of my suggestion from the suggestion and achievement awards committee. The training officials were most pleased with my idea and said it was the only comprehensive plan they had seen. They said the survey technique had a direct and immediate relevance, and they planned to make it a major part of the counterinsurgency training. At the request of the training director, I traveled down to Camp Peary several times to talk to both students and instructors about what they labeled the "McGehee method." One would think that now the Far East division might express some interest, but it did not.

Two months after my initial request for a tour in Vietnam, I was advised that the China desk would release me and that I was to report to the Vietnam desk as soon as possible. This was a great relief to me. I could get out of that do-nothing job, go overseas, and help win the war. But my experience had created serious doubts in my mind. I was just hoping against hope that I would not find the same Agency attitudes in Vietnam that had caused me so many problems in Thailand and at Headquarters. Little did I know that the reluctance to recognize reality about the insurgency in Thailand was nothing compared to the resistance I would encounter in Vietnam.

10.
THE CIA IN VIETNAM:
TRANSFORMING REALITY

I flew to Saigon with a jumble of American civilians and servicemen crammed into an American Category Z plane. As government travelers to Vietnam, we got a special rate but had to endure a long flight replete with cramped legs, harried stewardesses, and distressed kidneys.

I arrived in October 1968, a few months after the Tet offensive had seen armed Viet Cong raiding the sanctuary of the United States Embassy. Tan San Nhut Airport on the outskirts of Saigon did little to reassure me. The dilapidated terminal guarded by United States military police and Vietnamese soldiers was a swirl of bodies, luggage, and boxes of Hong Kong goodies purchased by privileged Vietnamese. A Vietnamese employee of the Agency held up a name sign "McGehee" and guided me through customs. Once through that mess, he drove me to the Agency's quarters, the Duc Hotel, located a short distance from the Presidential Palace. He said a shuttle bus would leave for the U.S. Embassy in the morning and gave me the name and phone number of the person I was to contact.

That afternoon I took the opportunity to walk around Saigon. I had visited the city in 1960 just before the influx of American military advisers. Saigon had been a peaceful city of tree-lined boulevards, a few three-wheeled cyclos and bicycles, the latter frequently ridden by Vietnamese women wearing the flowing *ao-dai* — a flared dress over satin trousers. The beauty of the city, the flower markets, and the exotic aromas of Vietnamese herbal cooking evoked a relaxed atmosphere of charm and grace.

The difference between the Saigon of 1960 and the

Saigon of 1968 was astonishing. Now military trucks filled with unkempt American soldiers, jeeps, motorcycles, ancient ratty-looking cabs of no discernible make, and small Japanese cars moved in exasperated tempo down the crammed streets. Trying to get a better view of the Presidential Palace, I forded the flow of traffic on Hong Thap Tu Street only to be waved back by two irate Vietnamese soldiers brandishing submachine guns. It was only then that I noticed that no pedestrians were allowed on the wide sidewalks next to the heavy fence around the Presidential Palace.

The politically significant twin-spiraled Catholic Church dominated the square opening on to Tu Do Street. Tu Do was awash with American soldiers, Vietnamese civilians and soldiers, Indian Sikhs, and Chinese businessmen intermingled in a hectic rush. Like the clouds of exhaust from the slow-moving vehicles, an atmosphere of hate permeated the air. Tu Do Street now housed the bars, the massage parlors, the trinket stores all catering to the American G.I. The open-front bars sheltered tough, haggard-looking girls casting come-on leers out at the strollers to entice them in to try their luck. Beggars pleaded for handouts, while one young Vietnamese asked if I wanted to exchange money "300 to 1" and another was openly hawking "barbits." The sounds of electronically boosted rock music crashed out from the bars, adding to the din of traffic and the malaise of the people. I began to question my decision to come to this God-forsaken city.

Backtracking down Hai Ba Trung to Thong Nhut Boulevard en route to the zoo, I ran into a group of young Vietnamese protesters scattering in all directions from tear gas fired by the Vietnamese police. Further down, I passed the U.S. Embassy with its ten-foot-high concrete fence, its circular gun turrets, its roof-top helicopter pad, and its thick white outer concrete shell designed to deflect any incoming artillery or rockets. All that it lacked to complete the picture of a medieval fortress under siege was a moat and a drawbridge.

Walking through the zoo, I overheard a conversation that spoiled the relative serenity of that park setting. "The basement of the zoo's central building was used during the Diem regime as an execution and torture chamber for political prisoners," one young American G.I. said to another. This was a deeply disturbing comment that I subsequently found out was all too true.

The next day I reported to the Agency offices in the Norodom complex, a few Quonset huts sitting within the fenced grounds of the embassy. This group of offices housed the less glamorous elements of the Agency, while the main Agency contingent was accommodated in the top three floors of the embassy building. I was assigned to the personnel pool. It was explained to me that because of the crush of people coming and going, all but the highest positions were filled by a draft system not too much different from that of the National Football League. While in this suspended status, we all were treated to a series of briefings by the station and other elements of the United States government contingent, especially the all-encompassing Civil Operations and Rural Development Support (CORDS) staff. This massive structure molded, or was supposed to mold, all of the disparate Vietnamese and American elements into one united pacification organization. On the American side, the CIA, the State Department, the Agency for International Development, the United States Information Agency, and selected military elements supplied people to CORDS. But all career employees owed their allegiance first, last, and always to their parent agencies, not to the jerry-built CORDS organization. And of course as with most things in Vietnam, the reality of the program was far different from the official illusion.

CORDS held a series of briefings in its two separate headquarters. Major portions of the briefings explained its organizational charter and its horrendously complicated acronyms. The CIA station management held its own separate briefings. The Agency's more than 700 employees were scattered throughout Saigon and upcountry, administering manpower in the tens of thousands. The station's breakdown for its internal command structure paralleled that of the Vietnamese and the U.S. Military Assistance Command for Vietnam (MACV) — from I (Eye) Corps in the North to the Southern Delta's IV Corps, with Saigon and Gia Dinh Province which surrounded it forming the critical V Corps region. The CIA called its supervisors of corps areas regional officers-in-charge or ROICs I through V.

The station's intelligence briefings on the situation in South Vietnam confirmed all my fears. Intelligence analysts giving the briefings talked only about the number of armed Viet Cong, the slowly increasing North Vietnamese regular army, and the occasional member of the "Communist infrastructure," i.e., the lone tax collector or party member who "terrorized" the population into cooperation with the Communists. They made no mention of the mass-based Farmers' Liberation Association, the Women's Liberation Association, or the Communist youth organizations, all of which in some areas certainly included entire populations.

The more I heard, the greater my disillusionment. While in Washington I had acquired a copy of *Viet Cong*, a book by Douglas Pike, the U.S. government's leading authority on the Viet Cong.[1] It described in great detail the farmers', women's, and youth organizations and how they were built. That book held the numbers of civilian members of these Communist front groups to ridiculously low levels. Even so, the station did not even acknowledge the existence of the associations. Michael Charles Conley's book, *The Communist Insurgent Infrastructure in South Vietnam*,[2] written under contract to the Department of the Army under the auspices of American University, set forth a detailed discussion of the mass-based civilian communist structures. Even though Conley must have been under tremendous pressure to keep his number of civilian members of the South Vietnamese communist movement low, he reported that there were probably more than a million — a million that did not exist anywhere in Agency reporting.

The Agency's briefers told us that there were several hundred thousand armed North and South Vietnamese communists in South Vietnam and that they had been badly demoralized by their losses during the Tet attacks in early 1968. That figure was obviously low. The reason that it had to be low was that U.S. policymakers had to sell the idea that the war in the South was being fought by a small minority of Communists opposed to the majority-supported democratic government of Nguyen Van Thieu. The situation, however, was the opposite, as I was to understand later. The United States was supporting Thieu's tiny oligarchy against a population largely organized, committed, and dedicated to a communist victory. But the numbers were not the only thing the United States policymakers lied about. The American people were not aware, and neither, I am sure, were my CIA briefers in Saigon, of the extent of CIA covert operations in Vietnam beginning as early as 1954. Only later did this tragic history come out, largely through the *Pentagon Papers*. It was only years after the publication of those papers during the research for this book that I began to appreciate fully the scope of CIA covert operations in Vietnam and the level of Agency deceits concerning the war.

The origins of the war dated back to 1858 when the French invaded and colonized Indochina. The French, utilizing the Vietnamese landlord class as their puppets, turned Vietnam into a marketplace for high-priced French manufactured goods and a source of cheap labor and raw materials for the "mother" country. At the time of the French invasion approximately 90 percent of the people lived and worked as farmers in the rural areas. The colonizers made laws that allowed them to confiscate peasant land, and as a result, over the ensuing decades, many peasants were left impoverished. The Indochinese Communist Party (ICP) was formed in 1930 to recapture control of the country from the French. This party evolved into Ho Chi Minh's Vietnam Workers Party. In its first manifesto in 1930 the ICP promised to "wipe out feudal remnants [the Vietnamese who cooperated with the French], to distribute land to the tillers, to overthrow imperialism, and to make Indochina completely independent."[3]

During the 1930s the ICP was divided by a series of internal battles about the proper way to fight the French, and at the same time was decimated by the French police.

In September 1939, World War II broke out in Europe and in September 1940 Japanese troops moved into Vietnam. During World War II the Japanese asserted control over the ports and airfields of Vietnam but allowed the French to continue to administer the local government. This cooperation ceased a few months before the end of World War II when the Japanese took control of all of Vietnam.

World War II was decisive for Ho's forces, for in 1941 he returned from China — where he had observed Mao's program of organizing the peasantry to overthrow Chiang — and formed the Viet Minh coalition to fight the Japanese and the French. A major element of Ho's program was reconfiscation of the land of the French and their Vietnamese puppets and distribution of that land to the peasantry.[4] Through his antiimperialism and land-reform programs, Ho built the Viet Minh into a committed, broadbased political organization, making him the only Vietnamese leader with a dedicated national following.

During World War II the American Office of Strategic Services (OSS), the predecessor of the CIA, recognized the strength of the Viet Minh and depended on it for intelligence and help in recovering downed pilots.[5] The OSS and the Viet Minh worked in close cooperation and the OSS provided 5,000 weapons, along with ammunition and training, to convert Ho's guerrillas into an organized army.[6] When the Japanese surrendered in August 1945, the Viet Minh marched into Hanoi and dozens of other cities in Vietnam and proclaimed the birth of the Democratic Republic of Vietnam (DRV). For a few weeks in September 1945, Vietnam was for the first time in recent history free of foreign domination. North and South were united under Ho.

Through a series of maneuvers, the French sought to re-colonize Vietnam and to destroy Ho's government. They installed a puppet, Bao Dai, and militarily tried to impose their will over the Vietnamese.[7] At first the United States was reluctant to accept this blatant French move, but the "loss" of China, the Korean War, and the deteriorating French position caused a reassessment. In 1950 the U.S. began providing direct military aid to French troops fighting in Vietnam as the struggle there was deemed an integral part of containing communism. By 1954 the U.S. was financing 78 percent of the war.[8]

The 1954 Geneva Conference to negotiate an end to the war concluded in July, only a few months after the French had been defeated at Dien Bien Phu. The accords reached at Geneva stated that there would be a cease-fire and a temporary military partition of Vietnam at the 17th parallel. Each side was given 300 days to complete the evacuation. The North was turned over to the Communists and the South to the French-backed Bao Dai. The final declaration said that North and South Vietnam were to be reunited on the basis of free elections to be held throughout the country on July 26, 1956 — elections that then Premier Ngo Dinh Diem and his American advisers later refused to hold.

U.S. policymakers decided the French had lost their will to fight in Vietnam and began to plan to assume the French role in that country. This approach was formalized on

August 20, 1954 in National Security Council memorandum NSC 5429/2, which said the U.S. must "disassociate France from levers of command, integrate land reform with refugee resettlement. . . . Give aid directly to the Vietnamese — not through France. . . . Diem must broaden the governmental base, elect an assembly, draft a constitution and legally dethrone Bao Dai."[9]

Once this decision was made, overnight the CIA's intelligence about the situation in Vietnam switched. The Agency now portrayed Diem as the miracle worker who was saving Vietnam. To make the illusion a reality, the CIA undertook a series of operations that helped turn South Vietnam into a vast police state. The purpose of these operations was to force the native South Vietnamese to accept the Catholic mandarin Diem, who had been selected by U.S. policymakers to provide an alternative to communism in Vietnam.[10] It was a strange choice. From 1950 to 1953, while Ho's forces were earning the loyalty of their people by fighting the French, Diem, a short, fussy bachelor, was living in the U.S. in Maryknoll seminaries in New Jersey and New York.

Diem arrived in Saigon in mid-1954 and was greeted by Colonel Edward Lansdale, the CIA's man in South Vietnam and the head of the Agency's Saigon Military Mission (SMM). Diem was opposed by virtually all elements of South Vietnamese society — Bao Dai's followers, the pro-French religious sects, the Buddhists, the remnant nationalist organizations, and, of course, the followers of Ho Chi Minh. He had no troops, no police, no government, and no means of enforcing his rule. What he did have was the complete support of Colonel Lansdale and all the money, manpower, weapons, training, propaganda, and political savvy in the CIA's covert-action war chest.

To create Diem's government, Lansdale's men, operating in teams in North Vietnam, stimulated North Vietnamese Catholics and the Catholic armies deserted by the French to flee south. SMM teams promised Catholic Vietnamese assistance and new opportunities if they would emigrate. To help them make up their minds, the teams circulated leaflets falsely attributed to the Viet Minh telling what was expected of citizens under the new government. The day following distribution of the leaflets, refugee registration tripled. The teams spread horror stories of Chinese Communist regiments raping Vietnamese girls and taking reprisals against villages. This confirmed fears of Chinese occupation under the Viet Minh. The teams distributed other pamphlets showing the circumference of destruction around Hanoi and other North Vietnamese cities should the United States decide to use atomic weapons. To those it induced to flee over the 300-day period the CIA provided free transportation on its airline, Civil Air Transport, and on ships of the U.S. Navy. Nearly a million North Vietnamese were scared and lured into moving to the South.

Lieutenant Tom Dooley, who operated with the U.S. Navy out of Haiphong, also helped to stimulate the flow of refugees to the South. At one point he organized a gathering of 35,000 Catholics to demand evacuation. A medical doctor, Dooley was a supreme propagandist whose message seemed aimed largely at the U.S. audience. He wrote three bestselling books, and numerous newspaper and magazine articles were written about him. Dr. Dooley's concocted tales of the Viet Minh disemboweling 1,000 pregnant women, beating a naked priest on the testicles with a bamboo club, and jamming chopsticks in the ears of children to keep them from hearing the word of God, aroused American citizens to anger and action.[11] Dr. Dooley's reputation remained unsullied until 1979, when his ties to the CIA were uncovered during a Roman Catholic sainthood investigation.[12]

The Agency's operation worked. It not only convinced the North Vietnamese Catholics to flee to the South, thereby providing Diem with a source of reliable political and military cadres, but it also duped the American people into believing that the flight of the refugees was a condemnation of the Viet Minh by the majority of Vietnamese.

Now the scene had been set and the forces defined. The picture drawn to justify U.S. involvement was that the Communist North was invading the Free World South. The CIA was ordered to sustain that illusion through propaganda and, through covert operations, to make the illusion a reality. Its intelligence, with an occasional minor exception, was only a convenient vehicle to sell the lie to the U.S. bureaucracy and people. Unfortunately, nearly everyone, including later policymakers, was deceived by this big lie. While the plan was never detailed in a single available document, an examination of the

Pentagon Papers, plus other related information, demands this conclusion.

A raft of Americans now descended upon Diem. The U.S. Army began training and arming his army. The CIA concentrated on building a government and a police for the new ruler. Colonel Lansdale formed the Freedom Company of the Philippines to send Filipinos to Vietnam under the guise of a private philanthropic organization to train Diem's palace guard, to organize the Vietnamese Veterans Legion, to help write the new constitution, to look for promising agent material to encadre the planned programs, and to assist the arriving North Vietnamese.[13]

Saigon and environs in the summer of 1954 were ruled by two pro-French religious-military sects (the Cao Dai and the Hoa Hao) and a bandit secular group (the Binh Xuyen). The U.S. stopped funding the French and funneled all its aid directly through Diem. The sect leaders were subverted by bribes, and when that didn't work, by killings. The Binh Xuyen did put up a show of force but were quickly defeated in a battle with Diem's units, which seized control of the capital.

Through the CIA, newspapers in the U.S. learned of Diem's victory, and stories about the miracle of Diem circulated around the globe. The CIA even wrote a Special National Intelligence Estimate that completely lied about what happened and concluded, "His [Diem's] success [was] achieved largely on his own initiative and with his own resources."[14]

Bao Dai was quickly removed from the scene by a rigged election that Diem won with 98 percent of the vote.

So, within little more than a year of Diem's return to Saigon, the CIA had completed the imposition of a Catholic premier and the importation of a Catholic encadred army and police to rule a nation that was primarily Buddhist. In 1956 the U.S. government and Diem tightened the new premier's control by calling off the elections for the reunification of North and South Vietnam that had been agreed upon in the Geneva Accords. They did this because they knew that if the elections had taken place, Ho Chi Minh would have won and the country would have been reunited under Communist rule. Even President Eisenhower admitted, "I have never talked . . . with a person knowledgable in Indochinese affairs who did not agree that . . . 80 percent of the population would have voted for the Communist Ho Chi Minh as their leader."[15]

Having thus established Diem's military control over Saigon, the CIA then went about imposing Diem's rule over rural South Vietnamese. In this process the Agency used people imported from the North to encadre its programs. For example, the Village Self-Defense Corps, a Colonel Lansdale concept, armed North Vietnamese refugees who had settled on land given them under Diem's land-reform program. The Village Self-Defense Corps years later was renamed the Popular Forces.[16]

The Agency sponsored another program recruiting young university men from the North to take a census of the population. The recruits soon forgot their census-taking responsibilities and concentrated on gathering intelligence on Communists.

To police the rural areas the CIA, along with teams from Michigan State University, created and trained the 50,000-man Civil Guard whose mission, according to CIA National Intelligence Estimate 63-56, was "to maintain law and order, collect intelligence, and conduct countersubversion operations at the provincial level in areas pacified by the army."[17]

The Agency helped Diem develop his political power through creation of the Can Lao Party. Ngo Dinh Nhu, Diem's brother, headed the party, which required members at all levels to serve as informants for its intelligence-collection programs. The party, as with all other CIA programs, became obsessed with detecting disloyalty and concentrated its efforts on the police function.

At the core of the intelligence-countersubversion network was Diem's dreaded Vietnamese Bureau of Investigation — a CIA-created security service.[18]

The rural, predominantly Buddhist South Vietnamese resisted Diem's unfair rule. The continual police operations to seek out disloyalty to Diem caused more and more peasants to join communist organizations for their own survival. Diem reacted to this perceived disloyalty by passing laws making it a crime to speak against the government or to spread rumors. Such crimes were punishable by death. Bernard Fall, in his book *Last Reflections on a War*, observed: "On May 6, 1959, the Diem regime passed Law 10/59, which provided for a system of drumhead courts capable of handing out death sentences for even trivial offenses. Thus *all* South Vietnamese opposition — whether Communist or not — had to become subversive, and did. . . . 'Four persons out of five became suspects and liable to be imprisoned if not executed.'"[19]

In reaction to Diem's campaign of death against his own people, the southern branch of the Communist Party pressured North Vietnam into supporting their armed revolution. Contrary to the impression generated by Agency propaganda, the war at this stage was not an "invasion from the North" but a local resistance to the despotic Diem regime. Numerous authorities have commented on this subject, and captured Communist documents also reveal this to be true.[20]

While the Agency was creating all of those "security" programs, it also had to estimate the strength of the communist forces. A captured Communist Party document containing the history of the party stated that its size in the South before Geneva was 60,000 party members (not including members of the mass organizations) with party members in nearly every village except those controlled by the religious sects and ethnic minorities.[21] The document said that at that time those in the South had the twofold mission of reorganizing the mass-based organizations and developing military units in absolute secrecy. Beginning with 15,000 dedicated hard-core party members — aided in their organizational efforts by Diem's ruthless oppression — the party began to rebuild itself from the ground up. Over the years it created an interwoven political, civilian, and military structure and honed it into a responsive revolutionary weapon. At the hamlet level nearly every man, woman, and child was recruited into some organization and motivated to fight Diem and his American backers.

By late 1963 the People's Revolutionary Party (PRP) and its National Liberation Front of South Vietnam (NLF) had declared that in their 30 different organizations they had a membership of 7 million, with the largest front groups being the Farmers' Liberation Association with 1.8 million members and the Women's Liberation Association with 1.2 million. These figures were undoubtedly inflated, but U.S. intelligence estimates ignored their existence. To understand the way U.S. intelligence estimated communist strength in South Vietnam at the time, it is useful to review the following chart, included in the *Pentagon Papers* and prepared by the RAND Corporation:

VIET CONG STRENGTH
1954 - 1964
(rounded to nearest thousand)

Year	Main & Local Forces (Regulars)	Guerrillas, Self-Defense Units, Secret Self-Defense Units (Irregulars)	Source
1955*	10,000	NA	NSC Briefing, 16 March 1956. Open sources give 5-10,000. *Weekly Intelligence Digest*, 18 May 1956, suggests 10,000 number should be revised to 6-8,000.
1956*	5,000-7,500	NA	*Weekly Intelligence Digest*, 10 August 1956.
1957*	1,000-2,000	2,000	*Weekly Intelligence Digest*, 30 May 1958; *Weekly Intelligence Digest*, 18 July 1958.
1958*	April—2,000	NA	*Weekly Intelligence Digest*, 19 December 1958.
1959*	2,000	NA	NIE 63-59, 26 May 1959.
1960*	April—4,000 Sept.—7,000 Dec.—10,000	3,000 (SNIE 63.1-60)	*Weekly Intelligence Digest*, 17 February 1961. SNIE 63.1-60, 3-5,000 regulars.
1961*	June—15,000 Sept.—16,000-17,000	NA	*Weekly Intelligence Digest*, 13 October 1961; *Weekly Intelligence Digest*, 20 October 1961.
1962*	23,000	NA	*Current Intelligence Weekly Summary*, OCI 2 November 1962.
1963* 1964**	June—25,000 June—31,000 Dec.—34,000	NA 72,000	*Southeast Asia Military Fact Book, DIA/JCS.* Based on MACV data. Data not retroactively adjusted.

*Estimate of Viet Cong strength for this period is subject to great uncertainty. The numbers here should be treated as order of magnitude.

**Add approximately 40,000 in the Viet Cong "infrastructure." The infrastructure is defined as the PRP, PRP Central Committee, and the NLF. See MACV, *Monthly Order of Battle Summaries*, for a discussion. Also add 23-25,000 in Administrative Service, i.e., staff and technical service units subordinate to various headquarters.[22]

The chart uses the term Viet Cong as the intelligence community's rather imprecise name for the Vietnamese communist movement in the South. The figures are based on both Agency and military estimates of the number of communists in the country, but those sourced to NIEs (National Intelligence Estimates), SNIEs (Special National Intelligence Estimates), and the *Current Intelligence Weekly Summary* of OCI (Office of Current Intelligence) most closely reflect the Agency's input.

The chart reveals a total lack of appreciation of the size of the movement. In 1954 French intelligence estimated that the communists controlled up to 90 percent of rural South Vietnam outside of the sect domains.[23] Yet, until 1964 U.S. intelligence only twice recorded any militia, guerrilla, or other irregular forces. Most glaringly, even after the communists announced the existence of the NLF and its multi-million-person structure, the estimates failed to include a single member of the farmers', the women's, or the youth groups. Until 1964 the chart also omits any reference to Communist Party members — the key element in the revolution. Those omissions reveal a lack of understanding of revolutionary methods and forces.

The Agency's erroneous assessment of the communist movement is best exemplified by a speech Colby gave in Vietnam. In his book, *Honorable Men*, he talks of a briefing he gave to American civilian and military chiefs in Vietnam in 1968: "To that audience I set forth something different from the usual rundown of Communist main- and local-force battalions. . . . I outlined instead the structure and functions of the Lao Dong Party and its southern section, named the People's Revolutionary Party, the National Liberation Front, the

Provisional Government of South Vietnam, the Liberation Committees and National Alliance of Democratic Forces, *which had made post-Tet* [1968] *appearances.* [Emphasis added.] I pointed out that these had *failed to attract much popular support* [emphasis added] but they nevertheless were the phantom political skeleton that the Communists would use in any negotiation for a peace treaty or cease-fire."[24]

After the war the U.S. government's leading authority on Vietnamese communism, Douglas Pike, tersely commented that earlier estimates by outsiders of the size of the party in the South had been consistently low. The party in the South (excluding the military and front groups) actually numbered at least 350,000 and may have had as many as 500,000 members.[25]

Although the CIA consistently underestimated communist strength in rural areas, its expanding and increasingly oppressive programs belied that false optimism. In 1959, William Colby, then chief of Saigon station, convinced Ngo Dinh Nhu, Diem's brother, to build self-defense forces in rural villages. This program utilized American Special Forces to form Catholic men and women into what were called Civilian Irregular Defense Groups (CIDG). Under this program 30,000 CIDG received arms and developed patrolling strike forces.[26]

Diem's police state found its programs unable to control the people. Beginning in 1959, with the assistance of the CIA, it sponsored a program to move villagers into organized communities for self defense. This concept, called "agrovilles," generated fierce resistance from the South Vietnamese who were forced to leave their homes to settle in the new sites.

Learning little from this experience, Diem's government, with the CIA in the lead, initiated the "strategic hamlet" program in late 1961. South Vietnamese were forcibly moved into fenced and guarded compounds, and the Special Police weeded out any Communists. An ideal strategic hamlet included a watch tower, a moat, fortifications, and barbed wire. The program infuriated the people whose homes were destroyed to force them into those confined sites. The strategic hamlet program died with the assassination of Diem.

The CIA was a most reluctant participant in Diem's removal, but other elements of our government demanded it. After several false starts, the coup group with U.S.

encouragement deposed Diem in early November 1963. Colby called the American-sponsored overthrow of Diem the worst mistake of the war. He said Buddhists had raised an essentially false issue of religious discrimination.[27]

Various coup governments took turns ruling South Vietnam following the assassination of Diem. There were six governments in the next 18 months alone.

The Agency continued to develop programs for rural security. First it developed the People's Action Teams — small teams of local armed men who provided security to the rural villages. This program soon expanded under the government of Nguyen Cao Ky, and its name was changed to Revolutionary Development. Ultimately 40,000 cadres were formed into 59-man Revolutionary Development Teams, which were directly funded and administered by the CIA.

The Agency also financed the construction of interrogation centers in all provinces and a National Interrogation Center in Saigon, all under the CIA-backed Central Intelligence Organization.[28]

In early 1964 President Johnson's national security advisers decided something was needed to overcome the U.S. public's apathy toward the war. To this purpose an entire series of U.S. provocations occurred in the Gulf of Tonkin. They included a July 31 attack on Hon Me Island by MACV-supported South Vietnamese Special Forces; the August 2 bombardment and strafing of North Vietnamese villages in the vicinity of Hon Me by aircraft, and the repeated feints of attack against Hon Me Island by the U.S. Navy destroyer *Maddox*. The ruse worked and North Vietnamese patrol boats, assuming the *Maddox* to be a part of the earlier South Vietnamese Special Forces attack, fired a few rounds at the destroyer. The next day the *Maddox* returned with a second destroyer and another so-called attack was launched at this two-ship patrol. Congress reacted immediately to what became known as the Tonkin Gulf incident. It passed a joint resolution of support and the American people responded to this "attack" on our sovereignty.[29]

However, in a few months U.S. policymakers needed additional evidence to justify the war to foreign and domestic audiences and to sustain the view that the insurgency was an invasion of the South by the North. To this end the State

Department issued a second White Paper. In 1961 it had already published the first one, "A Threat to the Peace: North Viet-Nam's Effort to Conquer South Viet-Nam." In 1965, just before the entry of U.S. combat troops into Vietnam and before the regular bombing of North Vietnam by American planes, the State Department issued "Aggression from the North: The Record of North Viet-Nam's Campaign to Conquer South Viet-Nam." Both papers relied on contrived CIA intelligence to support their arguments, and the second paper was based in part on evidence planted by the CIA.[30] The Agency conducted at least two covert operations to prove the paper's thesis. One involved an elaborate scheme to print large numbers of postage stamps showing the Viet Cong shooting down a U.S. helicopter. The highly professional production technique was meant to indicate that the stamp was produced in North Vietnam because the Viet Cong had no such capability. The Agency printed sheets of those stamps, wrote letters in Vietnamese, mailed them all over the world, and made copies available to U.S. journalists. A full-color blow-up of the "North Vietnamese Stamp" appeared on the cover of *Life* magazine on February 26, 1965, just two days before publication of the White Paper.[31]

The second covert operation entailed planting a weapons shipment and blaming it on the North Vietnamese. The Agency took tons of Communist-made weapons out of its warehouses, loaded them on a Vietnamese coastal vessel, faked a firefight, and then called in Western reporters and International Control Commission observers to "prove" North Vietnamese aid to the Viet Cong. The White Paper featured details of this operation under the headline, "Hanoi Supplies Weapons, Ammunition and Other War Material to Its Forces in the South." Seven pages of the White Paper were devoted to the CIA-planted evidence, including photographs of the beached Vietnamese junk and the assortment of ammunition it carried.[32] On March 6, 1965, just a week after the issuance of the White Paper, President Johnson ordered two Marine Corps battalion landing teams into Vietnam and the initiation of Operation Rolling Thunder, which consisted of the systematic bombing of North Vietnam.

U.S. combat troops in South Vietnam quickly discovered that the rural South Vietnamese, who were fighting for and supporting the Viet Cong, considered them the enemy. None-theless, the United States developed a simple plan to win — force the peasants by the millions into the cities and towns, turn the entire country into a massive police compound, and you deny those millions to the communists. Search-and-destroy missions, free-fire zones, and bombing of rural South Vietnam were all conducted to force the peasants out of their villages into the cities.

General Westmoreland put it this way: "So closely en-twined were some populated localities with the tentacles of the VC base areas . . . that the only way to establish control short of constant combat operations among the people was to remove the people."[33]

The CIA created a program of hunter-killer teams. Ac-cording to Marchetti and Marks, "In 1965 Colby . . . oversaw the founding in Vietnam of the Agency's Counter Terror (CT) program. In 1966 the Agency became wary of adverse public-ity surrounding the use of the word 'terror' and changed the name of the CT teams to the Provincial Reconnaissance Units (PRUs). . . . [The operation was described as] 'a unilateral American program, never recognized by the South Vietnamese government. CIA representatives recruited, organized, sup-plied, and directly paid CT teams, whose function was to use . . . techniques of terror — assassination, abuses, kidnappings and intimidation — against the Viet Cong leadership.'"[34]

All of the various civilian, military, and police programs were to contribute to the CORDS structure and programs. The primary CORDS program was the Phoenix operation. Under Phoenix, devised by Colby's office, all units coordinated "an attack against the Vietcong infrastructure. . . . Again CIA money was the catalyst. According to Colby's own testimony in 1971 before a congressional committee, 20,587 suspected Vietcong were killed under Phoenix in its first two and a half years. Figures provided by the South Vietnamese government credit Phoenix with 40,994 VC kills."[35]

Of course, when I arrived in Saigon in 1968 the Agency's briefers did not discuss this deplorable history. They probably were not aware of it themselves. I certainly wasn't. All I knew then was that our policy was based on "intelligence" reports of the numbers of communists in Vietnam that had nothing to do with reality. Either they were the result of unbelievable incompetence or they were deliberate lies created to dupe the American people. At that time I still didn't know which.

Hoping to correct the mistakes of the Agency's intelligence concerning the nature and scope of the Viet Cong movement, I immediately wrote a memorandum to the chief of station outlining my findings from the survey operation in Thailand, the details of the composition of the Viet Cong as set forth in the Pike and Conley books, and information from other scattered sources. The memorandum suggested that the Agency's coverage of the communist movement was somewhat incomplete and that the station ought to adopt a version of the Thailand survey operation to report more accurately on the mass-based communist movement and more effectively counter it. The memo was passed around for a week or two and then came back to me with no comment.

After a few weeks I was drafted to work in the fifth region or ROIC V. My initial assignment was as officer in charge of Gia Dinh, supervising the various Agency programs in that key province around Saigon. Several military officers detailed to the CIA came under my jurisdiction. They handled various action programs, particularly the Provincial Reconnaissance Units (PRU) that hunted out and killed or captured the communist infrastructure, one of the Agency's main contributions to the CORDS program of Rural Development Support.

The assignment to Gia Dinh gave me the opportunity to see how the Agency's intelligence program worked, or more accurately how it did not work, at that level. One- or two-sentence intelligence reports poured in, were translated, and were filed or thrown away. A typical report, one of hundreds like it received each week, said: "Two armed VC were seen moving south of the village of . . . this morning." A massive Agency/CORDS/Phoenix file system processed this daily flow of nonsense. Collation and analysis never applied. I wondered how this intelligence effort could possibly give our leaders and generals anything even approaching an accurate picture of what was going on. How could we ever defeat the communists if we were going about it like this?

Gia Dinh CORDS personnel attended weekly meetings

chaired by a kindly retired Army colonel. These amounted to several hours of trivia, a waste of the time of the entire large staff. Agency for International Development personnel devoted a good portion of their time to citing progress in removing garbage from Gia Dinh that had accumulated during the 1968 Communist Tet offensive. We should have devoted that time and more to removing the garbage from the Phoenix files.

The CORDS meetings, the killings by the CIA's assassination teams — the Provincial Reconnaissance Units — and the absurd intelligence-collection activities progressed as in a Greek tragedy. No one seemed to understand what was going on. Yet people died, reports flowed, meetings convened, and the gods frowned. That experience in Gia Dinh confirmed my worst fears about Vietnam.

A few weeks after I had been assigned to Gia Dinh a flash message signaled that my old boss William Colby, who had just recently been named by President Johnson to head CORDS, had ordered an immediate briefing by the Gia Dinh CORDS staff. The heads of various programs rushed over to the U.S. Army's bachelor officers' quarters, a large concrete and wooden frame building. As I arrived, hard-looking Vietnamese girls in tight leather mini-skirts were being rushed out.

Other officers of CORDS came scurrying in while reviewing their briefing notes. Within a matter of minutes Colby, trailed by a galaxy of aides and newspaper correspondents, burst into the gathering and we all jumped to attention. I could not believe the change in the man. The year before when he had come to Northeast Thailand he had moved slowly, seemed calm, relaxed, and exuded a concern for all. Now, in Gia Dinh, he looked and acted like a caricature, a harried, self-important, distracted bureaucrat on an important mission. Several of his aides carried massive notebooks, which they laid out for him at the head of the table.

We all sat down. Colby opened the books, looked up to see if everyone appreciated the gravity of that action, and began calling for statistics: "How many VC killed this month? How many captured? How many firefights?"

Each unit chief answered. Colby checked the replies against the figures in his book, and questioned each chief about discrepancies or outstanding figures. I sat quietly enjoying the spectacle and not knowing what to expect.

Unfortunately, true to his roots, he asked for an assessment of the situation from the CAS representative (Controlled American Source — the phrase used instead of CIA in government correspondence). I had been in Gia Dinh for just a few weeks and had been awash in two-sentence intelligence reports about the movements of one or two Viet Cong and had no files or prior assessments that would have allowed me to learn anything about the situation in Gia Dinh. Not being quick on my feet, I answered honestly that I had just arrived and at this point did not know the security situation in the province.

Finally after reviewing all the statistics, Colby adjourned the meeting to the adjacent bar for a cocktail party. I wondered as we moved into the next room just what had been accomplished.

At the party Colby made it a point to talk to me. Maybe he was lonely, and the others seemed to hang back from approaching this important official. I felt no awe, only anger. Here he was supposedly trying to understand the situation in Gia Dinh by digesting a mass of contrived statistics, yet in Northeast Thailand he had rejected undeniable intelligence on the situation there. If he understood what was happening in Thailand, he would have understood what was happening in Vietnam.

"How is your wife and family?" he asked.

"Okay. Norma has gone to work," I responded. "The two boys are in school in Herndon and my two girls are both in college." All the time I was thinking, you dumb, blind son of a bitch, do you believe all the garbage in your book of statistics? Don't you know that the Agency's intelligence is misleading everyone? Why can't you recognize this?

"What sort of office setup do you have here?" he asked. "Do you have any good operations with the special police?"

I gave all the appropriate answers, but I was thinking, here we are in the middle of an insane war, we all are running around shouting statistics that disprove the reality. Am I, is he, an inmate in this asylum or a keeper? Or is there any difference?

We continued to talk in this desultory manner for what seemed an interminable length of time — would he never go? I considered speaking my mind to force some reality into this fantasy, but I knew it would be futile. If a thousand reports in Northeast Thailand couldn't convince him, if the Vietnam War all around us couldn't convince him, then my lone voice certainly couldn't. And besides, it wasn't the proper situation. This was a cocktail party. How could I raise a fuss here? It would be so . . . inappropriate.

After Colby and his motorcade finally left, I returned to the CIA office-compound and made a large martini. I sat down and drank it while my mind raced to try to make some sense of the chaos of Vietnam. Here the U.S. was trying to fight an enemy it only slightly acknowledged. Why? What had happened to all the idealism, all the rules of getting and reporting intelligence? Why did the Agency blind itself while pretending to look for intelligence? Why did we insist on killing people instead of talking to them? How long would this insanity go on? I was depressed, confused, and in a state of agitated turmoil. I was also furious at Colby and furious at myself for not confronting him with the truth. The tension was unendurable. With all my strength I threw the martini glass at the nearest wall, smashing it and scattering glass everywhere.

After six weeks in Gia Dinh I was assigned as officer in charge of liaison activities with the chief of South Vietnam's Special Police. In this capacity I supervised other Agency case officers working with specific elements of the Special Police in and around Saigon.

My boss, Tom (fictitious name), was a strange bird whose general incompetence and constant harping had forced numerous case officers to transfer out of ROIC V. Fortunately, Tom left a few months after my arrival. He was replaced by Herman (another fictitious name), a model Aryan in his mid-forties, tall, slim, with a shock of snow-white hair. Herman had tremendous motivation, throwing himself into his job with a vengeance and decorating his office with pictures of dead Viet Cong. Usually he was quite formal, but occasionally he would loosen up and talk. "Ralph," he once told me, "those people in Headquarters didn't think it was a good idea for me to come out here. You see, my son was a Marine, and he was killed here. They didn't think I could bear up under the grief and maintain the proper perspective. They tried to discourage me from coming, but I just had to. I have to do my share."

For all his grief and obsession with avenging his son's death, Herman was a competent man. He was also a friend of the chief of station, Ted Shackley, so he got many important assignments. Herman in turn usually passed those jobs down to me. Numerous times each day he would buzz me to come down to his office where he would assign new tasks, check on the status of the previous day's requests, or bawl me out about past inadequacies.

Shortly after Herman became my boss, I gave him a copy of my memorandum explaining the composition of Communist insurgencies and suggested the Agency improve its coverage. Herman, who had spent most of his career in Europe, did not know what to think. But at least he talked to me and heard me out.

"Ralph, the rest of the world sees things differently," he said. "How can you be right?"

I understood his reaction. Here was a man new to Asia inundated with the same garbage briefings we had all endured. He had little background in Asia and knew zero about Asian Communist revolutions. How could he believe that one junior officer was better informed and had a clearer picture of the reality out there than all the rest of the Agency? If it had not been for my experience in Thailand, I would not have believed what I was saying either — simply because no one else was saying it, no intelligence reports mentioned it.

After a while I stopped agitating, and to escape, I buried myself in 12-hour work days, six days a week. (I worked only six hours on Sunday.) At the end of each long work day, I wearily returned to my small villa on Le Qui Don Street, or as it was commonly called, leaky dong. The villa sat next to the U.S. Information Agency's Abraham Lincoln Library and only a short distance from the Agency's Duc Hotel. I searched the various U.S. libraries in Saigon for books about Vietnam to read at home, but the shelves were full of nothing but pap and tales of earlier military victories. So I bought a small Japanese TV and spent the last hour or so of each evening watching the poor selection of programs broadcast by the Armed Forces network.

Under normal circumstances my job would have been an outstanding opportunity and challenge. But my earlier motivation no longer existed. I had once believed that although the United States followed self-interest in our overseas programs, we matched this interest with a concern for the people in the foreign countries. Now I did not know what to believe. I doubted the Agency's intelligence, its personnel, and even its integrity. Furthermore, my simplistic view of communists as the incarnation of evil and the United States as all good was slowly beginning to change. I seemed to be the only one around who realized we couldn't win. I knew by now that any careful examination of available information, let alone the survey, would prove that the vast majority of the Vietnamese people were fighting against the U.S. troops and for the NLF. They had chosen the kind of government they wanted, and all American war efforts were aimed at postponing the inevitable.

Every waking moment I fought an internal battle of doubts and contradictions. I couldn't sleep, my head ached all the time, the tension was terrible. My stomach reacted and sometimes I felt like vomiting. I had no one to talk to about my distress. Allen, for years a good friend, had been assigned to Vietnam by the Agency. We met a couple of times for dinner and drinks, but I could not relate to him. I was obsessed with what was happening to me, he could not really understand it, and small talk was impossible. So I spent all my time either at work or alone at home watching TV and drinking, hating it, longing for some human contact. All I wanted was to be home with my family and away from this awful place.

After six months I qualified for home visitation leave. I arrived in Herndon, Virginia, exhausted and high-strung from the unrelenting pressures of the job and my own mental agony. After several days of my incessant monologue about Vietnam and the Agency, Norma could take it no longer and I lapsed into relative silence. I began looking for another job, writing letters and making phone calls. But I had nothing to note on a resumé because I could not reveal that I worked for the CIA. Thus, these attempts failed.

I had been home a week when I received a telephone call from the secretary of William Nelson, the Far East division chief. She said that because the office of training had used my suggestion about the survey operation, I had been awarded $300 and a certificate of appreciation from CIA director Richard Helms. Nelson would present these to me at a staff meeting the next day if I could be present. I agreed.

I lay awake all night dreading the award ceremony. The irony of receiving the award from Nelson, who had threatened to ruin my career for submitting the proposal, was not lost on me. But of course he was required by regulations to make such ceremonial presentations. The six months in Vietnam had shown me the insanity of Agency programs there. An almost uncontrollable rage possessed me. I wanted to shout obscenities at the Agency for its blind intelligence and senseless killings. I feared the ceremony, for if it was necessary for me to speak, I knew I would lose control and the bottled-up rage would come bursting out.

The next day I went reluctantly to the Far East division's conference room located on the fifth floor. About a dozen of the division's top officials attended the meeting, and by the time I got there most had assembled. I took a seat on the couch in the rear while the others sat around a conference table. Some of the people in the room who had been my friends tried to engage me in conversation, but gave up when they saw my glare. Nelson began the meeting with the award ceremony. Petulantly he said, "Don't spend all 300 dollars. The tax hasn't been deducted yet." After reading part of the letter from the chief of the suggestion and achievement awards committee, he said, "That's enough here." He put the check and the letter and the certificate on the table in front of him, and I was forced to go up to him and pick them up. I grabbed them, turned, and without a word stomped out, slamming the door. My heart was pounding, and I was furious, but I had escaped without blowing up.

By about the tenth ·day of home leave I had begun to relax a little, only to feel the tension rising as I contemplated returning to Vietnam. I knew I ought to quit the Agency, but I was in a financial trap — four children in school, two of them in expensive colleges, a mortgage, no salable skills, and a mental condition ripe for an institution, not a new job. I justified staying by telling myself that I would continue to fight for the truth. If I quit, I would have no way to voice my views.

When I returned to Vietnam, I became ambitious. If I could not influence policy at my current middle level, GS-13, then I decided I would win promotions and work my way up in the bureaucracy where I could. I had not believed Nelson's earlier threat to block my promotions. I should have.

When Ted Shackley took over as chief of station, he notified all personnel that he based promotion recommendations on three criteria: the number of communists neutralized, the number of reports produced, and the number of unilateral recruitments achieved. Both Tom and Herman repeated over and over Shackley's message on promotion criteria.

My job as officer in charge, special police, would have been fascinating if I had believed in my work. Every major event in South Vietnam from January 1969 to July 1970 seemed to have at least some threads to my office. Until I was assigned to that position, however, the office had produced only one-half of one report a month. With three simple changes I increased the office's production 5,000 percent.

The first change in office procedure was to hire an adequate number of translators and interpreters. My case officers had frequently been standing in line waiting for a translator. Reports given to us for information or action would pile up and a month could go by before a necessary decision was made merely because of the translation backlog.

The second change was that I assumed a requirements and collation responsibility. I required case officers to route copies of all raw police reports to me. Frequently one report alone was not worthy of dissemination, but by combining a group of reports, significant and disseminable intelligence emerged. On one occasion I received a raw report that said all villagers had been warned by the communists to stay home for the next few days. Several other reports from the same vicinity indicated that the communists were planning something. I put these reports together into one collated report and noted that the various indicators suggested that the communists were planning an attack in that area. I sent my report to the station's report office, which disseminated it immediately. The attack occurred, but the government and U.S. troops were prepared and it was thwarted. Reports also frequently indicated a trend. By noting the trend, I suggested the kind of intelligence our people should be looking for. I was serving as an on-the-spot requirements and reports staff — a function normally performed by a rigid Headquarters bureaucracy back in Langley.

The last change merely amounted to placing square-shaped case officers in square jobs and round-shaped officers in round jobs. The case officers were talented but had not been slotted right. With them in proper assignments for their abilities, they began to produce.

Tom, my outgoing boss, suggested that I spread the office's production increase out over a longer period of time. He said the jump from one-half report a month to 25 within a two-month period made it appear as if he had not been doing his job, a correct assessment of the situation. In addition to the numerical increase, the reports were more substantive in content. It was a major coup to have a report published in the Agency's *Current Intelligence Digest*, but it became commonplace for us.

Our office handled what was probably the most important of the many spy cases in Vietnam — the Projectile operation. It had begun a year or more before I arrived and it was supposed to be providing information about the activities of a North Vietnamese spy net that had penetrated the highest levels of the Thieu government of South Vietnam. However, the information was so flimsy and our source had such dubious access that everyone doubted the story. I had followed the operational reports for a year. One of those said that Thieu's special assistant for political affairs, Huynh Van Trong, was a communist intelligence agent. Trong, in fact, according to the Projectile source, was a rather new member of the net and was less important than others in the group. The top man in the net was Vu Ngoc Nha, President Thieu's close friend, a respected Catholic intellectual, and an unofficial adviser on Catholic affairs. The Projectile source said the net included many other important government officials and military officers.

I received all of the special police reports from the CIA case officer working under my supervision. Every week or two I would prepare summaries of the operation for Herman and others in the station and occasionally a dispatch for

Headquarters.

The information began to predict the exact movement of the alleged communist spies. Police surveillance confirmed that they followed the schedules noted by the Projectile source. Weeks before the newspapers had the story, we learned from the source that President Thieu's special assistant for political affairs, Huynh Van Trong, was going to the United States on an extended trip to visit top-level officials there.

As confirmation piled on confirmation, I began to grow concerned. If, as it appeared, this was a communist intelligence net into the highest levels of Thieu's government, we should stop it. I broached the subject with the special police leadership, who seemed reluctant to end their best case. I then told Herman: "Look, we can no longer deny all of these accusations. If Huynh Van Trong is a communist spy and all the others are also, we should take some measures to roll up the net."

Herman, reflecting the prevailing wisdom, said, "It might be a communist deception operation. If the special police go out and arrest top government leaders and they're wrong, can you imagine the problems that would cause here and at home? Trong has just been to the U.S. He's just held talks with congressional and national security officials, so we've got to be careful. As a first step I want you to send a telepouch and get Headquarters' reaction to the idea."

The telepouch disturbed Headquarters. Its reply suggested the operation might be a communist deception and warned us to go slowly with plans to roll up the net. Any document from Headquarters came with the director's imprimatur and authority, though we had no way of knowing who was actually making the comments. As a result we all felt we were fighting a faceless bureaucracy.

When we received the reply from Headquarters, Herman buzzed me to come down. "I want you to do a full-scale review of the Projectile operation," he said. "I want to be absolutely sure of our position because if we are wrong, heads will roll. When you've finished with the summary analysis, we'll give copies to the special police and Headquarters. And if what we suspect is true, we will ask Langley for permission to arrest members of the net."

An amazing amount of paper — police and station reports, photos, and correspondence — had accumulated. One four-drawer filing cabinet contained most of the material. I vowed to resist Herman's pressure for immediate results, promising myself to take enough time to process the information thoroughly and to do a complete job.

I began by skimming through all of the material twice and eliminating three-fourths of it as repetitious or unessential. Next came the carding, a very tedious, time-consuming but necessary process. I carded to separate the information by individuals, to record links between people and events, and to record those in ways that would be easy to recall and locate. Carding the information required double processing — once to bring together the various scattered bits of information on individuals, and then to unite these into a discernible chronological or substantive pattern, much the way you would put together a jigsaw puzzle. As I compared the operation's information with police and Agency investigative material, most items checked out. Yet various explanations could account for the source's ability to predict the movement of government officials. Various explanations could account for any aspect of the operation's information. What was needed was some outside confirmation that this was, indeed, a communist intelligence net.

I had put off dealing with a discolored, ratty-looking old document that I had found in the back of the bottom drawer of our Projectile file cabinet. The document virtually defied understanding. It was an abominable translation from the Vietnamese of a report by an uneducated Vietnamese policeman. After postponing and procrastinating until everything else was done, I began to card the document. The language and syntax were terrible. It was as if someone had taken a box of phrases, like the old game of pick-up-sticks, and had thrown them out to fall where they may. Carding forced me to break the sentences down into component phrases and put them together again in an intelligible form. As I worked with the report, phrase by phrase, a form emerged.

The old document proved to be a gold mine. It described a communist intelligence operation in the South Vietnamese government. It was not unlike the net we were currently investigating, except there was one important difference. This operation had been directed at Diem's government years earlier. The document, dated circa 1962, showed that many members of the current Projectile net had held similar positions in that earlier communist intelligence group. With that information supporting what we got from Projectile, we had undeniable proof. I compiled a summary analysis, disseminated copies to various station elements, passed a copy to the special police, and telepouched copies to Headquarters.

Langley cabled acknowledgment of my summary. It acquiesced in our plans to roll up the net and again included a thinly disguised threat about what would happen if we were wrong. Herman and Shackley, convinced by my summary, backed efforts to roll up the net. But the police urged delay, as an important member of the net had left Saigon and might return.

One Agency case officer I shall call Vince had worked with President Thieu for years; his sole job was to maintain direct contact with Thieu. He carried all of the day-to-day messages that passed between the station and the embassy and Thieu, lessening the need for regular contact between Thieu and Shackley and Thieu and U.S. Ambassador Ellsworth Bunker. Over the years Vince and Thieu had come to understand and like each other and had become close friends. Shackley told Vince that he had to impress on Thieu the importance of arresting all the individuals in the net. Shackley could not justify continued CIA support when the top levels of the government were loaded with Communist spies.

Vince met with Thieu, who was extremely upset when he heard about the operation and our plans to arrest all of the members of the net. He claimed that if the story broke, the publicity would undermine his government. Thieu suggested delaying so that he could slowly and quietly dismiss those individuals in the net. Vince reported that for the first time he had to get nasty with Thieu. "I shook my fist under his nose," he said, "and asked him, 'How in hell can we justify further expenditure of American lives and money while communist spies are everywhere and you won't take action against them?'"

After a long argument, Thieu finally relented.

The colonel in charge of the special police took extreme precautions to ensure that word of the impending arrests would not leak out. His small secret police cadre prepared individual files on each person to be arrested. Late one afternoon, he called a task force in to his office, then cut them off from outside contact. He briefed each three-man arrest team separately and passed them copies of the file on their target individual. At midnight the police fanned out through Saigon and pulled in the net.

Herman had directed me to go to police headquarters that night and use a walkie-talkie radio to report the progress of the arrests to him. When the first arrests came in and the early information indicated that this was indeed a North Vietnamese intelligence net, I tried to call Herman. But because of the interference from the metal in the police buildings I couldn't get through, so I went out in the middle of the street in front of the police compound. In the daytime this pavement was a cacophonous swirl of cars, bicycles, and pedestrians. Now it was deserted, silent, and serene, a soft breeze blowing in the darkness. I called Herman and told him the good news. He was excited, and for the first time since coming to Vietnam I had a feeling of personal satisfaction.

I talked to Herman many times that night and the news got better and better. The operation had been a complete success. House searches by the police had uncovered a wide assortment of clandestine paraphernalia — microfilm of secret documents, document-copying cameras, one-time radio encoding and decoding pads, radios, secret ink, and a host of other material. The police also apprehended someone who had been visiting one of the targets. This visitor later turned out to be the head of a military intelligence net, providing my office with further work when that net was apprehended.

The police arrested more than 50 persons, 41 of whom ultimately were tried and convicted. The net had penetrated upper echelons of South Vietnamese society and government, including businessmen, military officers, teachers, students, and two top officials in the "open arms" program which was supposed to encourage Viet Cong to defect to the government. President Thieu's special assistant for political affairs, Huynh Van Trong, held the highest office. His Communist superior, however, Vu Ngoc Nha, possessed the most influence and was a close friend of President Thieu.

Nha confessed and said he had joined the Communist Party in 1949. In 1955 he came south in the CIA-generated refugee migration to set up an intelligence net, which had achieved some success before Diem's police rolled it up. Following Diem's fall in 1963 the new government released thousands of political prisoners, including Nha and all of his group. Nha arranged to have all record of his group's activities removed from police files and destroyed. The only report he did not get was the one old, tattered, English-language translation that had somehow ended up in the Projectile file cabinet. After a short cooling-off period, Nha rebuilt his net. The Catholics accepted him as a leading intellectual and made him an important member of their group. He served as President Thieu's adviser on Catholic affairs and was instrumental in having Thieu appoint Trong as his special assistant.

Trong confessed and said he attained that position through Nha's intercession with Thieu. Nha had recruited Trong by promising him the position of presidential special assistant. Trong understandably did not know where the power lay in Thieu's administration. Once, Trong had taken an official trip to the United States and held discussions over a period of weeks with top-level officials in our government. Upon returning to South Vietnam, he went directly to Thieu's office. Nha was with Thieu. Thieu ordered an immediate oral report of the trip. Trong said he was a little abashed to give his report simultaneously to the President and his own Communist superior. Later he compiled a written report for Thieu and gave a duplicate to Nha.

Our office wrote an intelligence report based on Trong's confession. Langley nit-picked and questioned its validity. We rechecked all details and forwarded those results to Headquarters. Langley finally permitted limited dissemination of that report to the U.S. intelligence community. While our Projectile operation had been successful beyond any of my dreams, this was obviously not the kind of success that the CIA's top officials wanted to see. For the report of the Projectile operation showed that our ally in this longest of wars had a government so riddled by enemy spies that they were able to operate under the nose of the President. It provided further evidence that the CIA had not only stubbornly refused to see the strength of the enemy but also had never acknowledged the weakness of our "friends." To me, it was obvious that we were bolstering a hopelessly corrupt government that had neither the support nor the respect of the Vietnamese people. This was not welcome news to the Agency or to U.S. policymakers who had invested so much money and human life in this futile struggle.

The success of the Projectile operation would seem at first glance to support William Colby's statement in his book, *Honorable Men*, that CIA officers in the early 1970s ". . . were getting more — and more accurate — reports from inside VCI [Viet Cong infrastructure] provincial committees and regional [Communist] party headquarters from brave Vietnamese holding high ranks in such groups. They had been first identified by people who knew them, then recruited by our intelligence officers."[36] But if I could reveal the identity of our source on the Projectile operation, it would lend no support to Colby's contention, which is pure fantasy. The truth is that never in the history of our work in Vietnam did we get one clear-cut, high-ranking Viet Cong agent. The Agency, in collaboration with the South Vietnamese intelligence services, developed hundreds of so-called access agents. Yet one purge of its agent lists saw more than 300 dropped for fabrication or lack of contact. Despite a single-minded determination to recruit a valid penetration of the Viet Cong, the Agency failed. The chief of station, desperate to prod his troops, offered an on-the-spot promotion to the officer able to recruit a province-level communist agent. No one earned that promotion. The fact that neither we, nor the South Vietnamese government, could produce one valid high-level reporting communist penetration agent is a comment on *Honorable Men* and on the South Vietnamese attitude toward the Diem, Ky, and Thieu regimes. The Viet Cong, on the other hand, had thousands of penetrations into the South Vietnamese government.

There were a few others within the Agency who were noticing the same things that I was. In May 1969 two analysts at Langley, Sam Adams and Robert Klein, using some of our Projectile material, began trying to estimate the number of spies in Thieu's government. Adams told a top official in the South Vietnam branch of the Directorate for Operations that he had discovered references in various documents indicating that there were more than 1,000 communist agents in Thieu's government. The official said: "For God's sake, don't open that Pandora's box. We have enough trouble as it is." In late November 1969, Klein and Adams compiled a report concluding that the total number of Viet Cong agents in the South

Vietnamese army and government was in the neighborhood of 30,000. If that report had been made public, it would have had enormous ramifications. How could we continue to support a government and army that were so widely infiltrated, that obviously had no hope of standing on their own? But the Agency forbade dissemination of that report. Both Adams and Klein later quit the CIA.

The follow-up to the serendipitous arrest of the head of another intelligence net during the roll-up of Nha's group occupied much of the time of the police and my office. That accidentally apprehended Communist intelligence officer, Van Khien, had led a North Vietnamese military intelligence operation into command elements of the South Vietnamese army (ARVN). Van Khien refused to talk, but careful checking, investigation, and police action located 10 members of his net. From that point we continued to unravel leads from Khien's and Nha's nets and other nets, arresting agents in two- and three-man increments.

Intelligence production from my office continued at an average of 25 reports a month. My officers were forbidden by the station from attempting to recruit their police liaison counterparts, so I had now more than fulfilled all of Shackley's requirements for promotion. Herman, before he left for a better job in the station, wrote a fitness report for me. It was highly complimentary but not enough so to bring about the automatic promotion as dictated by Shackley's guidelines. I gathered together the office logs and made an appointment with Herman.

I went over my accomplishments since taking over the job as officer in charge of special police — the increase in quantity and quality of reports, the Projectile net, the ARVN net. "You know my case officers are forbidden to attempt unilateral recruitments," I said, "but in Shackley's two remaining categories for promotion I have the best record in the station. I have more than fulfilled all the requirements you have been harping on, and now I deserve and expect a promotion."

"You know, Ralph," Herman said, "there are various people in this station younger than I am who are higher grades.

But I can't let this bother me. I just do my job the best I can. I recommend that you do the same."

"Are you telling me that you and Shackley have no intention of honoring your pledge?"

Herman was disconcerted by my question. He shifted uncomfortably in his chair and then responded, "Ralph, did you really believe he meant that? If you did, you are naive."

We talked for an hour, but he would not rewrite the fitness report. Months later Herman's deputy came to my office. He said that I was not in the just-completed round of GS-13 promotions but that I would be promoted the following year.

Herman was replaced by a Shackley protégé from the European division I shall call Harry. He had not particularly wanted to come to Vietnam and quickly proved to me that he was an incompetent flake. In a matter of weeks he destroyed all that I had so carefully built. He assigned key positions to officers from the European division who had been drafted for a tour in Vietnam. These new European case officers were inexperienced and not overly motivated. The old Vietnam hands, transferred to less attractive junior assignments, became bitter and uncooperative. The results were predictable and immediate. For the last three months of my tour we did not produce one intelligence report. Harry blamed me for the fall in production, but the trend continued for at least another year after I left. Harry, based on his unquestioning loyalty to Shackley, eventually attained supergrade rank and assignment to an important overseas post.

When it was time for me to go home, the head of the special police awarded me a medal and at the ceremony draped across my shoulders the Viet Cong flag that had flown over Saigon's central marketplace at the height of the Tet offensive. He entreated me to stay, and so did various station officers, but I couldn't wait to get out of that desolate country.

At the airport, I had an hour's wait before my plane took off. I sat down at a table in the dirty terminal restaurant and ordered a beer. A Eurasian who spoke fair English joined me. We exchanged casual conversation for a while, and then he asked if I would mind carrying a suspicious-looking package to the States for him. It struck me as absurd and ironic that the last thing I was being asked to do on my Vietnam tour was to transport heroin back to the United States. I told the man to go to hell.

My plane took off, and I sat by the window looking down at all the bomb pockmarks in the Vietnamese landscape. There seemed no hope for this poor, tortured country nor for ours. How many more Vietnamese and Americans would die here? How many more civilians would we kill, how many children would we napalm? Nothing seemed capable of stopping the U.S. juggernaut from pursuing its own fantasies. Certainly my own efforts to stop it had been in vain. The reality that I had seen and reported and urged my superiors to recognize had been totally rejected. The fantasies and illusions lived on.

I thought back to the time in Gia Dinh Province when I had planned to kill myself as a way of protesting all the things the Agency had done to create the bestial inhumanity of the Vietnam War. I had seen at first hand the ubiquitous refugee camps inhabited by scarred children and old people who had been bombed out of their villages and forced into those abysmal hovels. I again visualized the panic and pain of the children and could smell the stench of their burning flesh as they ran from the napalm. These things and others the CIA through its false information and covert operations had brought forth and, at that point in Gia Dinh, I had chosen to live by promising that some day I would expose the Agency's role in Vietnam. As I looked down on the battered countryside I renewed that promise and swore never to rest until I fulfilled that commitment.

I was glad to be going home. But I knew I would never be the same person again. All of my ideals of helping people, all my convictions about the processes of intelligence, all my respect for my work, all the feelings of joy in my life, all my concepts of honor, integrity, trust and love, all in fact that had made me what I was, had died in Vietnam. Through its blindness and its murders, the Agency had stolen my life and my soul. Full of anger, hatred, and fear, I bitterly contemplated a dismal future.

11.
COMING HOME

The director of the Agency for International Development, John Hannah, . . . "acknowledged today that the USAID program is being used as a cover for operations of the CIA. . . ."[1]

BEFORE leaving Saigon, I had asked for and been granted another tour in Thailand. I did not particularly want to go there or anywhere with the Agency, but if I had to remain with the CIA, being with my family overseas in Thailand seemed the least objectionable option.

I first had to return to Washington from Saigon [14 words deleted]. AID conducted several weeks of briefings in the old street-car barn just across Key Bridge in Georgetown for [one word deleted] and retired police officials recruited for overseas slots. I looked for a job during free periods between briefings and later during several weeks of home leave. Again security was an insurmountable problem. Unable to admit CIA employment and with no apparent salable talents, I could not find other employment.

The few weeks between my return from Saigon and our moving to Thailand were difficult for the family and me. Norma took my brooding silence personally. She had vehemently proclaimed so many times that she never wanted to go overseas again, especially to Thailand, and here we were making travel plans. Her attempts to talk with me about our problems got nowhere. I either shouted her down or, when that didn't work, rushed out of the house. It seemed that I had lost the ability to communicate with anyone.

I did not want my children damaged by my experiences, so I tried to protect them from the causes of my problems. In the years after we told the children I worked for the CIA, I had talked, even boasted, about the Agency and the good it was doing in the world. This was particularly true during my last tour in Thailand, where I constantly preached that we were fighting the communist murderers. The children had absorbed my teachings. Now I had changed but could not and would not explain this to them.

My older daughter, Peggy, thoroughly indoctrinated by me about the Agency and its benefits to the world, carried these views with her to college. She attended Wellesley College while I was serving in Vietnam. One day the professors and students held an anti-war protest, but Peggy refused to join them. Almost alone of the staff and students, she went to all her classes in a counter protest.

Scott, my older son, was 16 when I returned. He had the long hair, the raggedy clothes, and the contempt of all things parental and traditional that was typical of the era. He and his friends wanted nothing to do with school activities, working, studying, and all the things that my generation felt were so necessary. His long hair drove me wild. Did not tradition, wisdom, and custom dictate that a clean shave and a close-cropped head of hair embodied respectability and goodness?

One day Scott and I had a confrontation in our downstairs rec room, Scott standing on one side of our pool table and I on the other like a pair of reluctant combatants. He had cut school and had been seen driving around town in his combination clubhouse-van with his buddies. I had been away in Vietnam, and he was not used to my authority. When I told him I was taking away his privilege of driving the van — part of his identity — he reacted angrily. The tension was considerable, but each of us was puzzled by the other. We had grown distant in the past year and a half, and neither knew just what to do. Norma finally stepped in and suggested a compromise, which I welcomed.

I had ambivalent feelings. The long-haired hippies were protesting the war, something I now wanted to do. Yet I could not apply those feelings to my own family. If I could accept one, I should have been able to accept the other. But I could not.

One day while attending the AID briefings in Georgetown, I decided to take a walk on the extended lunch break.

It was a hot summer day, but I was dressed in a dark blue suit and a tie. I carried a briefcase with me and must have appeared the typical bureaucrat.

That area of Georgetown was the gathering place of hippies. Young people in various stages of dress hung out or sat on second- and third-story window ledges, watching the passing scene. Observing the new culture, I strolled down M Street to Wisconsin Avenue, where young people were walking, lounging in doorways, holding hands, passing out leaflets, and conducting serious discussions. I felt out of place yet in sympathy with them. I wished I could join them. Two young girls in long, peasant-style dresses came up and asked if I would attend a performance of live theatre being held around the corner. I looked at them, expecting mockery, but there was none. I could not say it, but I felt close to them. I wanted to say yes, I agree the war should be stopped, what we are doing is evil and wrong, I want to shed my protecting suit and put on jeans and be one of you. But all these things I could not say or do.

12.
DOWN AND OUT
IN THAILAND

IN late September 1970, Norma, Scott, Dan, and I flew
to Thailand, leaving the two girls behind in college. We soon
found an apartment building located not far from the International School of Bangkok. A large number of American
safe-haven families lived there to be near their husbands and
fathers in Vietnam.

The American high school reflected the unhappiness and
frustrations of the time for families. The school had earned a
reputation for its high academic standards and strict discipline.
On a previous tour our daughters had attended the school and
had received a good education in a healthy atmosphere. But
things had changed.

The school was now separated from the surrounding Thai
community by an eight-foot-high fence topped by barbed
wire. The shadow of the Vietnam War and the large military
presence in Thailand brought increasing numbers of unhappy
and alienated young people to the school. Many of them were
the sons and daughters of military officials carrying out the
war. Each morning these disaffected students had to endure
a clothing inspection, filing into the school compound through
a single narrow entrance. Those not properly dressed were
sent home. Drug use was common. GIs on leave were ready
sources, and directly outside the school, a vendor sold small
bags of pot from a tea cart. For $10 students bought gum
opium or vials of 98 percent pure heroin powder. Thai phar-
macies sold barbiturates and amphetamines.

One night Norma and I were relaxing in our apartment
just after dinner when a teenage girl started pounding at our
door, screaming that her friend, Mary, was threatening to jump

off the roof. I dashed out the door and up the stairs with Norma close behind. Mary was sitting near the railing in one corner and was strangely quiet. We approached carefully to avoid scaring her, but when she did not seem aware of our presence, we rushed forward and grabbed her. I carried her downstairs to the apartment and put her on the couch.

Mary, her friend explained, had taken some pills and freaked out. I went two floors down to her apartment and the maid told me that Mary's parents would not be home for some time. Back upstairs everything was wild. Mary was thrashing about, hollering and screaming that she wanted to go back on the roof. We tried to placate her, but refused to let her leave. Moaning and mumbling, looking wildly at nothing, Mary started hallucinating, pointing at the wall, and crying out. Norma restrained her while I tried to call the American doctor, who was not available. Finally she relaxed and slowly drifted off to sleep shortly before her parents came to pick her up.

A few weeks later, a high school student living above us, whose father was a much-decorated Marine colonel in Vietnam, convulsed from an overdose of drugs and was rushed to the U.S. Military's Fifth Field Hospital, where he almost died. It was only after these incidents that I discovered that the leaders of the American community had kept a lid on stories about drug-related problems. I learned that in the 1971-1972 school year, six students died from overdoses. More than 20 percent of all official American families in Thailand had to return to the States before the end of their tours because of drug problems.

Scott's attitude remained the same as it had been back in Herndon. He wanted nothing to do with school and the traditional life I had always taken for granted. He would board the school bus each morning, but frequently got off and spent the day drifting around the city. He hated the school and the atmosphere and was confused by the events occurring all around him. He tried to convince us to send him back to the States. Finally, after months of discussion and an invitation for him to stay in the home of friends in Herndon, we relented. It seemed that this was the only acceptable alternative.

On Scott's last day in Thailand I took him to school to pick up his report card, which showed he had earned grades from incomplete down to F. We sat in the car in the school parking lot and I tried to explain to him the necessity of an education.

"Scott," I said, "for thousands of years, billions of people have all had the same thoughts and ideas that you have now. They have all lived through the same feelings you have now. And yet they have recognized that education is important. Can't you entertain the idea that you might be wrong?"

I knew some of what he was feeling. My own experiences with the Agency often made me feel that I was the only one who was right and everyone else was wrong.

That night we took Scott to Don Muang airport. Norma, Dan, and I tried to be cheerful, while hiding our sorrow. The plane was announced and he departed, leaving a gaping hole in our life.

My job as deputy chief of the anti-Communist Party operations branch required that I help the chief of the branch supervise the activities of a number of persons, mostly case officers working in liaison. But I soon realized that nothing had changed except my perception about the CIA's work. We were doing the same old things as before, collecting intelligence designed to support U.S. policy goals in Thailand. This meant, of course, supporting the military dictatorship in power and ignoring problems caused by it. For the most part we got our intelligence directly from the leaders themselves or our liaison counterparts, who never, never reported derogatory information about the regime. We lived in a fantasy world; conversations sounded like the movies. We all had assigned roles and lines. To speak outside of the script was to bring down the wrath of all. Even now I have difficulty understanding how we played the game.

As in Iran, Vietnam, Latin America, and other areas of the world, we only wanted intelligence that told us our policies were correct. We did not want to know that the U.S.-backed dictators brutalized their people and that those people were angry.

To avoid hearing such news, the Agency did not allow its case officers to maintain direct contact with the general population. We sent case officers — only a few of whom knew the native language — on two-year tours. The case officers worked with the English-speaking members of the society's elite, never with the grubby working class. Although more than 80 percent of the Thai population are farmers, in 30 years there the Agency virtually never wrote an intelligence report based on an interview with a farmer (other than my survey reports). Instead it wrote reports on the problems government leaders-dictators were having with the rebellious people. If a language-qualified officer did develop contacts with the working classes and began getting information from them, he was immediately labeled derisively as having "gone native" and was soon on his way back to the States. I had seen the same pattern in Taiwan years before, but it hadn't occurred to me that anything was wrong. And we continue to see the same pattern today, as Agency bungling of intelligence in, among others, Iran and El Salvador in recent years have shown.

Thailand station was a large installation and its activities demonstrate many of the things that were wrong with the CIA. The station conducted a wide range of covert operations: counterinsurgency, psychological, paramilitary, external political and others. Here are some examples.

Counterinsurgency. Thailand station in 1970 performed as I expected in this field. [One 27-word sentence deleted.] Neither the station's operational efforts nor its reporting acknowledged the main focus of communist activity — the secret development of a massive rural political organization among the peasantry. No one seemed to know anything about the communist village organization.

A major problem was that top officials in the Thai station simply did not have the experience and knowledge necessary to run a decent operation. As an example, one day in early 1971 I attended a meeting with the head of a prominent counterinsurgency organization, whom I shall call General Chamnong, and several other officers. The purpose of the meeting was to permit the deputy chief of station to brief General Chamnong on his views of how Chamnong's organization should counter insurgency. [One 12-word sentence deleted.]

Since the deputy chief of station had called for this

special meeting, Chamnong expected some major pronounce-
ment. Instead the deputy chief of station, relatively new to
Southeast Asia, offered the full American litany on recommended counterinsurgency programs and actions. His main
point was that General Chamnong's unit should be used to cut
the links between the communist guerrillas and the villagers.
To emphasize his point, the deputy chief drew a representa-
tion of a village on a piece of paper and then encircled the
village — the circle representing that unit's "link-cutting"
operation. We older hands realized that in any province,
General Chamnong's organization had perhaps one effective
officer. That individual would be hard pressed just handling
his responsibilities in the capital of the province. Visiting numerous isolated villages and then cutting the links between the
villagers and the guerrillas was not even a remote possibility.

General Chamnong, never at a loss for words, regurgitated
the deputy chief's ritualistic counterinsurgency chant. That
weird exchange went on for about an hour. Later Chamnong
admitted the meeting had confused and worried him. He did
not know if the deputy chief was angry or if there was some
undecipherable message contained in his words. Mercifully,
Chamnong did not realize that the deputy chief had only presented his honest recommendation for a counterinsurgency
program.

Psychological Warfare Operations. To judge from press
accounts, Thailand station created a number of small disasters
in this area. Hoping to stimulate the Thai government to greater anti-communist efforts and simultaneously to trick the
Communist Party into believing its leadership was divided on
the question of armed versus peaceful revolution, the station
allegedly composed and wrote a letter to the Prime Minister.
According to accounts in both the American and Thai press,
the station in late 1973 sent a forged letter to the Prime Minister in the name of a leading official of the Communist Party
in Northeast Thailand. The letter offered an insulting cease-fire
to the Thai government in return for local autonomy in "liber-
ated areas" near Laos.[1] According to press accounts, the CIA
man in Sakorn Nakorn mailed it from there. **[Two sentences
for a total of 29 words deleted.]** When the Prime Minister received the letter, he vehemently and publicly rejected its offer
and decried the arrogance of the Communist Party in the

press. Apparently all was well and the operation a success. However, a reporter became suspicious. He acquired a copy of the letter and traced it back to Sakorn Nakorn. Tracing the letter was easy, because the man who mailed it had been impressed by the addressee and had decided it was too important to send by regular mail. He registered the return address to what the press referred to as the "CIA office" in Sakorn Nakorn. When the story broke, it created a barrage of anti-CIA articles in the Thai press, all indignant about the CIA's meddling in Thai affairs. That CIA operation accomplished what years of communist propaganda had been unable to do — it created anti-American demonstrations among normally pro-American Thais.

To top that bungled operation, a short while later one of our case officers attempted to recruit a Thai in a Bangkok coffee shop. The Thai man recorded and reported the attempted recruitment. The story broke and Thai-American relations fell to their lowest point. Not much later, Sam's principal agent, mentioned earlier, the former Communist Party central committee member who supposedly had created a splinter group to follow the peaceful path to revolution, decided to join the attack. He wrote a book about CIA activities in Thailand.[2] [One sentence of 19 words deleted.]

Another example of CIA image-bungling relates to one of its sore spots — the exposure of Agency personnel operating under various types of cover. The Agency howls at the exposure of its overseas personnel by its number one antagonist, Philip Agee, a former employee who writes books about the CIA. But the Agency often facilitates that identification. On one occasion in Thailand, the chief of station planned an all-employee party to be held in his home. It was a large house with a swimming pool known to all knowledgeable Thais as the home of the CIA's chief of station. The chief of one branch [one word deleted] of the station pleaded that his cover-sensitive subordinates should not be forced to attend. He noted that the local police guided the traffic and parking for the celebrants and that they most likely kept a record of the license plates of the attendees. He won the argument temporarily. But to his dismay the chief of station decided to hold two parties, one for those under light cover and another for those under deeper cover. What little concealment might have been provided by the single party was lost by this convenient separation into two groups.

Paramilitary. In the early 1950s the CIA's creation and support of the Police Aerial Reconnaissance Unit (PARU) in Thailand was a model for paramilitary operations. General Edward Lansdale's 1961 memorandum on unconventional warfare explained: "The PARU has a mission of undertaking clandestine operations in denied areas. 99 PARU personnel have been introduced covertly to assist the Meos [Hmong] in operations in Laos. . . . This is a special police unit supported by CIA . . . with a current strength of 300 being increased to 550 as rapidly as possible. . . . There are presently 13 PARU teams, totaling 99 men, operating with the Meo guerrillas in Laos."[3]

From Lansdale's description it is evident that the CIA used PARU as an extension of its own paramilitary officers and to conceal its own role. The CIA apparently could not motivate Laotians to fight for us, so it substituted the Hmong hill tribers. The CIA recruited those mountain tribesmen and used PARU to lead them in fighting the Communist Pathet Lao forces.

Over the years this "secret war" grew into a major conflagration. It became more a conventional war with artillery bombardments, aerial bombing, and big unit movements. All that effort was linked by a massive CIA support and transportation complex.

As in Vietnam the CIA refused to acknowledge the real nature of the Communist Pathet Lao. Through PARU and the Hmong it developed an army loyal to the United States and dependent upon the CIA. But without a commitment by the Laotians, the CIA's private army finally in 1975 succumbed to the reality of the overwhelmingly superior Pathet Lao forces. The Hmong who cooperated with the CIA are now a dying tribe. The war destroyed their young men. Remnants of their tribe now live an impoverished, uncertain existence in refugee camps in Thailand.

In another ill-fated paramilitary operation, the CIA supported the 4,500-man Border Patrol Police in Thailand. According to General Lansdale's memorandum cited above, the BPP's mission was "to cope with problems posed by foreign guerrilla elements using Thailand as a safe haven: the

Vietminh in eastern Thailand and the Chinese Communists along the Malayan border in the south."[4] But that rationale was specious because the Viet Minh had dissolved in the mid-1950s and even then it had never operated in eastern Thailand or anywhere at all in that country. The Chinese Communists also did not operate in Thailand or along the Malayan border.

As Lansdale noted in his memorandum, over the years the mission of the BPP changed to: "counter infiltration and subversion during peace-time, in addition to normal police duties, in the event of an armed invasion of Thailand, the BPP will operate as guerrilla forces in enemy-held areas, in support of regular Thai armed forces."[5]

Clearly all CIA rationale for supporting the BPP was based on false premises, not at all unusual in the secrecy-protected isolation of Agency bureaucracy.

External Operations. These were operations conducted in Thailand to gather information on third countries. [One word deleted] operations branch [one word deleted] of Thailand station conducted intelligence-collection activities aimed at the [one word deleted] Communist government.

Thailand station, bigger than many others, tried to recruit agents to go to [one word deleted] from among the extensive [two words deleted] community. [Three words deleted] case officers necessarily developed their own conceptual blindness. Locating a [two words deleted] traveling to [one word deleted], contacting, recruiting, training, and dispatching him is a difficult and time-consuming task, while the result of the total effort is negligible — a report on the situation in the agent's native village, the rice production, the attitude of the people, and sights seen traveling from the village. When balanced against the totality of [one word deleted], the information was valueless.

Political Commentary. The Thailand station was a top producer of political commentary, but this reporting created opportunities and pressures for unethical practices. I frequently saw case officers get a news tidbit, add a few references to earlier reports, and with flair and imagination embellish the item into a full-blown intelligence report. One of the most widespread abuses of this sort was coup reporting. The Thais' biennial semi-coups and the station's own creative activities caused Thailand station, like many others around the world, to fall into a reporting cycle on potential coups d'etat. In CIA reporting a group emerges, plans a coup, postpones the coup several times, and then fades from sight. Each stage in the coup cycle spawns its own series of intelligence reports. Most often no coup occurs, so in CIA reporting the same or a new coup group simply repeats the cycle. A case officer develops a symbiotic relationship with his agent, who perceives what information is wanted and may invent or create the necessary information. If, however, the information is genuine and a coup overturns the government, a station sometimes is caught by surprise in mid-cycle. With the new government comes a rash of counter-coup reports. Through this type of collection or imagination, a station's political officers always have the most reports.

But of course coup reporting can lead to absurdities like the one John Stockwell described in his book, *In Search of Enemies*. Stockwell said that as a case officer on an early first tour he found an agent, KRNEUTRON/1 (N-1), living a life of penniless indolence. Stockwell recruited N-1 to be his eyes and ears in the country. Stockwell pressed N-1 to produce intelligence. "Are you sure there is no coup plotting? What about your cousin, the late President's son?" asked Stockwell. N-1 talked to his cousin, and sure enough he was dissatisfied with the regime. From there a coup took root, and at least in Agency reporting, grew to large proportions. Headquarters was delighted with the intelligence and authorized bonuses, ignoring that the plotters were all immature youths. The plot was discovered by government authorities, and N-1 spent seven years in jail. Stockwell was young at the time and sincerely believed he was only collecting intelligence. It never occurred to him until later that he had formulated the plot.[6]

Stockwell's story is not unique. The same thing, with many variants, happened again and again throughout much of the world while the Agency reported volumes of self-contrived intelligence that made it look good to the President and his national security advisers.

I now recognized most of the Agency's problems in these various areas. Watching the fantasies of Agency "intelligence" operations caused my blood to boil. I was in a permanent state of distress, but I regarded my tour in Thailand as just a way to pass the time until I could retire. Sometimes I thought back to my football playing days at Notre Dame. Then I had been able to try my best, put my entire being into the game, feel the satisfaction of striving, working, and winning. But now on my job it was impossible to win. If you tried, you were beaten down by any one of many bureaucratic devices, and all you could do was swallow and pretend.

I still felt we should try to stop the spread of the Communist Party of Thailand and that to do so we first had to recognize its composition. Recognizing its true structure and nature, of course, would ultimately lead to acknowledging the true structures and natures of the Laotian, the Vietnamese, and by now also the Cambodian communist movements. If we did this, I now realized, the only sensible policy would be to withdraw our forces immediately from those countries — or to drop nuclear bombs on the people. I felt that if we were spending millions of dollars in Thailand building up the strength of the Thai military, we should at least try to report accurately on the communist insurgency it was supposed to be fighting. But having lost that battle before in Vietnam and earlier in Thailand, I decided to try to keep my peace and observe the ongoing fantasy.

Early on in this tour I met with some of the Thais who had worked with me three years earlier on the survey operations. A station officer asked me to visit his area upcountry to help him build good relations with the Thais, especially Colonel Chat Chai of the police, who had led the management team of the surveys. I traveled to Udorn in the Northeast, where a group of police officers were having a large dinner party for some Americans. It was held on a roof-garden of a local hotel with a small band providing the usual bad background music. Colonel Chat Chai seemed glad to see me and found a quiet table where he, the station officer, and I could talk. The colonel was a changed man. Before he had worked long, hard hours eschewing any diversions; now he was the opposite. The station officer had told me earlier that the colonel had a mistress and spent much of his time relaxing and enjoying life. The colonel was the first to admit the change.

"Before, the police collected intelligence on the

communists," he said. "Now that job has been taken away from us. If the communists cause an incident, I or one of my men will go out and walk around, and that's all. Others are supposed to take care of the problem, so I don't bother."

In becoming a cynic, Colonel Chat Chai had lost his giggle and had picked up some of the Thai evasions and circumlocutions. The all-powerful Thai military had taken over the responsibility for counterinsurgency and intelligence. This was the "others" he referred to.

He asked me, "What do you do? Any plans to start the surveys again?"

"Hell, I tried back at Headquarters and then in Vietnam to get the surveys going," I responded, "but people just aren't interested. So I just do what they tell me and pass the time of day the best I can. I started studying Thai again and it helps me keep my mind off what is going on."

We talked freely like this for hours. The CIA officer did not benefit from my visit and probably wished that I had stayed away. Colonel Chat Chai and I had both realized the futility of additional effort. We sadly wished each other goodbye.

One day Lieutenant Somboon, the leader of the survey teams, came to the station to see me. For security reasons, station employees were not allowed to bring foreign nationals into our offices, so Somboon and I went down to the first-floor cafeteria. Somboon was still searching for answers.

"I am stationed in the South now," he said, "and we have a big insurgency there. I try to tell the people about the surveys, but they don't pay any attention. The surveys did so good I don't sure why they stopped. I talked to your people, but they don't know about the surveys. Do you plan to get them started again?"

Lieutenant Somboon, who had been so full of energy, ideas, suggestions, and plans, now seemed only troubled. I could do nothing to help him. The Thais who looked to us for advice on counterinsurgency had dropped the surveys because we had. "But I can't do anything about it," I said, "because I lack influence."

I looked at the confusion on his face, and I assume he read the pain in mine. In other times we would have spent hours talking and planning; now there was nothing to say. After a half hour we parted.

Another day I was sitting in the downstairs cafeteria drinking coffee when I spotted Jimmy Moe, the model warrior from my paramilitary training years before, standing just outside the glass-paneled rear door. He appeared to be in abject misery. Here was the man of indefatigable energy looking totally defeated. I thought I knew why. I was sure that he had come to regard himself as a Judas goat. For like that stockyard villain, he had led his followers to their destruction. The Hmong, whom he had led in Laos during our long battle with the Pathet Lao, were a dying tribe. (I wonder how the CIA officers now leading the Miskito Indians to fight in Nicaragua will regard themselves in ten years.) The Laotian war decimated the young men of the Hmong, and at this point it was all but lost. Jimmy appeared so downcast and broken that I held back from jumping up and saying hello. He might have sensed my gaze, for he looked up at me and recognition flashed in his eyes, immediately followed by a return to the look of pain. We contemplated each other, and a thousand thoughts passed unspoken between us. To try to renew our friendship would be nothing but painful. He turned away as I got up to leave.

One day just before Christmas 1971, as Norma, Dan, and I were about to leave the apartment to go to the beach at Hua Hin, we decided to call Scott. We finally got through and it was good to hear his voice. I jokingly said, "Why don't you come on back?" He responded, "Oh, if I only could." Taken by surprise, I asked if he really meant it. He said, "Yes, things are different than I thought, and I'd like a second chance."

"Great!" I yelled. "I can't do anything for a few days, but as soon as we get back from Hua Hin, I will make arrangements here." We wished him a merry Christmas, and those few days at Hua Hin were filled with the joyful anticipation of getting our older son back.

Two weeks later he arrived at Don Muang Airport. The change in him was obvious. He was well-dressed, his hair was shorter, and he was in good spirits. Over the next few months he earned excellent grades in school. He met a young girl whose father was serving as the State Department representative in Bangladesh. Scott and Lisa became close friends and years later, after both had graduated from top universities, they married. It was only then that Scott told me that our talk in the car the day he had left Thailand had helped him to turn his life around.

From the time of my arrival in Thailand I had felt pains in my back and the back of my thigh that were growing progressively worse. On a doctor's recommendation, I had exercised daily for a year to alleviate the pain and to build up the muscles of my stomach, compensating for the back's weakness. The pain grew so intense that sometimes standing at a cocktail party was intolerable. Sweat would break out all over, I would feel faint, and I would have to sit down or pass out.

I visited doctors at the Fifth Field Hospital and the Seventh Day Adventist Hospital. All diagnosed the problem as a deteriorating spinal disk that only exercise would help. Sleep became almost impossible, as every movement woke me up. In the morning I would lie on my back contemplating how best to get dressed in a way that would cause the least pain.

Promotions to GS-14 were announced. I was not promoted as Shackley and his assistant in Saigon had guaranteed the year before. The lack of sleep, the physical pain, the mental agony came together, and my pent-up anger burst out. Over the next few days I composed a long, bitter memorandum explaining all that had happened to me — the circumstances surrounding my suggestion about the surveys, the failed intelligence, the broken promises. I let out all the anger, the frustration, the disappointment, the disbelief, and the disgust. I routed the memo to the chief of station, who called me in and sympathetically suggested that I present my grievances to the touring inspector general, Gordon Stewart, who was on a pre-retirement trip around the world that is traditional for supergrade bureaucrats. To justify the expense of this trip, he went through the motions of work, not expecting any major problems like mine to be presented to him.

A couple of days after sending him a copy of my memorandum, I was sitting in the cafeteria when my secretary ran up to me and said, "The inspector general wants to see you right now!" I went upstairs to his office. He angrily looked up from my memorandum on his desk and said, "Shut the door, sit down."

From here the meeting got worse. He said, "I have read your memorandum, and after consultation with the chief of station, I am putting you on probation."

Hardened by previous experiences, I was not surprised. I looked at him and asked, "Haven't I followed the correct procedure in bringing these problems to you? If so, why am I being put on probation?"

He waffled and gagged and finally admitted that I had followed correct procedure. "Nevertheless you are on probation," he said, "and the chief of station wants to talk to you at 10 tomorrow morning."

The next day the chief of station, a tall handsome man in his early fifties who let his secretary run the station, told me to sit down. He was visibly upset and acted so strange that I soon realized that he had the office bugged, hoping to catch me in some indiscretion.

He began uncertainly explaining his position while glancing furtively at his hidden microphone. He said, "There comes a time in the careers of some Agency case officers when they can no longer function as members of the team. You seem to have reached that stage, and I am now placing you on special probation. I will be watching you closely for the next three months."

He did not explain what would happen to me if I didn't measure up, but I was not too worried as he was such a weak man that I felt he would never fire me. I was right, for later I found out that no one in Headquarters had heard about my probationary status. The chief, or more likely his secretary, did write a telepouch to Headquarters suggesting that I needed counseling.

The back pains became intense, and a doctor at the Fifth Field Hospital told me to stop exercising and then return to see him. The next day I couldn't get out of bed. I finally crawled downstairs in my pajamas and lay in the back of the car while Norma drove me to the hospital.

After a series of new tests the doctor said I had a ruptured disk. He and a Thai doctor, a specialist who was the King's private doctor, scheduled an operation to remove the disk. But Norma insisted that I be returned to the States for the operation.

The trip back to Washington was a nightmare of confusion. The hospital in Bangkok gave me a large supply of Valium to keep me relaxed, and the medic told me to drink booze to further numb my pain — a combination that is now regarded as almost fatal. By the time the plane arrived in Honolulu I was flying high from martinis and pills. All passengers had to disembark to go through customs. I could not walk straight and kept veering to my right, jostling and bumping into people.

The customs inspector, a young woman, was conscientious and somewhat officious. Norma, recognizing the danger, tried to push me back while she handled everything, but I resisted. At one of the inspector's questions I exploded. We argued vehemently, while Norma kept trying to shove me away. The chief of customs came over. He probably had been forewarned that a CIA medical evacuee was on the plane, and he took over and gave us an immediate okay.

My daughter Jean and her husband Joe met us at Washington's Dulles Airport and took me directly to Georgetown Hospital. The doctors injected dye into my spinal column and discovered that the disk the Bangkok doctors were going to remove was okay, but another was ruptured. The operation was performed immediately, and fortunately it was a success.

13.
LIGHT AT THE END
OF THE TUNNEL

WHEN I returned to work after the back operation and several months of recovery, I checked in with East Asia (formerly Far East) division's personnel management officer, whom I shall call Blacky. He was a heavy-set Boston politician, a ward-healer, a cynic — he jokingly called the Saigon station Disneyland East — who adjusted his views to the prevailing operational winds in the division. He had received the telepouch from Thailand recommending that I be given counseling. "What the hell happened out there?" he asked.

I outlined briefly some of my problems and told him that I had left a full memorandum on the subject with the personnel officer back in Thailand. Blacky said he would send for a copy.

"In your reassignment questionnaire you said you wanted to get out of the Operations Directorate and into the Intelligence Directorate," he said. "I shopped your file with Intelligence but they weren't interested, so now I'll shop it around here."

Later when he received the memo from Bangkok station, his attitude changed radically. For in the memo I accused Shackley — soon to become Blacky's boss as division chief — of deliberate misrepresentation. Concentrating only on the issue of the promotion and ignoring all the other points in the memo, Blacky asked, "Who told you you were going to get promoted? They can't do that."

Blacky put out the word that I was a malcontent and wrote two critical memoranda for my personnel file. Naturally all East Asia branch offices turned me down for jobs. I finally was given a temporary assignment working on a research project in the basement in an out-of-the-way records office where elderly ladies shuffled through ancient files. The assignment was designed to humiliate me. One other division outcast joined me in the Langley Siberia. We had little in common except our misery, but it was good to have someone join me in cursing the Agency.

While in exile I composed a memorandum to William Colby, who had assumed the job of executive director comptroller of the Agency. I outlined how the Agency's intelligence in Vietnam was grossly flawed and cited a few books and studies that backed up my opinions about the composition of the communist movement. I attached copies of my earlier recommendation to the suggestion and achievement awards committee and proposed that the Agency take corrective action. I did not expect, nor did I receive, an answer from him. After a few days I forgot about it, but Colby apparently didn't. James Schlesinger, newly appointed as CIA director, was about to circulate his directive ordering all Agency employees to notify him of inappropriate or illegal Agency operations. The response to this request became known as the "family jewels." Just before Schlesinger's request circulated, I found myself going back overseas, amazingly enough, to Thailand on extended temporary duty. I never received Schlesinger's directive, and when I returned to Headquarters and found out about it, the deadline for actions on it had passed. I had been gotten out of town so my embarrassing story would not get on the list of "family jewels."

East Asia division finally placed me as its referent (representative) to the international communism branch (ICB) of the then infamous counterintelligence staff of the Directorate for Operations, which had just been decimated by James Schlesinger's firings. It was not a place from which to launch a new career. I remained with the Agency because all other options seemed closed. I needed the money, and I knew I might soon qualify for early retirement.

As the East Asia division referent I had virtually nothing to do. The lack of a real job gave me time to wallow in my woes. Everything now angered me. I openly laughed at the serious pronouncements made by Agency leaders, pointing out the fallacies beneath the rhetoric. The regular employees of ICB did not know what to make of me.

The next four years I spent in that assignment seemed like a prolonged confinement in the lower levels of Dante's hell. But I did think and observe and study. I ended up learning a great deal about communism and about the Agency.

All I was required to do at ICB was to review incoming material: Agency, State Department, and military cables, newspapers, and communist publications. Cabled intelligence reports covered general worldwide political developments. We selected the most relevant of these for inclusion in a daily clipboard that circulated to all officers. Communist publications received included English-language newspapers and journals and the United States Information Agency's daily booklets containing transcripts of communist radio broadcasts. Other material routed to ICB consisted of a booklet of daily news clippings and copies of *The Washington Post* and *The New York Times*.

One of the first things I noticed was that CIA intelligence reports and news reports were frequently similar. Sometimes a newspaper article preceded the intelligence report; sometimes the intelligence report came first; sometimes the two arrived simultaneously. Completeness of detail and accuracy of observation showed the same mixed results. Occasionally and ominously, a cabled intelligence report was identical to a newspaper item. My review of that variegated source material over the four years spent with the ICB indicated that the CIA, apart from its vast covert operations, had transformed itself largely into a government news service reporting only that information which justified those covert operations. In reporting on host country political developments, it not only competed with news correspondents, but also with State Department officers who through their official contacts possibly were more qualified to gather information on developments in the local government. To me, perhaps the most disturbing aspect of the CIA transforming itself into a government news service was that its true intelligence-gathering and analytical functions were relegated to distant secondary importance.

The Agency had hundreds of people working in various capacities in the world's news media from executives to stringers. Through them it disseminated propaganda designed to shape world opinion. Unfortunately there was no mechanism that prevented that disinformation from contaminating and spoiling the CIA's own information files. In my experience with ICB, where we had unusually widespread access to propaganda themes, I often read cabled instructions from Headquarters to the field on articles or themes to be placed by our local agents in foreign newspapers. Occasionally I could recognize and separate out the CIA-generated articles from others, but more often it was impossible to tell positively whether an item was genuine or planted. Many articles that I kept and filed, that served as background for studies I wrote, later turned out to be CIA propaganda.

As an example of this kind of disinformation operation, during the Cultural Revolution in China, the Agency's huge radio transmitters on Taiwan broadcast items as if they were continuations of mainland programs. Their broadcasts indicated the revolution was getting out of hand and was much more serious than it actually was. These broadcasts were picked up by the Agency's Foreign Broadcast Information Service and included in its daily booklets of transcriptions from the mainland. From there the information was picked up by other offices of the Agency and reported as hard intelligence.[1]

Planting a weapons shipment in Vietnam in February 1965 to prove outside support to the Viet Cong was another classic Agency disinformation operation. As noted earlier, after a staged firefight the shipment was "discovered," and the American press and the International Control Commission were called in to see the "proof." That event was picked up and replayed in a State Department White Paper. Immediately after the White Paper was published, President Johnson sent Marines into Vietnam. The U.S. military apparently believed the Agency disinformation and began patrolling off the shores of South Vietnam, looking for other shipments.

Here was a dangerous cycle. Agency disinformation, mistaken as fact, seeped into the files of U.S. government agencies and the CIA itself. It became fixed as fact in the minds of employees who had no idea where it had originated. That cycle in part created the disaster of Vietnam, especially when the Agency could not see through its own propaganda. That cycle continues today in El Salvador. The State Department, using documents "found" in El Salvador as its basis, issued in early 1981 a White Paper "proving" outside assistance to those opposed to the murderous government. Policymakers, the news media, and the Agency itself apparently believed these documents were real. Policy and public opinion were then molded on that assumption. Fortunately, some members of the public and the press are more skeptical now than they were during the Vietnam War, and the El Salvador White Paper was exposed in several publications, including *The Wall Street Journal*, as a sham.[2] I suspect, though I cannot prove it, that those documents on which the White Paper was based were forged and planted by the CIA.

Although I had been in the CIA for 20 years, I really never had attempted to understand communism on its own terms. Instead I relied on United States news organizations and CIA reporting for information about communist movements. This was true of everyone in the CIA. The limited two-year tours, the reliance on Agency "inside" information, and the prevailing fiercely anti-communist atmosphere all tended to give a distorted, one-sided view of any situation.

Early in my assignment to ICB a garrulous, friendly, energetic man in his late forties, whom I shall call John, contacted me. John had handled one of the Directorate for Operations' illegal domestic projects.[3] He had recruited, briefed, trained, and indoctrinated young American university students and used them to infiltrate leftist organizations on U.S. campuses. In what is called a "dangle operation," the students were to build up leftist credentials at home, so that when they were sent overseas by the Agency they would appear to foreign Communist parties to be genuinely leftist — good bait. These parties then might recruit them or confide in them. While building their leftist credentials in the United States, these young students were asked by John to gather information on U.S. leftist organizations — an activity then expressly forbidden by law.

John was now on the staff of East Asia division and wanted to brief me on his theories concerning the Sino-Soviet split. John would corner me and pitch his weird theories, but he was such a likable person I could not object. I found out that John knew more about Soviet and Chinese communism than almost anybody else in the Agency, and had a broad knowledge of communist terminology. Using primarily the dialectical methods and themes of Mao Tse-tung's brief thesis, "On Contradiction," John tried to convince me that the Chinese and the Soviets had secretly agreed to split in order to lull and conquer the rest of the world.

I liked to bait John. I asked him, if the Russians and Chinese were involved in a huge conspiracy, why had they been fighting each other on their border. "Everybody asks about that," he responded, "but you know the deception is more important than the fighting. So what if a few soldiers get killed if they can convince the rest of the world that they have really split? What's the loss?"

John's energy and enthusiasm outpaced his good sense. But the truth was that his theories were no crazier than what the entire U.S. intelligence community was saying about Vietnam.

Despite their skewed perspective, John's lectures provided the first break in my mental block. In those lectures John used communist writings, primarily Mao Tse-tung's, to explain their terms and the historical context from which they sprang. With his definitions I began to read and comprehend communist newspapers, journals, and broadcast transcripts. Then I began reading historical works and Chinese and Vietnamese revolutionary writings. Gradually, in an almost physically painful process, the accumulated facts and knowledge forced my mind to open to look at reality from the communists' perspective. To my amazement they had a case to make. Vietnam, of course, was the most dramatic example of this. For the first time now I had a chance to read the history of that war and for the first time I became aware that the Agency, in conjunction with the U.S. military and other elements of the U.S. government, had for 21 years attempted to deny the communists their legitimate claim to govern the people who overwhelmingly supported them.

The 1967 survey operation in Northeast Thailand had

taught me there were aspects of Asian communism about which the CIA dissembled. I now began to see that its ability to hide from reality went far beyond pretending not to notice in those areas. I began to realize that the CIA had a charter for action regarding Vietnam similar to *1984*'s Ministry of Truth. The Agency, however, unlike George Orwell's ministry, tried not only to obliterate and rewrite the past through its National Intelligence Estimates (supposedly the highest form of intelligence), but it also attempted via its covert operations to create the future.

I did not comprehend the CIA's deceits in a sudden burst of enlightenment; that knowledge came to me gradually over a period of years through direct, intense study and involvement. My final rejection of Agency "newspeak," however, was sudden. One day I came across an article by Sam Adams in the May 1975 issue of *Harper's* magazine. Entitled "Vietnam Cover-up: Playing War with Numbers, A CIA Conspiracy Against Its Own Intelligence,"[4] the article described a captured document from the Viet Cong high command showing that the VC controlled six million people! Adams had routed that report, and others, to the Agency's upper echelons — and had received no response. Adams, who had been the sole Agency analyst responsible for counting the number of armed communists in South Vietnam, described his long, unsuccessful battles with Agency authorities to force them to stop issuing false, low estimates of armed communists in South Vietnam. His battles earned him 30 threats of firing — finally in disgust he quit.

Here was someone else saying the same things that I had been saying. I was not alone. I was not crazy. Someone else had seen, had struggled, and had fought. But more importantly, here was the clue solving the mystery that had plagued me for years: why I had been dismissed from Thailand in 1967, why the survey operation had been cancelled, and why the information from the surveys had been muzzled.

Adams' article described a bitter battle being fought within the upper echelons of the CIA and U.S. military intelligence about the numbers of armed communists that we were up against in South Vietnam. In September 1967, just about the time Colby came to see me in Northeast Thailand, Adams — following numerous struggles within the Agency's hierarchy

— was finally allowed, alone of the Agency's legions, to try to persuade the U.S. military that its estimates of the number of armed communists in South Vietnam were ridiculously low. This fact, if acknowledged, would of course have shattered the basis for our entire policy. While Sam was fighting alone in Saigon and Washington without any real support from the CIA leadership, my survey reports were circulating at Langley. They showed that the armed element was only one facet of the many-sided Asian communist revolutionary organization. If the Agency would not tolerate Adams' figures on armed communists, it certainly could not acknowledge my revelations, which went a giant step further and assessed enemy strength as far greater than the mere number of armed units would ever lead anyone to believe.

Now I knew the answer to the puzzle. My survey reports had arrived at Langley at precisely the moment when the battle over the numbers of communists was coming to a climax. The reports proved exactly what the designers of U.S. policy in Vietnam refused to see or hear — that we had lost the war years before. To support their specious position, Agency leaders had to suppress the facts contained in the reports that contradicted it and had to make certain that neither I nor anyone else within the CIA could ever gather such information again.

All of my assigned duties in ICB consumed about one hour a day. After years of working long, hard hours, this sudden calm was strange. Former friends in the division avoided me and I them. I often sat and stared at the phone, wondering how in hell I could take the silent treatment for four more years until I might qualify for retirement.

One day it occurred to me that the job offered a real opportunity to study and write about Asian communism as no one in the CIA seemed to have done before. As a first step I checked the CIA's publication index for its studies of Asian revolutionary practices — there were none! I next began to gather think-tank studies and books and to set up files for the project. After a few months I prepared a memo to the East Asia division chief, Shackley, asking his approval to continue the project. He did not answer that memo. Realizing the division would never agree to the study and determined to go ahead, I transferred permanently to ICB. Jake, my boss, favored the study, so now I had approval to continue.

It soon became obvious that the various books and think-tank studies in the CIA library only brought together all of the many misconceptions within the military-intelligence community about "insurgency-counterinsurgency." Totally ignored by the Agency were four basic data banks about Asian communism: French writings on the Vietnamese revolution; State Department "China hands" reports from China in the 1940s; works by American scholars and newsmen with access to Chinese Communist source material; and, amazingly, writings on revolution by Mao Tse-tung, Ho Chi Minh, Lin Piao, and General Vo Nguyen Giap. To read these documents would have meant rejecting all of the pet theories floating around in the think-tanks and counterinsurgency schools. These organizations needed a different sort of war, so they invented one and ignored what the enemy was saying about his own forces. While 700 Agency staff employees were paid large salaries to gather information on the nature and strengths of the Viet Cong, not one person was assigned to read the books by the communist leaders that laid out clearly all that the Agency wanted to know. Just one intelligent analysis of that source material over the two decades would have exposed the terrible inadequacies of the CIA's intelligence and foretold our inevitable defeat in Vietnam.

But the Agency's ability to hide its head in the sand went far beyond ignoring this obvious source material, which thousands of students on campuses in the U.S. were reading voluntarily. In addition the CIA ignored the content of Vietnamese Communist radio broadcasts that its subsidiary office, the Foreign Broadcast Information Service, monitored, translated, and distributed in booklet form every day. In the broadcasts the Communist leaders addressed themselves at great length and gave instructions to the various liberation associations operating in Vietnam. Yet the Agency pretended that the liberation associations with membership in the millions did not exist.

The Agency's refusal to see what was right in front of its face went even further. From the 1950s to the 1960s, China provided training for Third World revolutionaries. Over the years we spied on returning trainees and stole copies of their notes and other training material. Happy case officers would submit that material for intelligence dissemination. Gasps would emit from the China reports office: those stupid Chinese taught their brother revolutionaries the same things they broadcast to the world. The stolen training material, although slightly more specific, based itself on publicly available Chinese revolutionary writings. Lin Piao's highly publicized pamphlet, "Long Live the Victory of People's War," epitomized the entire training curriculum. Yet the China reports office would stamp "Do Not Disseminate" across those captured training manuals. George Orwell's fictional Ministry of Truth had its counterpart in reality.

As I began to understand Vietnamese Communist terminology and to learn the movement's historical development, it became even more apparent that our reporting failed to include the basics of that movement. In early 1974, I prepared another memo for the chief of East Asia division noting the inaccuracies of our reporting of the communist movement not only in Vietnam but also in the Philippines, Thailand, Malaysia, Laos, Cambodia, and Singapore. I requested Shackley's permission to brief division personnel, both in Headquarters and overseas, on the realities of Asian communism. As always, Shackley did not bother to respond. A few months later I sent him another memorandum and again requested permission to talk to someone, but the only answer I got was silence.

In November 1974 two draft intelligence reports came across my desk indicating that the government of South Vietnam was disintegrating. The reports originated from the station's southern regional base called ROIC IV. Normally, cabled intelligence reports, except for those requiring immediate dissemination, were routed through and cleared by the Saigon station. But in this case, in order to avoid the station chief's censorship, two brave case officers, supported by the regional officer in charge, cabled their reports directly to Headquarters. Copies of these cables came to me. I read them in amazement, as they contradicted everything the station was trying to sell regarding the situation in Vietnam. The first report gave a year's statistics on the number of South Vietnamese military personnel and civilian government employees from one province who either defected to the Viet Cong or deserted — one-third of them in one year. The second report said government forces in one southern province controlled only the capital of the province, with all the remaining area controlled by the communists.

When he heard what had happened, Tom Polgar, the chief of Saigon station, fired off priority cables to Headquarters virtually ordering it not to disseminate the information in the cables; it did not. He also wrote cables, which I read, to the authors of the reports, ridiculing them for submitting unsubstantiated, poorly sourced, gloomy, inaccurate information and laying out guidelines that would make further such reporting impossible. Among these guidelines was an instruction that the case officer must personally travel to every area he claimed was controlled by the communists to verify his statement. Of course, had the officer attempted this, the Viet Cong would have captured or killed him.

When I saw the intelligence reports and Polgar's angry reaction, I did not jump up and charge into Shackley's office to try to force him to recognize what was happening. Shackley was reading the same cables. He knew what was going on, and he must have acquiesced. I did, however, try to call attention to the information in the reports. I extrapolated it to apply to a lesser or greater degree to other areas of Vietnam and included my own assessment of the strength of South Vietnamese Communist organizations and North Vietnamese forces. I put all of this in an end-of-year 1974 report that was disseminated only to the deputy director for operations and the chief of the East Asia division. My report said that the government of South Vietnam was in grave danger of imminent collapse. As always, I received no response.

Only a few months later, in April 1975, the Thieu government collapsed. I sat at home and watched the eerie television images of helicopters evacuating people from the top of the U.S. Embassy fortress in Saigon. This seemed so preventable. From the first days in 1954 to the last minutes in April 1975 all the evidence was there. There were no Russian soldiers in Vietnam, no Chinese; the victorious forces were all Vietnamese. In anger I watched it all, knowing that as soon as we recovered from this disaster, we would go charging off again somewhere else, chasing the lead of false Agency intelligence bolstered by disinformation operations.

The wave of exposures of illegal Agency operations peaked in 1975 with investigations by the House of Representatives' Pike Committee and the Senate's Church Committee. The Pike Committee's final report was classified and not released to the public. Portions of it were leaked, however, and appeared in the February 16, 1976 issue of *The Village Voice*. The report recorded the Agency's intelligence performance in six major crises, and in each situation the CIA's intelligence ranged from seriously flawed to non-existent. The report noted that during Tet 1968, the CIA failed to predict the communist attack throughout all of South Vietnam. In August 1968 in Czechoslovakia the Agency "lost" an invading Russian army for two weeks. On October 6, 1973 Egypt and Syria launched an attack on Israel that the Agency failed to predict. It concentrated all of its efforts on following the progress of the war, yet it so miscalculated subsequent events that it "contributed to a U.S.-Soviet confrontation . . . on October 24, 1973. . . . Poor intelligence had brought America to the brink of war."[5] The Pike Committee also cited flawed Agency information concerning a coup in Portugal in 1974, India's detonation of a nuclear device the same year, and the confrontation between Greece and Turkey over Cyprus in July 1974.

The Church Committee, after an exhaustive review, concluded that the Agency acted more as the covert action arm of the Presidency than as an intelligence gatherer and collator. Its final report said the CIA was heavily involved in covertly sponsoring the publication of books and that over the years until 1967 it had in some way been responsible for the publication of well over 1,000 books — a fifth of these in the English language. According to the Church Committee, the Agency was running news services, had employees working for major press organizations, and was illegally releasing and planting stories directly into the U.S. media. Frequently these stories were false and were designed to support the Agency's covert action goals.

Pictures of CIA director William Colby testifying and holding up a poison dart gun, details of CIA failures to destroy biological warfare chemicals under direct orders, information on the Agency's illegal opening of the mail of U.S. citizens, specifics of the Agency's years-long preoccupation with trying to overthrow the government of Chile, sordid details of Agency officers providing drugs to customers of prostitutes in order to film their reactions, and facts about numerous other illegal operations revealed during the congressional investigations all created a depressing atmosphere around Langley.

The morale of CIA employees in this period was at an all-time low. Surprisingly, few seemed particularly bothered by the activities themselves, just upset at having them exposed. There was no remorse, just bitterness. The true believers held to the position that if the general public knew what we knew, then it would understand and support the Agency's activities.

The Church Committee's observation that the Agency was more the covert action arm of the President than an intelligence gatherer confirmed all my suspicions about the true purpose of the Agency: it existed under the name of the Central Intelligence Agency only as a cover for its covert operations. Its intelligence was not much more than one weapon in its arsenal of disinformation — a difficult concept to accept. But with these revelations I began to see where my experience in Southeast Asia had broader ramifications. The Agency refused or was unable to report the truth not only about Asian revolutions; it was doing the same wherever it operated.

To confirm this observation I began reviewing current events in Latin America, the Middle East, and Africa and saw the same patterns of Agency disinformation operations, including its intelligence supporting its covert operations. This convinced me. The Agency is not, nor was it ever meant to have been, an intelligence agency. It was created slightly after the United Nations. It was the United States' substitute for gun-boat diplomacy that was no longer feasible under the scrutiny of that world organization. The Agency was to do covertly that which was once done openly with the Army, the Navy, and the Marines. The Central Intelligence Agency, I now knew, was in truth a Central Covert Action Agency.

After the 1976 Christmas holiday season I returned to work. I walked into our vaulted area where we kept the coffee pot. There on the bulletin board was a memorandum from the deputy director for operations, William Wells. The memorandum said the Agency was currently overstaffed and that operations officers with a minimum of five years overseas and a total of 25 years of service could volunteer for early retirement. I tore the memo off the board and raced around yelling, "I can retire, I can retire."

I ran into my office and called Norma. Then I walked into the office of the chief of ICB, Jake, and told him of my decision, just in case he had not heard my yelling. He asked me to think the decision over for a day or so. "No need," I said, "no need."

Some weeks later, the awards office notified me that based on Jake's recommendation, I had been awarded the Agency's Career Intelligence Medal. I agreed to accept it for three reasons: to give my children an occasion to be proud of their father, not to embarrass Jake, and to lend credibility to any criticisms of the Agency I might make in the future. Otherwise I very much wanted to say, "Take your medal and shove it."

My wife, my four children, one son-in-law, and a grandson all gathered for the awards ceremony. I was deeply moved by my family's presence there with me. I had lived through 25 years of illusion, the last decade of which had been filled with anger, bitterness, self-doubts, mistrust, disbelief, disgust, and struggle. That I had emerged with my sanity intact was a testimonial to their backing and loyalty.

William ("Wild Willie") Wells made the presentation in a room off of the director's office on the seventh floor. He read the award citation aloud. As with nearly everything else touched by the Agency, its intelligence was flawed. It said that the Agency gave me the medal, in part, for my excellent work in Malaysia — a country I had never even visited.

14.
CONCLUSION

THE CIA is not now nor has it ever been a central intelligence agency. It is the covert action arm of the President's foreign policy advisers. In that capacity it overthrows or supports foreign governments while reporting "intelligence" justifying those activities. It shapes its intelligence, even in such critical areas as Soviet nuclear weapon capability, to support presidential policy. Disinformation is a large part of its covert action responsibility, and the American people are the primary target audience of its lies.

As noted in the Church Committee's final report, the Agency's task is to develop an international anti-communist ideology. The CIA then links every egalitarian political movement to the scourge of international communism. This then prepares the American people and many in the world community for the second stage, the destruction of those movements. For egalitarianism is the enemy and it must not be allowed to exist.

The Vietnam War was the Agency's greatest and longest disinformation operation. From 1954 until we were ejected in 1975, the Agency lied in its intelligence while propagandizing the American people. It planted a weapons shipment, forged documents, deceived everyone about the Tonkin Gulf incident, and lied continually about the composition and motivation of the South Vietnamese communists. Even now Agency historians and ex-employees try to perpetuate the propaganda themes through which it tried first to win and later to maintain American support for the war. As recently as April 22, 1981, former CIA director William Colby wrote an article for *The Washington Post*, portraying the Vietnam

War — even in light of the *Pentagon Papers* disclosures — as the altruistic U.S. coming to the assistance of the South Vietnamese people. He had the audacity to recommend the period from 1968 to 1972 — the era of CIA assassination teams — as a model for use in El Salvador.

Not much has changed since I left the Agency. It follows all the same patterns and uses the same techniques. We have seen this in relation to El Salvador, where it fabricated evidence for a White Paper[1] the same way it did in Vietnam in 1961 and 1965.[2] We have seen it in Iran, where it cut itself off from all contact with potential revolutionary groups to support the Shah.[3] We have seen it in the recruitment ads seeking ex-military personnel to man its paramilitary programs. We have seen it in relation to Nicaragua, where it arms Miskito Indians in an attempt to overthrow the Nicaraguan government.[4] In this case it again exploits a naive minority people who will be discarded as soon as their usefulness ends, as happened with the Hmong in Laos. We have seen it in its attempts to rewrite and censor the truth. I personally have experienced this kind of Agency effort recently when it censored an article I wrote about its successful operation to overthrow the government of Achmed Sukarno of Indonesia in 1965.[5] Its operations under President Reagan have become so outrageous that even the House of Representatives Intelligence Committee protested its plans to overthrow Qaddafi of Libya.[6]

As long as the CIA continues to run these kinds of operations, it will not and cannot gather and collate intelligence as its charter says it must do. This leaves our government without that essential service. The most powerful and potentially most dangerous nation in the world is forced to rely on CIA disinformation rather than genuine intelligence because currently there is no alternative. This situation in today's world of poised doomsday weapons is not acceptable.

But the danger looms even greater. The Reagan Administration has taken steps to strengthen the Agency's position. On December 4, 1981, in Executive Order 12333 entitled "United States Intelligence Activities," the President gave the CIA the right to conduct its illegal operations in the United States, and on April 2, 1982, in Executive Order 12356 entitled "National Security Information," he limited the public's access to government documents, thereby increasing the CIA's ability to hide from public scrutiny. The President wants the Agency free of the constraints of public exposure so that it can gather and fabricate its disinformation unharried by criticisms and so that it can overthrow governments without the knowledge of the American people. Such activities, of course, are not in the best interests of the vast majority of Americans. For example, whenever another factory moves to a foreign country whose leader is kept in power through Agency operations, more American jobs are lost. Only the rich American increases his profits. It is for this reason that I believe that President Reagan acts as the representative of wealthy America and, as his executive agency, the CIA acts to benefit the rich.

Even after the Agency's conspicuous failures in Vietnam, Cuba, the Middle East, and elsewhere, the fable that the CIA gathers real intelligence dies hard. But if the Agency actually reported the truth about the Third World, what would it say? It would say that the United States installs foreign leaders, arms their armies, and empowers their police all to help those leaders repress an angry, defiant people; that the CIA-empowered leaders represent only a small fraction who kill, torture, and impoverish their own people to maintain their position of privilege. This is true intelligence, but who wants it? So instead of providing true intelligence the Agency, often ignorant of its real role, labels the oppressed as lackeys of Soviet or Cuban or Vietnamese communism fighting not for their lives but for their communist masters. It is difficult to sell this story when the facts are otherwise, so the Agency plants weapons shipments, forges documents, broadcasts false propaganda, and transforms reality. Thus it creates a new reality that it then believes.

Efforts to create a workable intelligence service must begin by abolishing the CIA. For a host of reasons I believe the CIA as it now exists cannot be salvaged. The fundamental problem is that Presidents and their National Security Councils want the CIA as a covert action agency, not an intelligence agency. As long as the CIA is subject to such politically oriented control, it cannot produce accurate intelligence. Because the CIA has been and is a covert action agency, all of its operating practices have been adopted to facilitate such operations while its intelligence-collection activities have been tailored to the requirements of these covert efforts. The

Agency's difficulties begin with the selection of personnel who are chosen based on personality characteristics essential for covert operations, not intelligence. The problem continues with the formation of operating rules that serve to foil the production of accurate intelligence while facilitating the implementation of covert operations. Until those factors are altered, the CIA cannot function as an intelligence agency.

Covert operations must be removed from the CIA and placed in an entirely separate government agency. I would prefer recommending the total abolishment of covert operations, but that is impossible given the current world political realities. However, if a new covert action agency consisted of a handful of knowledgeable people who could, in emergency situations, pull together the necessary manpower to conduct a specific covert operation, then the chance of its duplicating the abuses of the CIA would be lessened.

If an administration at any point decided it wanted a true intelligence service, it could be easily created. But it would not be enough merely to separate covert operations from intelligence. Accurate intelligence demands an atmosphere free of political pressure. One obvious solution revolves around identifying individuals possessing recognized ability, integrity, and flexibility and giving such individuals lifetime or long-term non-renewable appointments to a board controlling intelligence requirements and production. That board, augmented by top graduates of political science schools in one-year clerkships, would provide the independent analytical judgment necessary for valid intelligence. Expecting our system to grant that independent authority may be unrealistic. But trained analysts, working with all-source information, overseen by a "Supreme Court" of intelligence, would help to guarantee the production of accurate intelligence. Establishing a truly effective intelligence agency is no problem. The only problem is getting our leaders to want one, and that problem may be insurmountable.

APPENDIX.
THIS BOOK AND
THE SECRECY AGREEMENT

The secrecy agreement that I signed when I joined the CIA allows the Agency to review prior to publication all writings of present and former employees to ensure that classified information relating to national security is not revealed. This provision seems logical and necessary to protect legitimate secrets. However, my experiences in getting this book approved show that the CIA uses the agreement not so much to protect national security as to prevent revelations and criticisms of its immoral, illegal, and ineffective operations. To that end, it uses all possible maneuvers, legal and illegal. Had I not been represented by my attorney, Mark Lynch of the American Civil Liberties Union (ACLU), and had I not developed a massive catalogue of information already cleared by the Agency's publications review board (PRB), this book could not have been published. The review of my manuscript came in two basic stages, first on an initial manuscript that I wrote without editorial assistance, and second on a revised manuscript written following an editor's advice.

On February 26, 1980, I submitted the first version of the manuscript to the Agency for review and on March 21, several days before the mandatory 30-day review period expired, John Peyton, a lawyer of the Agency's general counsel staff who served concurrently as the PRB's legal adviser, called and asked that I come to a meeting on March 26. He moaned audibly when I advised him that Mark Lynch of the ACLU would accompany me to the meeting. At the meeting, held in the general counsel's office on the seventh floor of the Headquarters building in Langley, the government's side was represented by five attorneys – three from the general counsel's office and two from the Justice Department. Had I come to the meeting alone, I would have been the lamb ready for slaughter. Because of his participation in other sensitive Agency cases, Lynch had earlier been granted a high-level "Q" clearance, but even so the Agency required him to sign an agreement before he could participate in that meeting. Peyton then explained that the publications review board had made 397 deletions in my manuscript. I was surprised, because I had been extremely careful not to use classified information in the manuscript. Those 397 deletions exceeded even the 339 passages excised from *The CIA and the Cult of Intelligence*, a book by John Marks and Victor Marchetti that deliberately set out to expose Agency secrets. I later learned that the 397 deletions represented only a fraction of those initially demanded by the Agency's Directorate for Operations. When I notified Peyton that I would be represented by the ACLU, the Agency had quickly retracted its more capricious deletions, resulting in the final list of 397 items.

Lynch suggested that he and I first be permitted to adjourn to a private room to review each item. When we finished the review, the full group reconvened. I said that almost all deletions appeared in some form in the *Pentagon Papers*. Ernest Mayerfeld, deputy general counsel, said if that was true he could not object to their inclusion in the book. The lawyers said that I should get together the next day with the Agency's freedom of information officer, Bob, to consider specific deletions.

After lunch and later at home I reviewed the Agency's deletions and matched each item with my source documents. I was overjoyed: all significant deletions were covered by supporting public data. My joy was premature.

Early the next day I met Bob, who during my last few years with the Agency had served as my boss once removed. A dedicated cold warrior, Bob was a tall, stocky, impressive man in his late fifties who had achieved supergrade status in the Agency and had served as chief of station **[19 words deleted]**.

Bob seemed as agitated as I, and it was obvious that he felt he was soiling himself by dealing with me. In less civilized circumstances we probably would have been happier fighting rather than talking. Early on Bob set the tone. "It's too bad you didn't work for the Israeli intelligence service," he said. "They know how to deal with people like you. They'd take you out and shoot you."

Bob then launched into a long monologue covering the vagaries of the secrecy laws, including details of the Carter administration's Official Disclosure Law, the Freedom of Information Act, and the various problems in their application. I impatiently endured this speech. I was most anxious to get on with the review, to produce my public documents, and to get the hell out of there.

We finally moved to the review of the specific deletions. The very first item caused trouble. Inexplicably the publications review board had deleted a reference indicating that the CIA conducted joint operations with Thai authorities. That relationship was so well known that books had been written about it, academic studies discussed it, pictures of CIA station chiefs appeared in the Thai press, and high-level Thai officials openly bragged in the media about CIA support for their organizations. Needless to say, I had not anticipated that the CIA would consider that relationship secret. If I could not admit that such a relationship existed, there was no point to the book since most of my observations were based on my six years with the Agency in Thailand. Fortunately I recalled a document from *The New York Times* edition of the *Pentagon Papers* entitled "The Lansdale Memorandum for Taylor on Unconventional Warfare," which discussed specific CIA operations conducted jointly with Thai organizations.

When I told Bob about the Lansdale memorandum being in the *Pentagon Papers*, he appeared to be surprised. But he recovered quickly and said there was only one official version of the papers – the Department of Defense's 12-volume edition. After numerous phone calls a secretary brought in 11 of the 12 volumes – the one missing volume, according to the index, was the one that most likely would include the Lansdale memo. This really shook Bob. He suspected that someone had removed the critical volume. Later we did get that volume, but the Lansdale memo was not in it. I argued that the Supreme Court's decision in the *Pentagon Papers* case had placed that information in the public domain, and it certainly could no longer be considered secret. We argued back and forth and finally agreed to postpone decisions on this and other items relating to CIA joint operations with Thai organizations.

Many deletions caused little problem. In some cases, where an ex-CIA official's affiliation with the Agency was well known, I had used that person's true name. The Agency objected. I felt the point was unimportant and agreed to substitute titles or aliases.

At one point I really became worried. Bob said that I must produce the document from which I had taken a direct quote. If I could not produce it, he warned that I would be accused of stealing secret documents. I had not deigned to steal any of the Agency's classified fantasy, but I was not sure that I could relocate that precise quote. Luck was with me that day, and a short scan of the research materials I had brought with me produced that quoted passage.

We referred the question of joint operations with the Thai police to the general counsel's office, which conceded that such information was probably not deletable. We continued our review based on the premise that I could discuss joint intelligence and counterinsurgency programs with the Thais. Even so, I could not mention my participation in programs with specifically named Thai organizations although I could substitute phrases to describe them. Also I was allowed, via footnoting, to replace a deleted item with information from a source document. By juxtaposition I hoped my meaning would be clear.

The next day I objected to the deletion of my very negative assessment of the Agency's long-term operations against mainland China. I produced a book, *Sub Rosa*, in which a former Hong Kong station chief, Peer de Silva, set forth his own lengthy, negative evaluation of those operations. I said Peer's book had been approved by the PRB and it had permitted him to state his opinion; therefore, I should be given the same privilege. Bob agreed and my critical comments, in modified version, were reinstated. From that point on I searched through books written by former Agency officials and cleared by the CIA, to locate items similar to deletions made in my book. By this tactic I was successful in reinstating numerous deletions.

We had a problem over naming specific CIA stations and bases – other than those already acknowledged – even though those installations were well known. The Agency's objection had nothing to do with secrecy. It instead applied to administering the Freedom of Information Act. Whenever the Agency acknowledged the existence of a station or base, the public could, under the act, demand documents relating to the facility. Although it seldom releases documents in response to such appeals, the Agency must by law physically check all such documents. By not allowing anyone to admit that a station or base exists, it avoids those requests.

Bob and I agreed to a modified version of my book. That weekend I made all the changes. On Monday morning I reviewed those changes with Mark Lynch and submitted the book to the deputy general counsel, Mayerfeld. In the interim Mayerfeld's office had reversed itself. He said *The New York Times'* Pentagon Papers had not been officially released, that the Supreme Court only ruled that it could not enjoin publication of those documents. Therefore, my discussion of liaison programs with Thai organizations might again encounter opposition.

That night I searched through the edition of the *Pentagon Papers* that Senator Mike Gravel of Alaska had entered in the official records of the Senate. I found that it included the Lansdale memorandum and therefore supposed that that constituted official disclosure. The next morning I happily relayed the news to Bob. He said members of Congress could say anything, so the Gravel edition did not count.

Official disclosure only occurs when a member of the executive branch of government performs that function. But how finely the Agency interpreted that statement I was yet to find out.

I immediately went to the Reston Regional Library to look for statements made by members of the executive branch relating to CIA operations with Thai organizations. I spent the day going through *The New York Times Index*, reviewing all entries under Thailand from the present back to 1954. The index mentioned one well-publicized incident, allegedly caused by the CIA, that generated riots in Thailand. Because of the furor, numerous American officials were forced to comment on CIA operations in Thailand. Some press accounts sourced their information to CIA officials in Langley and the United States Embassy. I felt those references constituted executive branch disclosure of CIA activities in Thailand. I called Bob. He asked if the articles named specific American officials – a mere reference to a CIA official in Langley did not count. I said that Ambassador William Kinter had made a statement. He asked if the statement was in quotes. He said reporters could write anything, and if the statement was not in quotes it did not constitute official disclosure. (Later after completing the review process I found a reference to a high-level CIA official making a direct statement concerning CIA operations in Thailand.[1] I called Bob and asked if that did not constitute that ever-elusive official disclosure. He said no. That person had probably spoken unofficially and could be prosecuted for violating his secrecy agreement.) But as I continued to accumulate public evidence of the CIA's relationship with Thai organizations, Bob began to concede that I might retain relevant items in my book.

On Tuesday, April 8, I went to the Agency to rework the items deleted from my resubmitted version. I was not surprised to see that the Directorate for Operations had reversed itself in several key areas. Where its original deletions did not hold up, it merely changed its objections to apply to previously approved information.

China desk had changed its objection to my negative evaluation of its operations. The desk now claimed that the technique itself was classified. That technique, recruiting persons from the other side, was just slightly newer and less well known than prostitution. Of course if I could not discuss the technique, my evaluation would be meaningless. That night I went back to the Reston Library and cleaned out its shelf of books written by ex-Agency officials. Those books, some undoubtedly written at the behest of the CIA, discussed that "forbidden" technique in detail. By adding footnotes to those books, I was allowed to retain my discussion of that technique.

The Thai desk had also changed its position on material not initially marked for deletion – namely, the rural village survey program that I directed with Thai officials. The desk's original objection pertained only to my mention of working in liaison with Thais. When it became apparent it could not maintain that objection, the desk then claimed the technique itself was classified and must be deleted. This was ridiculous. Over the years I had lectured and passed out unclassified handouts describing the method. When documents reporting on those training sessions were located, the Thai desk had to drop its objection.

Forty-six days after I submitted the book, the Agency returned the manuscript with a letter saying that it had no security objections to the publication of that version. Throughout the review one central issue had been in question: reference to CIA operations with Thai organizations. What terrible secret was the CIA so vehemently attempting to hide? On October 6, 1976, Thai security forces over-threw the civilian, democratically elected government in a violent bloodbath. A study by Dr. E. Thadeus Flood published by the Indochina Resource Center said of that bloodbath: "This activist agency [CIA] took the lead in developing a strong apparatus in Thailand. . . . It should be mentioned that in their training, the CIA placed special stress on the Thai Border Patrol Police (BPP). News reports from Bangkok during and after the recent coup indicate that it was the Thai BPP who levelled their heavy weapons at unarmed Thai students, boys and girls, waving white flags, and raked them with fire."[2]

Thomas Lobe describes what happened in more detail: "On that horrible day in October 1976, then, the CIA/OPS-trained Border Patrol Police, with some units of the OPS-trained riot squads of the Metropolitan Police, burst into Thammasat University to crush the unarmed students and their fury knew no bounds . . . in meting out humiliations, in mutilations brutally inflicted, in burning a student alive, and in simple wholesale murder. Thousands of unarmed students were killed, injured, or arrested, and a few days later, most of the liberal to left journalists, scholars, and intellectuals were also rounded up and put in prison or 'rehabilitation camps.' "[3]

After receiving the approved version of the manuscript, I signed a contract with a publisher who wanted extensive rewrites.

I began rewriting the manuscript and submitting each chapter as it was completed. On February 4, 1982, Paul Schilling, a young lawyer on the general counsel's staff, called and asked me to come to the Agency the next day for a meeting to discuss the first chapter. I was annoyed because everything in the chapter had either been approved before, was quoted from the Senate's Church Committee report, or was personal. I prepared myself with documents and met with Paul in one of the little anterooms off the main reception area. Some of the objections were to information that the Agency had declassified and released to the Church Committee, which I easily documented. But the other objections concerned details of my training in espionage and paramilitary operations and details of psychological tests the Agency uses to help identify a specific personality type for possible employment. I was not prepared to rebut those arguments. Paul and I agreed that I would return home and call in the appropriate references.

The rest of the day I phoned around to all Fairfax County libraries to get copies of books by William Colby, Ray Cline, Allen Dulles, Lyman Kirkpatrick, David Phillips, and other pro-Agency authors whose works had received formal CIA approval if not sponsorship. Almost all discussed information that the PRB now claimed was classified. I phoned the citations in to Paul Schilling. I thought that would take care of the matter. A few days later Paul called and asked if I would come in for another meeting. On February 11 we met again in one of the cubbyholes off the packed main reception area. Paul apologized for asking me in again and said that the PRB had agreed that the information I had taken from the Church Committee report was not classified. I relaxed. The PRB was merely recognizing reality.

Paul then said, "But the other material on your training and the psychological test is classified. The board said it had made a mistake earlier when it had approved that information."

To the shock of the people in the reception area I bellowed, "That's tough shit. It can't reclassify information." After calming down, I pointed out that the

Agency had cleared similar information on training for its friendly former officers such as Colby, Phillips, Cline, Dulles, Kirkpatrick, and others.

"Yes," Paul said, "but the PRB made mistakes."

I noted that in at least one case the CIA had helped a former officer write his book, and the book contained numerous references to training.

Paul responded, "The Agency's relationship with an author is that the PRB reviews material written by the author, nothing else."

"That's not the case with [the book in question]. It was written as a covert action project by the Agency. I know it was."

Paul continued, "The Agency's relationship with an author. . . ."

I then cited facts relating to the writing of that book.

Paul retorted, "The Agency's relationship with an author. . . ."

Schilling recommended that I consider an appeal to the deputy director of the CIA, Admiral Bobby Inman.

That weekend I called Paul at home and advised him that Executive Order 12065 on classification, Section 1-607, reads: "Classification may not be restored to a document already declassified and released to the public under this order or prior orders." Paul said, "Oh, we're operating under a new order." What Paul was referring to was a draft executive order then being proposed by the Reagan Administration. That order, only later put into effect, allows officials to reclassify information previously declassified and disclosed if it is determined in writing "that the information requires protection in the interest of national security and if the information may be reasonably recovered." The manuscript obviously could not be "reasonably recovered," since I had sent copies to my publisher, my editor, and numerous others.

Paul quickly realized he had jumped the gun on the new executive order and shifted instead to the position that Agency officials had again and again made mistakes in declassifying information in my original manuscript and in other books.

After consultation with Mark Lynch, I prepared and submitted my 35-page appeal on February 19, 1982, noting that many of the deleted items had been approved in the first manuscript, had appeared in the approved writings of other pro-Agency officers, or were available in numerous other publications. On March 12, 1982, I received a letter from the general counsel's office saying, "The DDCI [deputy director of central intelligence] has reversed the board with respect to all . . . passages contested in the appeal," except that, "the DDCI has upheld the board's decision to delete five sentences . . . unless Mr. McGehee can show the Agency has previously cleared such information."

I immediately scanned four approved books and found 24 references to equivalent or identical material as contained in the five sentences. I sent these references to the general counsel. The PRB acted quickly and, rather embarrassed, acknowledged that my five sentences were not classified.

I thought, well, now I have been vindicated and my problems are over. But this was not to be. On March 23, I received another letter informing me that chapter two was so sensitive that it was impossible to identify specific items and the PRB had rejected the entire chapter. I had had enough and contacted George Lardner, Jr., a journalist with *The Washington Post*. He wrote a long article entitled "CIA Veteran Decries Effort to Reclassify Material for His Book." This public embarrassment forced the Agency to reconsider its actions. On April 29, I received a registered letter offering me the services of Bob – my old antagonist – to work together to produce an approved version of the manuscript.

I accepted the offer. We held three long sessions at my office, so we would have instant access to my books and files. The battle over chapter one had been completed, so we concentrated on the remaining chapters that I had turned over in the preceding months. Chapter two, dealing with my tours in Japan and the Philippines, according to the earlier PRB decision could not be used, but in the interim I had stumbled upon one of the lesser-known books by ex-CIA officials, Howard Hunt's *Undercover*. In it, to my joy, was a chapter dealing with his assignment as a case officer to Japan; the same chapter also discussed the Agency's base at Subic Bay in the Philippines. His book had been approved by the Agency and when I pointed this out to Bob he agreed that I should also be permitted to discuss my activities in those countries. Even so, I was not allowed to include details of my work. I could only give information no more explicit than that given in *Undercover*.

Chapter three also presented major problems. Many of my specific designations for places were deemed classified, but by making minor changes I was allowed to retain some points. The discussions of my work at Headquarters processing clearances and file traces were marked classified and many sentences had to be deleted. Although the Marchetti-Marks and Colby books had discussed the requirements for clearances and traces, they had not gone into any detail. Unable to locate other coverage of these procedures, I could not retain my material. But I was allowed to quote information on that topic given in Philip Agee's book, *Inside the Company*.

Chapter four, about my tour on Taiwan, gave information in general terms of an agent operation directed at mainland China. Someone had objected to this major element of the chapter. I protested that other approved Agency authors had been allowed to discuss agent operations, some with a great deal more specificity than my account. This argument was finally accepted.

Bob and I reviewed each of the many points in the remaining chapters. In this process I conceded a number of points where the law was clearly on my side. I did this to speed the clearance process and to avoid a long, time-consuming lawsuit.

John Marks and Victor Marchetti's book *The CIA and the Cult of Intelligence*, published in 1974, was the last approved critical book written about the Agency by an ex-employee. In light of my own experiences the reason is obvious: the secrecy agreement and the way it is abused by the Agency. It is virtually impossible to write in an atmosphere where everything is secret until it is deemed otherwise. The PRB, taking its responsibilities seriously, labels just about everything secret until an author who is critical of the Agency can prove this not to be the case. But the situation for ex-employees who are advocates of the CIA is the opposite. They are given almost *carte blanche* to discuss operations and techniques, and in some instances they are assisted in the research and writing of their works.

Does the secrecy agreement work to protect legitimate classified information? Probably to some small degree it does. But the price we pay for this minor protection is enormous. The Vietnam War is a prime example. This Agency-produced disaster was sold to the American people through massive disinformation operations. Would it not have been better if we had known the truth at an early stage? Similarly, would the American people not be better off knowing the truth about the CIA's current secret war in Latin America? Don't we deserve to know about reckless and phony covert operations, including Agency-planted "Communist" documents, that help determine our foreign policy?

It is clear that the secrecy agreement does not halt the flow of information to our enemies, for it does not affect the CIA employee who sells information. Look, for example, at England, which has a strict official secrets act and probably the most porous security service in the western world. What the CIA's secrecy agreement does quite effectively, however, is to stop critics of the Agency from explaining to the American public what the CIA is and does. It is sad to say, but the truth is that the primary purpose of the secrecy agreement is to suppress information that the American people are legitimately entitled to. For this reason, I am opposed to the secrecy agreement as it is now written and administered.

Because the major portion of my CIA career revolved around Southeast Asia, where CIA operations were well publicized and even officially disclosed, the Agency could not stop release of much of the information in this book. But my experience should sound a warning. Agency officials show no hesitation in trying to censor embarrassing, critical, or merely annoying information. I cannot speak for the legal aspects of the various laws, but it is obvious that national security has little to do with how the Agency administers the secrecy agreement. As the CIA becomes more adept at applying the law under President Reagan's executive order on classification that went into effect August 1, 1982, all critical information about the Agency will probably be forbidden.

I do not expect that the executive branch or the Supreme Court will be upset by the Agency's attempts to censor information that the public is entitled to. The American people, however, should be worried. Once the Agency is unleashed and the iron curtain of official disclosure falls, we will all suffer its consequences.

SOURCES

1. Gung Ho !

1. Victor Marchetti and John D. Marks, *The CIA and the Cult of Intelligence* (New York: Alfred A. Knopf, 1974), p. 281.

2. Japan and the Philippines: Innocents Abroad

1. U.S. Congress, Select Committee to Study Governmental Operations with Respect to Intelligence Activities, *Foreign and Military Intelligence*, 94th Congress, 2nd sess., 1976. (Hereafter cited as Church Committee.) Book IV, p. 50.
2. *Ibid.*, pp. 49-50.
3. *Ibid.*, p. 49.
4. Victor Marchetti and John D. Marks, *The CIA and the Cult of Intelligence* (New York: Alfred A. Knopf, 1974), p. 167.
5. Jerrold L. Walden, "Proselytes for Espionage – The CIA and Domestic Fronts," *Journal of Public Law 19*, No. 2 (1970), pp. 195-196.
6. Harry Rositzke, *CIA's Secret Operations: espionage, counterespionage and covert action* (New York: Reader's Digest Press, 1977), pp. 168-169.
7. *Ibid.*, pp. 169-171.
8. *Ibid.*, pp. 171-173.
9. William R. Corson, *The Armies of Ignorance* (New York: The Dial Press/ James Wade, 1977), pp. 369-370.
10. *Ibid.*, p. 371.
11. Center for National Security Studies, *CIA's Covert Operations Vs. Human Rights* (Washington, D.C.), p. 12.
12. Robert Borosage and John D. Marks (eds.), *The CIA File* (New York: Grossman Publishers, 1976), p. 23.
13. Church Committee, *op. cit.*, p. 36.
14. David Wise and Thomas B. Ross, *The Invisible Government* (New York: Bantam Books, 1964), p. 115.
15. Thomas Lobe, *United States Security Policy and Aid to the Thailand Police* (University of Denver Graduate School of International Studies:

Monograph Series in World Affairs, Vol. 14, No. 2, Denver: University of Denver, Colorado Seminary, 1977), *passim*.

16. Christopher Robbins, *Air America: The Story of the CIA's Secret Airlines* (New York: G. P. Putnam's Sons, 1979), pp. 85-86.
17. *Ibid.*, p. 86.
18. Lobe, *op. cit., passim*.
19. Edward Geary Lansdale, Major General, United States Air Force (Ret.), *In the Midst of Wars: An American's Mission to Southeast Asia* (New York: Harper & Row, 1972), *passim*.
20. Center for National Security Studies, *op. cit.*, p. 13.
21. Borosage and Marks, *op. cit.*, p. 21.
22. *Ibid.*
23. Robbins, *op. cit.*, p. 18.
24. Andrew Tully, *CIA: The Inside Story* (New York: William Morrow and Company, 1962), pp. 60-67.
25. Wise and Ross, *op. cit.*, pp. 127-128.
26. Borosage and Marks, *op. cit.*, p. 21.
27. Kermit Roosevelt, *Countercoup: The Struggle for Control of Iran* (New York: McGraw-Hill Book Company, 1979), *passim*.
28. Wilbur Crane Eveland, *Ropes of Sand: America's Failure in the Middle East* (New York: W. W. Norton, 1980), *passim*.
29. Center for National Security Studies, *op. cit.*, p. 13.
30. Rositzke, *op. cit.*, p. 162.
31. Church Committee, *op. cit.*, Book IV, p. 49.
32. *Ibid.*, p. 55.
33. Center for National Security Studies, *op. cit.*, p. 12.
34. Corson, *op. cit.*, p. 132.
35. Center for National Security Studies, *op. cit.*, p. 12.
36. Thomas W. Braden, "I'm Glad the CIA is 'Immoral'," *The Saturday Evening Post*, May 20, 1967, pp. 10, 12, 14.
37. Sol Stern, "NSA and the CIA," *Ramparts* 5, March 1967, pp. 29-38.
38. William E. Colby, "Statement before the Senate Armed Services Committee," January 15, 1975, as quoted in *The Washington Post*, January 16, 1975, p. A18.
39. *The Washington Post*, January 16, 1975, p. A18.
40. Church Committee, *op. cit.*, Book I, p. 193.
41. *Ibid.*
42. *Ibid.*, p. 192.
43. *Ibid.*, p. 199.
44. Carl Bernstein, "The CIA and the Media," *Rolling Stone*, October 20, 1977, p. 55.

3. Washington: Fun in the Files

1. Philip Agee, *Inside the Company: CIA Diary* (New York: Stonehill Publishing Company, 1975), pp. 56-58.

5. Life at Langley

1. U.S. Congress, Select Committee to Study Governmental Operations with Respect to Intelligence Activities, *Foreign and Military Intelligence*, 94th Congress, 2nd sess., 1976. (Hereafter cited as Church Committee.) Book IV, p. 64.
2. *Ibid.*, p. 65.
3. *Ibid.*, pp. 66-67.
4. *Ibid.*, p. 67.
5. *Ibid.*
6. *Ibid.*, pp. 67-68.
7. *Ibid.*, p. 68.
8. Victor Marchetti and John D. Marks, *The CIA and the Cult of Intelligence* (New York: Alfred A. Knopf, 1974), pp. 31-32, 297.
9. Ralph W. McGehee, "Foreign Policy By Forgery: The C.I.A. and the White Paper on El Salvador," *The Nation*, April 11, 1981, pp. 423-434. Deletions in original.
10. Thomas Lobe, *United States National Security Policy and Aid to the Thailand Police* (University of Denver Graduate School of International Studies: Monograph Series in World Affairs, Vol. 14, No. 2, Denver: University of Denver, Colorado Seminary, 1977), *passim.*
11. Center for National Security Studies, *CIA's Covert Operations Vs. Human Rights* (Washington, D.C.), p. 13.
12. *The Washington Post*, January 18, 1971, p. B7.
13. Andrew Tully, *CIA: The Inside Story* (New York: William Morrow and Company, 1962), pp. 88-89, 97. See also Warren Hinckle and William Turner, *The Fish Is Red* (New York: Harper & Row, 1982).
14. Marchetti and Marks, *op. cit.*, pp. 298-299.
15. *Newsweek* 84, September 30, 1974, p. 37. See also Philip Agee, *Inside the Company: CIA Diary* (New York: Stonehill Publishing Company, 1975).
16. *The Washington Post*, April 6, 1973, pp. A1, A12.
17. U.S. Congress, Select Committee to Study Governmental Operations with Respect to Intelligence Activities, *Covert Action in Chile*, 94th Congress, 1st sess., 1975.
18. Center for National Security Studies, *op. cit.*, p. 12.
19. *Ibid.*
20. Marchetti and Marks, *op. cit.*, pp. 124-125.
21. *Ibid.*, pp. 126-131.
22. Center for National Security Studies, *op. cit.*, p. 12.
23. Church Committee, *op. cit.*, Book IV, p. 68.
24. Center for National Security Studies, *op. cit.*, p. 12. See also John Stockwell, *In Search of Enemies* (New York: W. W. Norton, 1978).
25. Center for National Security Studies, *op. cit.*, p. 13. See also John Stockwell, *op. cit.*
26. *Newsweek* 78, November 22, 1971, p. 37. *The New York Times*, September 22, 1974, Section 4, p. 1. Marchetti and Marks, *op. cit.*, pp. 31, 117.
27. Center for National Security Studies, *op. cit.*, p. 13. See also Gordon Winter, *Inside BOSS* (London: Penguin, 1982).
28. Church Committee, *op. cit.*, Book IV, p. 69.

29. *The New York Times*, January 4, 1975, p. 8.
30. *The New York Times*, December 31, 1974, p. 1.
31. William E. Colby, "Statement before the Senate Armed Services Committee," January 15, 1975, as quoted in *The Washington Post*, January 16, 1975, p. A18. (Hereafter cited as "Colby Statement.")
32. *Congressional Quarterly*, February 24, 1967, pp. 271-272.
33. Colby Statement, *loc. cit.*
34. Center for National Security Studies, "CIA Domestic Spying More Extensive," September 10, 1979.
35. Colby Statement, *loc. cit.*
36. *Ibid.*
37. *Ibid.*
38. *The Washington Post*, January 16, 1975, pp. A1, A18.
39. *The New York Times*, December 17, 1972, p. 23.
40. Nina Adams and Alfred McCoy, *Laos: War and Revolution* (New York: Harper and Row, 1970), pp. 155-178.

6. North Thailand: Saving the Hill Tribes

1. Thomas Lobe, *United States National Security Policy and Aid to the Thailand Police* (University of Denver Graduate School of International Studies: Monograph Series in World Affairs, Vol. 14, No. 2, Denver: University of Denver, Colorado Seminary, 1977), p. 24.
2. Douglas S. Blaufarb, *The Counterinsurgency Era* (New York: The Free Press, 1977), p. 195.
3. Christopher Robbins, *Air America: The Story of the CIA's Secret Airlines* (New York: G. P. Putnam's Sons, 1979), p. 19.

7. Headquarters: Duping Congress

1. Frank Snepp, *Decent Interval* (New York: Random House, 1977), *passim.*
2. *The New York Times*, July 29, 1965, p. 11.

8. In Search of Reds

1. Douglas S. Blaufarb, *The Counterinsurgency Era* (New York: The Free Press, 1977), pp. 196, 183, 197.
2. Chawin Sarakham, *Unmasking the CIA* (Bangkok: Kribisak and Thapthiuami, 1974). This book describes the operation. (This footnote was required by the Agency during the review process.)

9. Headquarters: Ghosts in the Halls

1. See for example, Miles Copeland, *Without Cloak and Dagger* (New York: Simon and Schuster, 1974), p. 320; and Harry Rositzke, *CIA's Secret*

Operations (New York: Reader's Digest Press, 1977), p. 51 and following.

2. Peer de Silva, *Sub Rosa: The CIA and the Uses of Intelligence* (New York: Times Books, 1978), pp. 193-194.

10. The CIA in Vietnam: Transforming Reality

1. Douglas Pike, *Viet Cong: The Organization and Techniques of the National Liberation Front of South Vietnam* (Cambridge, Mass.: The M.I.T. Press, 1966).

2. Michael Charles Conley, *The Communist Insurgent Infrastructure in South Vietnam: A Study of Organization and Strategy* (Washington, D.C.: The American University, 1967).

3. Vietnam Lao Dong Party, *Thirty Years of Struggle of the Party* (Hanoi: Foreign Language Publishing House, 1960), p. 26.

4. *Ibid.*, p. 71. See also Jeffrey Race, *War Comes to Long An* (Berkeley: University of California Press, 1972), *passim.*

5. Senator Mike Gravel, *The Pentagon Papers* (Boston: Beacon Press, 1971), Vol. I, p. 45.

6. Alexander Kendrick, *The Wound Within* (Boston: Little, Brown and Company, 1974), p. 35.

7. Gravel, *op. cit.*, p. 53.

8. Gravel, *op. cit.*, p. 78.

9. Gravel, *op. cit.*, p. 204.

10. Philippe Devillers and Jean Lacouture, *End of a War: Indochina, 1954* (New York: Frederick A. Praeger, 1969), p. 224. The footnote on page 342 re this topic is sourced to *The London Times*, December 15, 1965.

11. Dr. Tom Dooley, *Three Great Books* (New York: Farrar, Straus and Cudahy, Inc., 1960), pp. 48, 98, 100.

12. Jim Winters, "Tom Dooley the Forgotten Hero," *Notre Dame Magazine*, May 1979, pp. 10-17.

13. Joseph B. Smith, *Portrait of a Cold Warrior* (New York: G. P. Putnam's Sons, 1976), pp. 252, 255.

14. Department of Defense, *United States Vietnam Relations 1945-1967* (Washington, D.C.: United States Government Printing Office, 1971) (Hereafter referred to as the Department of Defense Pentagon Papers.), Vol. 10, p. 958.

15. Dwight D. Eisenhower, *Mandate for Change: 1953-1956* (New York: Doubleday and Company, Inc., 1963), p. 372.

16. Edward Geary Lansdale, Major General, United States Air Force (Ret.), *In the Midst of Wars* (New York: Harper & Row, 1972), p. 327.

17. Department of Defense Pentagon Papers, *op. cit.*, Vol. 10, p. 1077.

18. Warren Hinckle, Robert Scheer, and Sol Stern, "The University on the Make," *Ramparts*, special edition, 1969, p. 54.

19. Bernard B. Fall, *Last Reflections on a War* (Garden City, New York: Doubleday, 1967), pp. 201-202, in part quoting Jean Lacouture.

20. Philippe Devillers, "The Struggle for the Unification of Vietnam," *China Quarterly*, No. 9, January-March 1962, pp. 15-16. Noam Chomsky, *At War with Asia* (New York: Pantheon Books, 1970), p. 41. Arthur Schlesinger,

Jr., *The Bitter Heritage* (New York: Houghton Mifflin, 1966), pp. 34-35. And others.

21. Robert F. Turner, *Vietnamese Communism* (Stanford: Hoover Institution Press, 1975), p. 172.
22. Department of Defense Pentagon Papers, *op. cit.*, Vol. II, Section IV, A. 5, Tab 4.
23. Gravel, *op. cit.*, Vol. I, p. 252.
24. William Colby and Peter Forbath, *Honorable Men: My Life in the CIA* (New York: Simon & Schuster, 1978), pp. 256-257.
25. Douglas Pike, *History of Vietnamese Communism, 1925-1976* (Stanford: Hoover Institution Press, 1978), p. 15.
26. Colby, *op. cit.*, p. 169.
27. Colby, *op. cit.*, pp. 203, 206.
28. Victor Marchetti and John D. Marks, *The CIA and the Cult of Intelligence* (New York: Alfred A. Knopf, 1974), pp. 245-246.
29. For accounts of the events surrounding the Tonkin Gulf incident, see for example: Eugene G. Winchy, *Tonkin Gulf* (New York: Doubleday, 1971); Anthony Austin, *President's War* (Philadelphia: Lippincott, 1971); Peter Dale Scott, *The War Conspiracy* (New York: The Bobbs-Merrill Company, Inc., 1972); Joseph C. Goulden, *Truth Is the First Casualty* (Chicago: Rand McNally, 1969); and Ralph Stavins et al., *Washington Plans an Aggressive War* (New York: Random House, 1971).
30. *The Washington Post*, "CIA Fakes '65 Evidence on War in Vietnam, Ex-Officer [Philip Liechty] Charges," March 20, 1982, p. A19.
31. *Ibid.*
32. *Ibid.*
33. General William Childs Westmoreland, *A Soldier Reports* (New York: Doubleday and Company, 1976), p. 152.
34. Marchetti and Marks, *op. cit.*, p. 245.
35. *Ibid.*, p. 246.
36. Colby, *op. cit.*, p. 269.

11. Coming Home

1. Nina S. Adams and Alfred W. McCoy (eds.), *Laos: War and Revolution* (New York: Harper & Row, 1970), pp. 380-381, in part quoting Associated Press dispatch of June 8, 1970.

12. Down and Out in Thailand

1. *The New York Times*, January 6, 1974, p. 4.
2. Chawin Sarakham, *Unmasking the CIA* (Bangkok: Kribisak and Thapthiuami, 1974). This book describes the operation. (This footnote was required by the Agency during the review process.)
3. The New York Times, *The Pentagon Papers* (Toronto: Bantam Books, Inc., 1971), p. 133.
4. *Ibid.*, p. 134.

5. *Ibid.*, p. 133.
6. John Stockwell, *In Search of Enemies* (New York: W. W. Norton & Company, Inc., 1978), p. 32.

13. Light at the End of the Tunnel

1. Victor Marchetti and John D. Marks, *The CIA and the Cult of Intelligence* (New York: Alfred A. Knopf, 1974), pp. 158-160.
2. *The Wall Street Journal*, "Tarnished Report?" June 8, 1981, p. 1. See also Philip Agee, *White Paper? Whitewash!* (New York: Deep Cover Publications, 1981).
3. Commission on CIA Activities within the United States, June 1975 (Washington, D.C.: U.S. Government Printing Office, 1975). Beginning on page 137.
4. Sam Adams, "Vietnam Cover-up: Playing War with Numbers, A CIA Conspiracy Against its Own Intelligence," *Harper's*, May 1975, pp. 41-73.
5. Reprinted in Facts on File, *The CIA and the Security Debate: 1975-1976* (New York: Facts on File, 1977), p. 86.

14. Conclusion

1. Philip Agee, *White Paper? Whitewash!* (New York: Deep Cover Publications, 1981).
2. *The Washington Post*, "CIA Faked '65 Evidence on War in Vietnam, Ex-Officer Charges," March 20, 1982, p. A19.
3. United States House of Representatives, "Iran: Evaluation of U.S. Intelligence Performance Prior to November 1978" (Washington, D.C.: U.S. Government Printing Office, 1979).
4. Saul Landau and Craig Nelson, "The CIA Rides Again," *The Nation*, March 6, 1982.
5. See Ralph W. McGehee, "Foreign Policy By Forgery: The C.I.A. and the White Paper on El Salvador," *The Nation*, April 11, 1981.
6. *Newsweek*, "A Plan to Overthrow Kaddafi," August 3, 1981, p. 19.

Appendix: This Book and the Secrecy Agreement

1. Thomas Lobe, *United States National Security Policy and Aid to the Thailand Police* (University of Denver Graduate School of International Studies: Monograph Series in World Affairs. Vol. 14, No. 2, Denver: University of Denver, Colorado Seminary, 1977).
2. Dr. E. Thadeus Flood, "The United States and the Military Coup in Thailand," Indochina Resource Center publication, undated, p. 1.
3. Thomas Lobe, *op. cit.*, p. 117.

GLOSSARY

Agent: A foreign national who supplies information or performs other functions for the CIA case officer.

Border Patrol Police (BPP): A Thai paramilitary organization.

Case officer: An American staff officer working at any level in the Directorate for Operations and serving as intelligence gatherer, propaganda writer, or covert operator.

Census Aspiration Cadre (CA): United States program in Northeast Thailand to provide information on the Communist Party of Thailand.

China activities: Headquarters element in the Far East division that directed the CIA's worldwide intelligence collection and covert operations against Communist China.

Civil Air Transport (CAT): The Agency's first airline in the Far East based initially and primarily on Taiwan.

Civil Operations and Rural Development Support (CORDS): A united organization of American and Vietnamese governmental elements to pacify the Vietnamese.

Civilian, Police, Military (CPM): Thai provincial structure for countering the Communist Party of Thailand. CPM-1 was a military camp in Sakorn Nakorn Province in Northeast Thailand that conducted military operations against the CPT in the Northeast.

Communist Suppression Operations Command (CSOC): The Thai central headquarters for all reporting, planning, and operations against the Communist Party of Thailand.

Dead drop: A device for maintaining contact between clandestine operatives – where money or messages can be left for pick-up; e.g., a hole behind a loose brick in a wall.

Directorate for Administration (DDA): CIA element responsible for personnel, budget, security, medical services, and logistical support for overseas operations; established in 1950.

Directorate for Intelligence (DDI): Agency element created in 1952; responsible for the production of finished intelligence (excluding scientific and technical) and for the collection of overt information. Renamed the National Foreign Assessment Center (NFAC).

Directorate for Operations: Responsible for clandestine collection, counter-intelligence, and covert operations. Formerly named Directorate for Plans; renamed Directorate for Operations in 1973. It is common practice within the CIA to refer to the head of this unit as the DDO or formerly as the DDP.

Directorate for Plans (DDP): A CIA element created in 1952, also known as the clandestine services. Responsible for clandestine collection, counter-intelligence, and covert operations. Renamed the Directorate for Operations (DDO) in 1973. It is common practice within the Agency to refer to the head of this unit as the DDO.

Director of Central Intelligence (DCI): Chief officer of the CIA.

East Asia division (EA): Headquarters element of the Directorate for Operations that directs the Agency's worldwide intelligence collection and covert operations relating to Asia. Formerly called the Far East division.

Farmers' Liberation Association (FLA): Basic Communist structure in rural villages. First stage in developing a revolutionary organization.

Intelligence assistants (IAs): CIA employees who handle routine paperwork, run file traces, and perform tasks for case officers.

International communism branch (ICB): A subordinate element of the counter-intelligence staff of the Directorate for Operations that provides expertise in the field of international communism.

International organizations division: Coordinated the Directorate for Operations' clandestine activities aimed at developing an international anti-Communist ideology.

Joint Security Centers (JSCs): Regional Thai intelligence offices that collated information on the Communist Party of Thailand.

Live drop: A person traveling regularly who carries money, messages, and material between elements in a clandestine network.

Mail drop: An accommodation address used to prevent a direct link between elements of a clandestine network.

Mongoose Operation: CIA program of clandestine collection, paramilitary, sabotage, and political activities aimed at toppling the Castro government.

Nai amphur: Thai equivalent of an American sheriff.

National Security Council (NSC): The senior foreign policymaking body of the executive branch established in 1947.

Office of Current Intelligence (OCI): A component of the Directorate for Intelligence established in 1951. Responsible for the production of current intelligence in numerous areas.

Office of Strategic Services (OSS): U.S. intelligence agency from 1942 to 1945. Responsibilities included research, analysis, espionage, and overseas operations.

Officer in charge of liaison Special Police (OICSP): Chief CIA official working in liaison with the Vietnamese Special Police.

Paramilitary (PM): Military activities used as an element of the CIA's covert action function. Can include demolitions to full-scale wars such as the secret war in Laos.

People's Action Teams (PAT): Agency-sponsored program in Vietnam, consisting of small teams of armed men assigned to protect rural villagers from the Communists.

Permanent change of station (PCS): Usually a two-year assignment of Agency personnel overseas.

Personal record questionnaires (PRQ): Forms filled out by case officers for prospective agents. PRQ Part I provides basic biographic data while PRQ Part II describes operational use of the agent. PRQs were forwarded to Headquarters to obtain required approvals to use agents.

Phoenix program: Agency-sponsored program in Vietnam to seek out and capture or kill members of the Communist organization in South Vietnam.

Police Aerial Reconnaissance Unit (PARU): A Thai paramilitary organization used in Laos to fight that secret war.

Province officer in charge (POIC): Chief Agency official assigned to work in a Vietnamese province.

Provincial Reconnaissance Units: An Agency-sponsored organization in Vietnam designed to seek out and capture or kill members of the Vietnamese Communist infrastructure.

Records integration division (RID): Headquarters Directorate for Operations element that maintained files and name indices.

Regional officer in charge (ROIC): The Agency's chief official assigned to the various regions in Vietnam.

Sea Supply Company: A large commercial firm said to have been used to cover CIA activities in Thailand.

Special assistant for counterinsurgency: Office in the United States Embassy in Thailand responsible for coordinating all American programs designed to counter insurgency.

Temporary duty assignment (TDY): CIA assignment to a task or area for a short, specific period.

Western Enterprises: A commercial firm said to have been used to cover CIA activities based on Taiwan.

INDEX

"Abbott, Dave" (deputy station chief, Thailand), 63-64, 74-75, 80, 86, 88-89, 92, 117
Abraham Lincoln Library, Saigon, 146
Abzug, Bella, 62
Adams, Nina S., 207, 209
Adams, Sam, 156-157, 184-185, 210
Adoula, Cyril, 60
Africa, 56
  CIA operations in, 28, 60, 190
AFL-CIO, 59
AFSCME, 59
Agee, Philip, 35-36, 168, 202, 205-206, 210
Agency for International Development (AID), 59-60, 95-96, 127, 143, 160-161
  police training mission (CIA cover), 60
agrovilles, 138
Air America, 27, 71, 78, 95
Air America: The Story of the CIA's Secret Airlines (Robbins), 205, 207
Air Asia, 27
Albania
  CIA operations in, 24
"Allen" (McGehee's colleague), 41-44, 147
Allende, Salvador, 59
American Civil Liberties Union, [vi], 196
American dissidents, 63
American University, 128
amphetamines, 163

Anderson, Jack, 63
Andres, Monica, [vi]
Angola
  CIA operations in, 60
anti-American demonstrations, 168
anti-communist witchhunt, 3
antiwar movement, 62, 161
Arbenz, Jacobo, 27
Arlington, Virginia, 18
Armee Clandestine, L', 57
Armies of Ignorance, The (Corson), 204-205
Arosemena, Carlos Julio, 59
ARVN, 157
Asian communism
  see communism
Asian revolutions, 116, 190
Associated Press, 209
At War with Asia (Chomsky), 208
atomic weapons, 132
Austin, Anthony, 209

Bangkok, Thailand, 66-67, 69, 87, 90, 93, 98, 100, 102, 109, 163-165, 177
Bangladesh, 174
Bao Dai, 130-131, 133
barbiturates, 163
"Bart" (Thai desk chief), 122-123
"Barton, Al" (McGehee's boss in Taiwan), 45
Batista, Fulgencio, 27
Bay of Pigs invasion, 54-56, 58, 61
Bernstein, Carl, 31, 205

Bhumibol, King, 76, 87, 176
"big brother" concept, 103
Binh Xuyen, 133
biological warfare chemicals, 190
Bitter Heritage, The (Schlesinger),
    208-209
blackmail, 11
"Blacky" (personnel management
    officer), 179
Blaufarb, Douglas S., 69, 87-88, 207
Bo Daeng, 109-110
Bob (ex-station chief, FOIA officer),
    197-199, 201-202
Bolivia
    CIA operations in, 59-60
Bolivian rangers, 59
bombing of Vietnam, 140-141
books
    sponsored by CIA, 30-31, 58,
        200-201
    written by ex-CIA officials,
        198-202
Border Patrol Police, Thailand, 26, 69,
    87, 169-170, 200, 211 (defined)
Borosage, Robert, 204-205
BOSS (South African secret police), 60
Boston, Massachusetts, 178
    police trained by CIA, 63
Boys Day, Japan, 32
Braden, Thomas W., 29, 205
Brazil
    CIA operations in, 59
British authorities in Hong Kong
    cooperation with CIA, 21
British authorities in Malaya, 99
British Guiana
    CIA operations in, 59
British security forces, 203
Buddhists, 131, 133-134, 139
bugging, 176
Bunker, Ellsworth, 153
Burma
    CIA operations in, 25-26, 70
Burnham, Forbes, 59
Buro de Represion Actividades
    Comunista (BRAC), Cuba, 27-28

Cambodia
    CIA operations in, 58
    communist movement in, 172, 187
Camp Dale, Colorado
    secret CIA base at, 27

Camp Peary ("The Farm"), 12-16, 43,
    73
Can Lao Party, 134
Cao Dai sect, 133
"Carson, Rob" (instructor, later
    McGehee's colleague in Thailand),
    14, 73, 76
Carter administration, 197
Castillo-Armas, Carlos, 27, 58
Castro, Fidel, 58, 213
Catholic Vietnamese, 131-133, 138,
    150, 155
Celebes fighting, Indonesia, 27
Census Aspiration Cadre, Thailand,
    107, 111-112
census taking, 107, 134
Center for National Security Studies,
    [vi], 59, 204-207
"Chamnong, General," 166-167
CHAOS, Operation, 62
"Chat Chai, Colonel" (Thai police
    intelligence head), 96-103, 107,
    172-173
Chawin Sarakham, 207, 209
Cherry Street, Vienna, Virginia, 45
Cherrydale, Virginia, 18-19
Chiang Ching-kuo, 51
Chiang Ching-kuo, Mrs., 51
Chiang Kai-shek, 9, 50
Chicago, Illinois, 1-2
    police trained by CIA, 63
Chieng Khong, Thailand, 71
Chile
    CIA operations in, 59, 190
China (People's Republic of), 9, 50,
    86, 130, 183
    CIA intelligence collection in, 62
    CIA mail surveillance operation on,
        30
    CIA operations in, 13, 21-22, 25-
        26, 32-41, 43, 117-121, 181,
        186-187, 198, 202
    communist movement in, 132,
        170, 186-187
    foreign policy of, 120-121
    language of, 37-38
    McGehee's plane flies over, 71
    newspapers in, 39
China hands, 186
China operations group (CIA)
    see CIA – China operations group
China Quarterly, 208
"Chinese James Bond," 48
Chinese names, 37-38

Chinese Nationalists, 25-26, 46-53, 64
  see also Taiwan
Chinmen Island
  see Quemoy Island
Chomsky, Noam, 208
Christian Democratic Party, Italy, 24
Chulalongkorn University, Thailand,
  101
Church Committee *Report*, 22-23, 25,
  28-31, 56, 60, 62, 189-190, 192,
  200, 204-206
CIA (Central Intelligence Agency)
  and academia, 29-30
  access agents, 156
  Africa division, 60
  agents, 11, 22, 38-40, 47-50, 156,
    211 (defined)
  agents – recruitment of, 11, 29,
    35-36, 38-40, 48, 89-90, 118-
    119, 121, 134, 156-157, 168,
    170
  and AID cover, 60
  airline holdings, 27
  assassination operations, 58, 60;
    see also CIA – Provincial
    Reconnaissance Units; CIA –
    Phoenix program
  awards office, 191
  bases, 21, 198
  and biological warfare, 190
  "Bold Easterners" in, 12, 32
  and book publishing, 30-31, 58,
    189, 200-201
  break-ins, 61-62
  briefings, 82-84, 120, 127-128,
    137-138, 187
  Career Intelligence Medal, 191
  case officers, 10-11, 43, 57, 81-82,
    117-121, 149-150, 157-158,
    165-166, 168, 170-171, 174,
    187, 211 (defined), 213
  censorship – and McGehee's article
    in *The Nation*, 193
  censorship – specific deletions
    from this book, 19, 36, 57-58,
    87, 110, 117, 160, 166-168,
    170, 197
  censorship – and this book, 35-36,
    196-203, 207, 209
  Central Reference Service, 36
  CHAOS, Operation, 62
  Charter, 193
  China activities, 44-56, 117-124,
    211 (defined)

China activities – records unit,
  34-41, 43
China desk, 118-120, 124, 199
China operations group, 21-22,
  32-33
China reports office, 187
  and Chinese names, 37-38
Civilian Operations and Rural
  Development Support
  (CORDS), 127, 141-142,
  211 (defined)
  and Congressional briefings, 82-84
Counter Terror program, Vietnam,
  141
counterespionage review, 39
counterinsurgency operations, 56,
  59, 61, 76-81, 86-106, 112-124,
  166-177, 186-188
counterinsurgency training, 124
counterintelligence office, 62
counterintelligence/operational
  approval branch, 35-36
coup reporting, 170-171
cover, 6, 60, 65, 160, 168-169;
  see also CIA – secrecy agreement
covert action capability, 194-195;
  see also specific countries
Cuban counterintelligence office,
  61
*Current Intelligence Weekly Sum-
  mary*, 136-137
"dangle operation," 182
deception of Congress, 82-84
demolition course, 15
deputy directors, 191, 201
deputy station chiefs, 74-75, 86
desk officers, 82
destabilization operations, 59;
  see also CIA – governmental
  overthrow operations
destruction of documents, 41
Directorate for Administration,
  8, 212 (defined)
Directorate for Intelligence, 8, 36,
  40, 109, 115, 178, 212 (defined), 213
Directorate for Operations, 84,
  156, 178-179, 188, 191, 196,
  199, 211, 212 (defined), 213
Directorate for Plans, 7-10, 35-36,
  40, 56, 84, 212 (defined)
directors, 23, 28, 55, 212 (defined);
  see also specific individuals

CIA (Central Intelligence Agency),
continued
  disinformation and propaganda
    operations, 23-24, 28, 30-31,
    82-84, 131-133, 139-140,
    180-182, 189-190, 192-193,
    203
    – in Africa, 190
    – in China, 181
    – in Eastern Europe, 23-24
    – in El Salvador, 182, 193
    – in Latin America, 190
    – in the Middle East, 190
    – in the Third World, 28
    – in the U.S., 82-84, 189
    – in Vietnam, 131-133, 139-
      140, 181, 192-193
  district surveys, 101-116, 121-124,
    142, 147-148, 172-173, 183-184
  domestic operations, 60-63, 82-84,
    182, 189-190
  East Asia division, 92, 178-179,
    183, 185, 187-188, 212 (de-
    fined); *see also* CIA – Far
    East division
  employee morale, 190
  employee orientation, 7-10
  established (1947), 12
  European division, 60, 158
  European division – German
    branch, 23
  expenditures, 23-24, 56-57, 59, 62
  "family jewels," 179
  Far East division, 34, 40, 81-82,
    109, 115-116, 121-124, 147-
    148, 211-212; *see also* CIA –
    East Asia division
  field reassignment questionnaire, 32
  file traces, 34-40, 41, 202
  Foreign Broadcast Information
    Service, 181, 186
  and foreign intelligence liaison,
    28-29, 60, 120
  funding of organizations, 23-24,
    30, 61
  funding of political parties, 59
  general counsel's office, 196,
    200-201
  governmental overthrow operations
    – in Albania, 24
    – in Brazil, 59
    – in British Guiana, 59
    – in Chile, 59, 190
    – in Costa Rica, 27

    – in Cuba, 56-58
    – in Czechoslovakia, 24
    – in Ecuador, 59
    – in Hungary, 24
    – in Indonesia, 27, 57-58
    – in Iran, 28
    – in Libya, 193
    – in Rumania, 24
    – in Syria, 28
  Headquarters, 54-56, 63, 73-74,
    151, 153, 155, 171, 176, 179,
    181, 187-188, 196
    – McGehee at, 34-43, 54-56,
      63-65, 81-86, 117-124,
      147-148, 160-162, 178-191
  and indexing of names, 36-41
  infiltration of U.S. left groups, 182
  informants, 61
  inspector general, 175-176
  intelligence analysis, 81-82, 149-
    150, 157, 184-190; *see also*
    CIA – coup reporting; CIA –
    district surveys
  intelligence assistants, 10-11,
    212 (defined)
  intelligence collection, 28-29, 76,
    89-91, 142, 170, 186-190, 192,
    194-195
  international communism branch,
    91, 179-182, 185, 191, 212
    (defined)
  international organizations division,
    22-23, 29-30, 212 (defined)
  interrogation techniques, 105-107
  invasion operations, 25-26, 54-56,
    58, 61
  J Building, 34
  K Building, 4
  and labor unions, 24, 30, 59
  Lao desk, 82
  library, 186
  lie detector test, 5-6
  mail surveillance, 30, 190
  manipulation of elections, 23
  maps, 83
  Medal of Intelligence, 91
  media fabrications – *see* CIA –
    disinformation and propaganda
    operations
  Middle Eastern division, 60
  Mongoose Operation, 212-213
    (defined)
  National Foreign Assessment
    Center, 212

CIA (Central Intelligence Agency),
continued
National Intelligence Estimates,
134, 137, 184
news services, 31
office of current intelligence,
136-137, 213 (defined)
office of policy coordination, 25
office of security, 62
office of training, 147
officer in charge of liaison, Special
Police, 145, 157, 213 (defined)
official disclosure, 198-199, 203
operations – *see* specific countries,
regions, projects; *see also* CIA –
counterinsurgency operations;
CIA – disinformation and
propaganda operations; CIA –
governmental overthrow operations; CIA – invasion operations; CIA – paramilitary
operations
operations training, 10-11
parachute training, 14-15
paramilitary officers, 12-16
paramilitary operations, 13, 27-28,
54, 56-60, 76-80, 169-170, 193,
213 (defined)
paramilitary training, 11-16, 57,
200-201
People's Action Teams, Vietnam,
139, 213 (defined)
permanent change of station, 110,
213 (defined)
personal record questionnaire,
35-36, 213 (defined)
personality/intelligence tests, 6-7,
200
Phoenix program, 141-142, 213
(defined)
planting of phony documents,
see CIA – disinformation and
propaganda operations
and political parties, 24
project cryptonyms, 36
proprietaries, 25, 27, 29, 31
province officer in charge, 110,
142, 213 (defined)
Provincial Reconnaissance Units,
141-143, 213 (defined)
provisional operational approval by,
36
"Prudent Professionals" in, 12
psychological warfare operations,

167-169
publication index, 185
publications review board, 196-198,
200-201
radio operators, 39
radio stations, 23-24, 181
record keeping, 22, 32-41, 43, 179
records integration division, 36,
213 (defined)
recruitment and selection, 2-7, 193,
195, 199; *see also* CIA – agents
– recruitment of
recruitment of students, 29-30,
134, 182
regional officer in charge, 127, 142,
145, 214 (defined)
and resistance movements, 13, 24
retirement plan, 191
Revolutionary Development Teams,
Vietnam, 139
Saigon Military Mission, 131
salary and fringe benefits, 18, 20
secrecy agreement
– effect on families, 17-21, 32,
45-46, 66-69
– prosecution threatened under,
199
– and this book, 196-203
see also CIA – censorship
security clearances, 34-41, 196, 202
701 (RIF) program, 54-55
and sexism, 10-11, 34, 51
special assistant for counterinsurgency, 89, 214 (defined)
Special National Intelligence
Estimates, 137
special operations division, 59
station chiefs
– in Hong Kong (de Silva),
119, 198
– in the Philippines (Fitz-
Gerald), 32
– in Saigon (Shackley), 149,
156
– in Thailand, 72-73, 81, 86,
109-111, 114, 168-169,
175-176
stations
– in Africa, 60
– in Hong Kong, 21, 119, 198
– in the Philippines, 32-33
– in Saigon, 125, 127, 141-147,
149-159, 178, 187-188
– in Taipei, 21, 44-53

CIA (Central Intelligence Agency), continued
  stations, continued
    – in Thailand, 66, 71-75, 81, 86-89, 93-95, 165-176, 178
    – in Tokyo, 21-22, 31
    – in West Berlin, 23
    – isolated from local people, 51-53, 165-166
    – problems with disclosure, 198
  suggestion and achievement awards committee, 121-124, 148, 179
  surveillance of Americans, 61, 63
  temporary duty assignment, 92, 121, 214 (defined)
  Thai desk, 81-84, 90-91, 122, 199
  training, 11-16, 22, 57, 124, 200-201
    – of foreign troops, 59
    – of local police, 60, 63, 102, 134, 138
    – of Tibetan guerrillas in Colorado, 27
  training division, 74-75
  201 file, 36
  and underestimating enemy strength, 127, 135-138, 140, 184-185
  and use of drugs, 190
  and use of journalists, 28, 30-31, 180-181, 189
  and use of mercenaries, 60
  and use of pseudonyms, 35-36
  Vietnam desk, 124
  Weekly Intelligence Digest, 136, 150
  women in, 10-11, 34, 51, 121
  see also Camp Dale, Colorado; Camp Peary; Katzenbach Committee; specific individuals, organizations, and countries
CIA and the Cult of Intelligence, The (Marchetti/Marks), 5, 35, 196, 200, 204, 206, 209-210
CIA and the Security Debate: 1975-1976, The (Facts on File), 210
CIA File, The (Borosage/Marks), 204-205
CIA: The Inside Story (Tully), 205-206
CIA's Covert Operations vs. Human Rights (CNSS), 204-206
CIA's Secret Operations (Rositzke), 204-205, 207-208

Civil Air Transport, 25, 27, 132, 211 (defined)
Civilian, Police, Military (CPM)
  see Thailand – Civilian, Police, Military (CPM)
Cline, Ray, 51-52, 200-201
clipping service, 39, 50
Colby, William E., 35, 62, 81-83, 111-116, 137-139, 141, 143-145, 156, 179, 184, 190, 192, 200-202, 205, 207, 209
Cold War, 56
Colorado
  secret CIA base in, 27
COMINFORM, 9
COMINTERN, 9
Commission on CIA Activities within the United States, U.S., 210
communism, 3, 8-10, 22-23, 42-43, 50, 70, 83, 85, 89, 91-92, 102-103, 112-113, 123-124, 146, 172, 180, 182-188, 192, 194; see also communist movements; Communist Party of Thailand; Communist Party, U.S.A.; communist press; communist youth movement; Farmers' Liberation Association; Pathet Lao; PKI; Thailand – Communist Suppression Operations Command; Viet Minh; Women's Liberation Association
Communist Insurgent Infrastructure in South Vietnam, The (Conley), 128, 208
communist movements
  in Cambodia, 172, 187
  in China, 132, 170, 186-187
  in Indonesia, 57-58
  in Laos, 64, 70-71, 83, 169, 172, 187
  in Malaya, 99
  in Malaysia, 187
  in the Philippines, 187
  in Singapore, 187
  in Thailand, 87-92, 95-116, 121-124, 165-173, 187
  in Vietnam, 127-147, 149-159, 172, 179, 181, 183-189, 192-193
Communist Party of Thailand, 81, 89-92, 108, 112-113, 167-168, 172, 211
  Masses Mobilization Unit, 112-113
Communist Party, U.S.A., 8
communist press, 180

Communist Suppression Operations
Command
    see Thailand – Communist Sup-
        pression Operations Command
communist youth movement, Vietnam,
    128
Congo
    CIA operations in, 60
Congress, U.S., 198
    CIA deception of, 82-84
    Gulf of Tonkin resolution, 139
Congress of Cultural Freedom, 24
Congressional Quarterly, 207
Conley, Michael Charles, 128, 142, 208
contract with publisher, 200
"Controlled American Source" (CIA),
    144
Cooper, Chester L., 61
Copeland, Miles, 207
CORDS
    see Vietnam – Civil Operations and
        Rural Development Support
        (CORDS)
Corson, William R., 204-205
Costa Rica
    CIA operations in, 27
Countercoup: The Struggle for Control
    of Iran (K. Roosevelt), 28, 205
Counterinsurgency Era, The (Blau-
    farb), 87-88, 207
Covert Action in Chile (U.S. Senate),
    206
Cuba, 59-60
    Bay of Pigs invasion, 54-56, 58, 61
    CIA operations in, 27-28, 54, 56-58,
        61, 194
    Mongoose Operation, 212 (defined)
Cuban Americans
    CIA surveillance of, 61
Cuban exiles, 58, 60-61
Cultural Revolution, China, 181
customs inspection, U.S., 177
Cyprus, 189
Czechoslovakia
    CIA operations in, 24, 189

Dalai Lama, 27
de Silva, Peer, 119, 198, 208
dead drop, 11, 211 (defined)
death penalty, 134-135
deaths, 57-58, 200
    from Phoenix program, 141

Decent Interval (Snepp), 84, 207
Defense Department, U.S., 197,
    208-209
Dellums, Ronald, 62
Democratic Republic of Vietnam
    established, 130
    see also Vietnam
destabilization
    see CIA – destabilization opera-
        tions; CIA – governmental
        overthrow operations
Devillers, Philippe, 208
DIA (Defense Intelligence Agency),
    136
Dien Bien Phu, Vietnam, 130
Doi Su Thep Mountain, 72, 76
domino theory, 70
Don Muang Airport, Bangkok, 165,
    174
Donovan, William ("Wild Bill") J., 12
Dooley, Tom, 132, 208
Downey, Thomas, 25
drug use, 5, 35, 163-164, 190
Duc Hotel, Saigon, x, 125, 146
Dulles Airport, Washington, D.C., 177
Dulles, Allen, 23, 28, 40, 54-55,
    200-201
Dulles, John Foster, 23

East Fork Baptist Church cemetery, 1
Eastern Europe
    CIA operations in, 13, 23-24
    see also specific countries
Ecuador
    CIA operations in, 59
Egypt, 28, 189
Eisenhower, Dwight D., 23, 50,
    133-134, 208
El Salvador
    CIA operations in, 166, 182, 193
electoral politics, 23
End of a War: Indochina, 1954
    (Devillers/Lacouture), 208
ERA (Externalized, Regulated, Adap-
    tive) personality, 6
Eurasian (at Saigon airport), 158
European security services, 120
Eveland, Wilbur Crane, 205
executive branch, U.S., 199, 202
Executive Order 12065 (1978), 201,
    203
Executive Order 12333 (1981), xi, 193

Executive Order 12356 (1982), 193,
    201, 203

Facts on File, 210
Fairfax County, Virginia
    libraries, 200
    police trained by CIA, 63
Fall, Bernard B., 134-135, 208
Far East, 12
    CIA operations in, 23-27
    see also specific countries
farmers, 129, 166
Farmers' Liberation Association,
    Thailand, 104-108, 112-113,
    212 (defined)
Farmers' Liberation Association,
    Vietnam, 35, 37, 128, 212
    (defined)
FBI (Federal Bureau of Investigation),
    4-5, 8, 63
Fecteau, Richard, 25
Federal Republic of Germany
    CIA operations in, 24
    CIA station (West Berlin), 23
Figueres, Jose, 27
Filipinos, 133
films, 5, 8
Fish is Red, The (Hinckle/Turner), 206
FitzGerald, Desmond, 32
Flood, E. Thadeus, 200, 210
Florida
    CIA operations in, 61
Forbath, Peter, 209
Foreign and Military Intelligence
    see Church Committee Report
foreign nationals, 173
    see also CIA – agents
France, 129-131, 133
    CIA operations in, 24
    intelligence service, 137
Francis, Al, 109
Freedom Company of the Philippines,
    133
"freedom fighters," 24
Freedom of Information Act, 197-198
free-fire zones, 103, 141
Frei, Eduardo, 59
Fuentes, Miguel Ydigoras, 58-59

Gardner, John, 61

gaseous-diffusion plant, China, 119
Geneva Conference (1954), 130, 133,
    135
Geneva Conference (1961-1962), 64
Georgetown Hospital, Washington,
    D.C., 177
Georgetown, Washington, D.C.,
    160-162
Germans, 42
Getler, Michael, 63
Gia Dinh Province, Vietnam, ix-x,
    127, 142-145
G.I.'s, 125-126, 163
Goldwater, Barry, 61
Goulart, Joao, 59
Goulden, Joseph C., 209
government credibility, 3
Gravel, Mike, 198, 208-209
Greece, 9, 189
Green Bay Packers, 2, 18
Green Berets, 59
Guatemala
    CIA operations in, 27, 58-59
Guevara, Ernesto "Che," 60
Gulf of Tonkin incident, 139, 192,
    209
gun-boat diplomacy, 190
Guyana
    CIA operations in, 59

Had Yai, Thailand, 96-97
Haiphong, Vietnam, 132
Hale, Nathan, 4
Hanayo (McGehee's maid), 21
Haneda Airport, Tokyo, 17
Hannah, John, 160
Hanoi, Vietnam, 130, 132
Harper's, 184, 210
"Harry" (McGehee's boss in Saigon),
    158
Haw, the, 71
Hayama, Japan, 20
Health, Education and Welfare Depart-
    ment, U.S., 61
Helms, Richard, 61-62, 147
"Herman" (McGehee's boss in Saigon),
    145-146, 149-154, 157-158
Herndon, Virginia, 81, 92, 144, 147,
    164
heroin, 158, 163
Hill, Rey, 95
hill tribes, 70-71, 76-80

Hinckle, Warren, 206, 208
hippies, 161-162
History of Vietnamese Communism, 1925-1976 (Pike), 209
Hitler, Adolph, 85
Hmong, the, 47, 71, 83, 169, 174, 193
Ho Chi Minh, 70, 129-131, 133-134, 186
Hoa Hao sect, 133
Hollywood, California, 3
Hon Me Island, Vietnam, 139
Hong Kong, 125
    CIA operations in, 21, 119, 198
    ex-station chief (de Silva), 119, 198
Honolulu, Hawaii, 177
Honorable Men (Colby/Forbath), 35, 137, 156, 209
House of Representatives, U.S., 189, 210
    Intelligence Committee, 193
    UnAmerican Activities Committee, 3
Hoxha, Enver, 24
Hua Hin, Thailand, 174
Huk insurgency, 26
Hungarian uprising (1956), 24
Hungarian Workers' Party, 24
Hungary
    CIA operations in, 24
Hunt, E. Howard, 61, 202
Huston Plan, 62-63
Huynh Van Trong, 150-151, 154-155

I Was a Communist for the FBI (film), 8
Ibarra, Jose Velasco, 59
In Search of Enemies (Stockwell), 171, 206, 209
In The Midst of Wars: An American's Mission to Southeast Asia (Landsdale), 205, 208
India, 189
Indochina, 129
Indochina Resource Center, 200, 210
Indochinese Communist Party, 129
Indonesia
    Army, 57
    CIA operations in, 27, 57-58, 193
    massacres, 57-58
Indonesia – 1965: The Coup that Backfired, 58
Inman, Bobby, 201

Inside BOSS (Winter), 206
Inside the Company: CIA Diary (Agee), 35-36, 202, 205-206
International Control Commission, 140, 181
international organizations
    CIA operations in, 29-30
International School of Bangkok, 92, 110, 163
International Telephone and Telegraph, 59
interrogation centers, 139
Invisible Government, The (Wise/Ross), 204
IQ test, 7
Iran, 9, 165-166, 210
    CIA operations in, 28, 193
"Iron Curtain," 3, 9, 15, 23-24
Israel, 189
Israeli intelligence service
    cooperation with CIA, 28
Israeli invasion of Egypt, 28
Israeli troops, 28
Italy
    CIA operations in, 24
Ivy League schools, 12

Jagan, Cheddi, 59
"Jake" (McGehee's boss in ICB), 186, 191
Japan, 129-130
    CIA operations in, 21-22, 31-32, 202
    McGehee in, 17, 20-22, 31-32
Japanese communists, 17
"Jason" (McGehee's colleague in Thailand), 88-89
Joe (Jean McGehee's husband), 177
"John" (McGehee's boss in Thailand), 74
"John" (from domestic operations), 182-183
Johnson, Lyndon Baines, 61, 85, 139-140, 181
"Johnson, Rod" (station chief, Thailand), 72, 74, 81, 86, 109-110, 114-117
Joint Chiefs of Staff, U.S., 136
Joint United States Military Advisory Group, 71
Journal of Public Law, 204
Justice Department, U.S., 196

Kadar, Janos, 24
Kaddafi, Muammar
    see Qaddafi, Muammar
Karens, the, 70
Katzenbach Committee, 61
Katzenbach, Nicholas, 61
Kendrick, Alexander, 208
Kennedy administration, 60
Kennedy, John F., 25, 54, 75-76
Kennedy-Nixon debates (1960), 25
Kennedy, Robert F., 62
Kentwood, Louisiana, 1
Khrushchev, Nikita, 24, 42
King, Martin Luther, Jr., 62
Kinter, William, 199
Kirkpatrick, Lyman, 200-201
Klein, Robert, 156-157
Korea
    CIA operations in, 13, 21, 25
Korean War, 3, 7, 21, 25, 130

L/1 (agent in China), 47-50
labor unions, 24
Lacouture, Jean, 208
land reform, 129-130, 134
Landau, Saul, 210
Landsdale, Edward Geary, 26, 131,
    133-134, 205, 208
    memorandum on unconventional
        warfare of, 169-170, 197-198
Langchow, China, 119
Langley, Virginia, 54-55, 150, 190
Lao border area, 77-80, 86
Lao Dong Party, 137, 208
Laos
    CIA operations in, 47, 56, 58, 64,
        70-71, 83-84, 169, 174, 187,
        193
    see also Police Aerial Reconnais-
        sance Unit
Laos: War and Revolution (Adams/
    McCoy), 207, 209
Lardner, George, Jr., 201
Last Reflections on a War (Fall),
    134-135, 208
Latin America
    CIA operations in, 27-28, 58-59,
        165, 190, 203
    see also specific countries

Le Qui Don Street, Saigon, 146
Leahy, Frank, 2
LFBOOKLET (agent in Saigon),
    38-40, 50
Li Mi, 25-26
libraries
    CIA Library, 186
    in Fairfax County, Virginia,
        199-200
    in Saigon, 146
Libya
    CIA operations in, 193
lie detector test, 5-6
Liechty, Philip, 209
Life magazine, 140
Lin Piao, 186-187
Lisa (Scott McGehee's wife), 174-175
Lisu, the, 71
live drop, 11, 212 (defined)
Lobe, Thomas, 69, 200, 204-206, 210
London Times, 208
Los Angeles, California
    CIA operations in, 61
Lumumba, Patrice, 60
Lynch, Mark, [vi], 196, 198, 201

MACV
    see United States – Military Assist-
        ance Command in Vietnam
McCarthy, Joseph, 3
McCoy, Alfred W., 207, 209
McGehee, Daniel, [vi], 46, 69, 92,
    144, 163, 165, 174, 191
McGehee, Jean, [vi], 20-21, 44-46,
    68-69, 92, 144, 177, 191
McGehee, Norma, [vi], 17-22, 31-32,
    44-46, 64-69, 75, 92, 110, 124,
    144, 147, 160, 165, 174, 176-177,
    191
McGehee, Peggy, [vi], 20-21, 44-46,
    66, 68-69, 92, 110, 144, 161, 191
McGehee, Ralph W. (father), 1
McGehee, Ralph W., Jr.
    acknowledgements, [viii]
    reasons for writing book, ix-xiii
    childhood, youth, college, 1-2
    as football coach, 2
    recruited by CIA, 2-3
    goes to Washington, D.C., 3-4
    processed by CIA, 4-7
    CIA orientation, 7-10
    basic operations training, 10-11

McGehee, Ralph W., Jr., *continued*
  paramilitary training at Camp
    Peary, 11-16
  in Japan with China operations
    group, 17, 20-22, 31-32
  secrecy agreement and effect on
    family, 17-21, 32, 45-46, 66-69
  son Scott born, 31-32
  in Philippines, 32-33
  back at HQ (1956-1958), 34-43
  as case officer in Taiwan, 44-53, 64
  at HQ (1961), 54-56, 63-65
  goes to Thailand, 66-80
  at HQ (Thai desk), 81-86
  back in Thailand, 87-116
  illness, 92-95
  assigned to Taiwan, 114-115
  assignment cancelled, 117
  at HQ (1967-1968), 117-124
  in Vietnam, 125-128, 141-159
  growing disillusionment with CIA,
    144-148, 159, 171-172
  seeks other jobs, 147, 160-162
  home visitation, 147-148
  in Thailand, 163-177
  back pains and operation, 175-177
  final assignment at HQ, 178-191
  awarded Career Intelligence Medal,
    191
  secrecy agreement and this book,
    196-203
  El Salvador article cited, 206, 210
McGehee, Scott, [vi], 31-32, 42-46,
    69, 76, 92, 110, 144, 161, 163-165,
    174-175, 191
McLean, Virginia, 85, 118
McNamara, Robert, 64
Maddox (U.S. destroyer), 139
Mae Rim, Thailand, 79
Mafia, the, 58
Magsaysay, Ramon, 26
mail drop, 11, 212 (defined)
Malaya, 99, 170
  mailbox operation in, 99, 101
Malaysia, 187, 191
Mandate for Change (Eisenhower), 208
Mao Tse-tung, 9, 25, 50, 70, 118, 129,
    183, 186
Marchetti, Victor, 5, 35, 63, 141, 196,
    202, 204, 206, 209-210
Marks, John D., 5, 35, 141, 196, 202,
    204-206, 209-210
Marshall Plan, 1
Martin, Ambassador Graham, 109

Marxist-Leninist movement, 120
Mary (teenager in Bangkok), 163-164
Maryknoll seminaries, 131
mass media, 28, 30-31
massacres, 57-58, 141, 200
May Day (1953), 17
Mayerfeld, Ernest, 197-198
medical examination, 5
Mekong River, 64
Meo, the
  see Hmong, the
Michigan State University, 134
Middle East
  CIA operations in, 28, 190, 194
  see also specific countries
Miskito Indians, 174, 193
mobile strike forces, 84
Mobutu, Joseph, 60
"Moe, Jimmy" (case officer), 13-14,
    16, 47, 83, 174
Moline, Illinois, 1
Montgomery County, Maryland
  police trained by CIA, 63
Montgomery Ward, 2, 18
Monthly Order of Battle Summaries
    (MACV), 136
Mossadegh, Mohammed, 28
Mount Fuji, Japan, 21
MPLA, 60
"Munson, Mr." (head of personnel
    pool), 4-7

N-1 (Stockwell's agent), 171
nai amphur, 100-103, 111, 213
    (defined)
Nam Tha, Laos, 64
napalm, ix, 80
Nation, The, 57, 206, 210
National Alliance of Democratic
    Forces, Vietnam, 138
National Liberation Front of South
    Vietnam, 135-137, 147
national security, 196, 201, 203
national security advisors, U.S., 80,
    139, 171
National Security Council, U.S., 8, 64,
    131, 136, 194, 213 (defined)
National Student Association, 30, 62
NATO, 120
Nelson, Craig, 210
Nelson, William E., 121-122, 147-148
New Jersey, 131

New York City, 30
  CIA operations in, 61, 63
  police trained by CIA, 63
New York State, 131
New York Times, 3, 180, 197, 199,
  206-207, 209
  Index, 199
news services, 31, 189
Newsweek, 206, 210
Ngo Dinh Diem, 26, 126, 130-135,
  138-139, 152, 155-156
Ngo Dinh Nhu, 134
Nguyen Cao Ky, 139, 156
Nguyen Van Thieu, 128, 150, 153,
  155-156, 188
Nicaragua
  CIA operations in, 174, 193
1984 (Orwell), 184
Nixon, Richard M., 25, 62, 120
Normal Park Presbyterian Church,
  Chicago, 18
Notre Dame Magazine, 208
nuclear explosion, India, 189

Office of Strategic Services
  see OSS
Official Disclosure Law, U.S., 197
Official Secrets Act, U.K., 203
Okinawa
  CIA base in, 21
opium, 26, 76, 78-79, 163
OPS, 200
Orwell, George, 184, 187
OSS (Office of Strategic Services),
  12, 29, 130, 213 (defined)
Osyka, Mississippi, 1

Pacific Corporation, 27
Pahlavi, Mohammed Reza, 28, 193
Panmunjom, Korea, 3
Pao Tou, China, 119
Pathet Lao, 64, 83, 169
  see also communist movements —
  in Laos
Pattalung Province, Thailand, 90, 96
Pearl Harbor, Hawaii, 42
Pentagon Papers, The, 26, 69, 129,
  133, 135, 193, 197-198, 208-209
People's Action Teams, Thailand,
  107-108, 111-112

People's Action Teams, Vietnam,
  139, 213 (defined)
People's Progressive Party, Guyana, 59
People's Revolutionary Party,
  Vietnam, 135-137
personality profile, 6-7
Peru
  CIA operations in, 59
Peyton, John, 196
Phao Siyanon, 26
Philippines, the
  CIA operations in, 26, 32-33, 187,
  202
  communist movement in, 187
  Huk insurgency in, 26
  McGehee in, 32-33
Phillips, David Atlee, 200-201
Phoenix program, 141-143, 213
  (defined)
Phoumi Nosavan, 64
Phu Phan mountain range, Thailand,
  100
Pickering, Larry, 71
Pike Committee, 189
Pike, Douglas, 128, 138, 142, 208-209
PKI (Communist Party of Indonesia),
  57-58
plutonium plant, China, 119
poison dart gun, 190
Poland
  CIA operations in, 24
Polgar, Tom, 188
police
  CIA training of, 60, 63, 102, 134,
  138
  see also specific countries
Police Aerial Reconnaissance Unit,
  26, 58, 69, 169, 213 (defined)
Polish Freedom Movement, 24
Polish security forces, 24
political parties, 24
Portrait of a Cold Warrior (Smith), 208
Portugal
  CIA operations in, 24, 189
Praphat Carusathien, 72, 87, 109
Praphat-Thanom clique, 111-112
President, U.S., 171, 190, 192-194
presidential campaign, U.S. (1964), 61
President's War (Austin), 209
Projectile Operation, 150-157
prostitutes, 190
Puerto Rico
  CIA operations in, 61

Qaddafi, Muammar, 193, 210
Quemoy Island, 25, 46-47, 50

Race, Jeffrey, 208
radio codes, 11
Radio Free Europe, 23-24
radio interception, 39
Radio Liberty, 23
Ramparts, 61, 205, 208
RAND Corporation, 135
rape, 132
Ratner, Michael, [vi]
Ray, Ellen, [vi]
Reagan administration, 201
Reagan, Ronald, xi, 193-194, 203
reclassification, 201
Red Lahu, the, 70
red scare, 3
"Red Sox/Red Cap," 24
religion, 9-10
resistance movements, 13, 24, 46
Reston, Virginia, Regional Library, 199
retired police officers, 160
Reuther, Walter, 30
Revolutionary Development Teams,
    Vietnam, 139
revolutionary movements, 56
    see also communist movements
Rhodes Scholar, former, 40
rich Americans, 194
RIF (reduction in force), 54-55
riots, 59, 200
Robbins, Christopher, 205, 207
Rolling Stone, 205
Rolling Thunder Operation, 140
Roosevelt, Franklin Delano, 12
Roosevelt, Kermit, 205
*Ropes of Sand: America's Failure in
    the Middle East* (Eveland), 205
Rositzke, Harry, 28, 204-205, 207
Ross, Thomas B., 204
Rumania
    CIA operations in, 24

Saigon, Vietnam, 38-40, 50, 125-127,
    131, 133-134, 141-142, 145-146,
    158, 160, 188

sainthood, 132
Saiyut Kerdpol, 109-110, 116
Sakorn Nakorn Province, Thailand,
    109, 167-168, 211
"Sam" (McGehee's colleague in Thai-
    land), 74, 91-92
Sammy (McGehee's gardener), 21
San Francisco, California, 30
San Juan, Puerto Rico
    CIA operations in, 61
Sarit Thanarat, 71-72
satellites, 41-42
    photography from, 119
Saturday Evening Post, 205
Schaap, William, [vi]
Scheer, Robert, 208
Schilling, Paul, 200-201
Schlesinger, Arthur, Jr., 208-209
Schlesinger, James, 179
Scott, Peter Dale, 209
Scott, Walter, 4
Sea Supply Company, Thailand,
    26, 214 (defined)
search and destroy missions, 141
secrecy
    see CIA – secrecy agreement;
    Executive Order 12065;
    Executive Order 12356;
    reclassification
secret writing, 11
security clearances, 34-41, 196, 202
Senate, U.S.
    Armed Services Committee, 205,
        207
    Select Committee to Study Govern-
        mental Operations with Respect
        to Intelligence Activities, 206;
        see also Church Committee
        Report
    Subcommittee on Internal Security,
        3
Seoul, Korea, 21
Seventh Day Adventist Hospital,
    Bangkok, 93-95, 175
sex, 5, 13
Shackley, Ted, 146, 149, 153, 156-
    158, 175, 178, 185-188
Shan State Independence Army, 70
Siberia, 9
Sihanouk, Norodom, 58
Sinatra, Nancy, ix
Singapore communists, 187
Sino-Soviet split, 183
Sirikhit, Queen, 76, 87

Sklar, Zachary, [vi]
Smith, Joseph B., 208
"Smith, Mr." (orientation instructor), 8-10
Snepp, Frank, 84, 207
Soldier Reports, A (Westmoreland), 209
"Somboon, Lieutenant" (in Thailand), 101, 103-106, 110-111, 173
"Song, Captain" (in Thailand), 70
South Africa
    CIA operations in, 60
South Korean paramilitary troops, 25
Southeast Asia, 70, 92, 203
    CIA operations in, 56-58, 190
    see also specific countries
Southeast Asia Military Fact Book (DIA/JCS), 136
Soviet Ukraine
    CIA operations in, 24
Soviet Union, 9, 23-24, 41, 56, 120, 183, 194
    army, 189
    CIA intelligence collection on, 62
    CIA mail surveillance on, 30
    communism of, 8-10
    nuclear capability, 192
Sputnik 1 (satellite), 41
Stalin, Joseph, 9-10
State Department, U.S., 3, 59, 71, 109, 127, 174, 180, 186
    White Paper on El Salvador, 182, 193
    White Papers on Vietnam, 139-140, 181, 193
Stavins, Ralph, 209
Stern, Sol, 205, 208
Stewart, Gordon, 175-176
Stockwell, John, 171, 206, 210
strategic hamlet program, Vietnam, 138
strikes, 59
Sub Rosa: The CIA and the Uses of Intelligence (de Silva), 119, 198, 208
Subic Bay, the Philippines, 32-33, 39
Suharto, General, 57
Sukarno, Achmed, 27, 57, 193
Supreme Court, U.S., 197, 203
surveillance photography, 29
surveillance techniques, 11
Syria, 189
    CIA operations in, 28

Taipei American School, 46
Taipei, Taiwan, 43-47, 50, 64
Taiwan
    CIA operations in, 21, 25-26, 46-50, 166, 181, 202
    CIA station in, 21, 44-53, 114-115, 166
    CIA station chief (Cline) in, 51-52
    Eisenhower's visit (1960) to, 50
    intelligence service, 44, 46-50, 64
    McGehee in, 44-53, 63
    McGehee assigned to, 114-115
    McGehee's assignment cancelled, 117
    Western Enterprises Company, 25-26, 214 (defined)
Taiwanese, 51-52
Tan San Nhut airport, Saigon, 125
telephone books, 37
Tet offensive (1968), 125, 128, 138, 143, 158, 189
Thailand
    Border Patrol Police, 26, 69, 87, 169-170, 200, 211 (defined)
    Border Security Volunteer Teams, 69
    Census Aspiration Cadre, 107, 111-112
    CIA district surveys in, 101-116, 121-124, 142, 172-173, 183-184
    CIA operations in, 25-26, 58, 69-116, 121-124, 142, 165-177, 183-184, 187, 197-200
    CIA station in, 66, 71-75, 81, 86, 89
    Civilian, Police, Military (CPM), 87-88, 101-102, 108, 112, 116, 211 (defined)
    communist movement in, 87-92, 95-116, 121-124, 165-173, 187
    Communist Suppression Operations Command, 87-88, 102, 109-110, 211 (defined)
    coup d'etat (1976) in, 200
    farmers in, 166
    intelligence service, 88-89, 98
    International School of Bangkok in, 92, 110, 163
    Joint Security Centers in, 101, 212 (defined)
    language of, 73, 86, 173

Thailand, *continued*
  McGehee in, 66-80, 87-116,
    163-177
  mercenaries in, 57
  military, 87, 90, 108, 170, 172-173
  people of, 75-76, 80, 166
  People's Action Teams, 107-108,
    111-112
  police, 26, 58, 69, 87, 90, 95-116,
    168-170, 172-173, 198, 200,
    213
  Police Aerial Reconnaissance Unit,
    26, 58, 69, 169, 213 (defined)
  press in, 167-168
  Remote Area Security Program, 69
  Sea Supply Company, 26, 214
    (defined)
  Special Branch, 87
  students in, 200
  U.S. Embassy in, 67, 214
  Volunteer Defense Corps, 107
  see also Communist Party of
    Thailand
Thailand Independence Movement, 86
Thammasat University, Bangkok, 200
Thanom Kittikachorn, 72, 87
Third World, 194
  CIA propaganda operations in, 28
  see also specific countries
Third World revolutionaries, 187
Thirty Years of Struggle of the Party
  (Lao Dong Party), 208
"Thompson, Charles" (records task
  force head), 40-41
Three Great Books (Dooley), 208
Tibet
  CIA operations in, 27
  secret base for training Tibetan
    guerrillas in Colorado, 27
Tidewater, Virginia, 12
Tilden Technical High School, Chicago,
  1
Time magazine, 3
Tokyo, Japan, 17
"Tom" (McGehee's colleague in
  Taiwan), 44, 50
"Tom" (McGehee's boss in Vietnam),
  145, 149-150
Tonkin Gulf (Winchy), 209
torture, 103, 105-106, 126-127, 194
training films, 5, 8
Truscott, Lucian, 24
Truth is the First Casualty (Goulden),
  209

Tu Do Street, Saigon, 126
Tully, Andrew, 205-206
Turkey, 9, 189
Turner, Robert F., 209
Turner, William, 206

U-2 spy plane, 29
Udorn, Thailand, 109, 115, 172
Undercover (Hunt), 202
United Auto Workers, 30
United Kingdom, 21, 24, 99, 203
United Nations, 190
United States
  Armed Forces Radio, 146
  Army, 59, 128, 133, 190
  CIA mail surveillance operation in,
    30
  CIA operations in, 27, 29-31,
    60-63, 182
  CIA training of Tibetan guerrillas
    in Colorado, 27
  Huynh Van Trong's visit, 151, 155
  Information Agency, 127, 146, 180
  invasion of Cambodia, 58
  Marine Corps, 16, 140, 145, 164,
    181, 190
  military, 17, 140-142, 149, 163-
    164, 180, 183-184
  Military Assistance Command in
    Thailand, 64
  Military Assistance Command in
    Vietnam, 127, 136, 139
  military – Fifth Field Hospital,
    Bangkok, 164, 175-177, 181
  military police, 125
  Navy, 5, 12, 51, 132, 190
  police training by CIA, 63
  press in, 167, 180-182, 189
  sends troops to Thailand, 64
  Special Forces, 138
  use of atomic weapons discussed,
    132
  see also specific cities and states
*United States Security Policy and Aid
  to the Thailand Police* (Lobe),
  204-206, 210
*United States Vietnam Relations
  1945-1967* (Defense Department)
  see Pentagon Papers, The
University of Dayton Flyers, 2, 18
University of Notre Dame, 1-3, 18,
  118, 172

Unmasking the CIA (Chawin), 207,
    209
Uruguay
    CIA operations in, 60

Valium, 177
Van Khien, 157
vices, 35
Vienna, Virginia, 45
"Viet Cong" strength, 127, 135-138,
    140, 184-185
*Viet Cong: The Organization and
    Techniques of the National Libera-
    tion Front of South Vietnam*
    (Pike), 128
Viet Minh, 129-132, 170
    see also Vietnam – communist
        movement in
Vietnam, 109, 114, 116, 161, 164,
    179, 183
    agrovilles in, 138
    Buddhists in, 131, 133-134, 139
    Bureau of Investigation, 134
    businessmen in, 154
    Catholics in, 133, 138, 150, 155
    Central Intelligence Organization,
        139
    CIA operations in, ix-xi, 26-27,
        56-57, 84, 103, 107, 125-159,
        165, 181, 187-188, 194
    Civil Guard, 134
    Civilian Irregular Defense Groups,
        138
    communist movement in, 127-147,
        149-159, 172, 179, 181, 183-
        189, 192-193
    communist radio in, 186
    CORDS (Civil Operations and Rural
        Development Support), 127,
        141-142, 211 (defined)
    elections in, 130, 133
    Law 10/59, 134-135
    McGehee in, ix-xii, 125-159
    "Open Arms" program in, 154
    people of, 155
    People's Action Teams, 139,
        213 (defined)
    Phoenix program in, 141-143,
        213 (defined)
    police, 126, 134, 138, 144-145,
        149-158, 213
    police surveillance in, 151
    political prisoners in, 126-127, 155
    Popular Forces, 134
    postage stamp fabrication in, 140
    protestors in, 126
    Provincial Reconnaissance Units,
        141-143, 213 (defined)
    refugees in, 100, 131-132, 134
    Revolutionary Development
        Teams, 139
    soldiers, 125-126, 154, 187-188
    Special Police, 144-145, 149-158,
        213
    spy scandal in, 150-157
    strategic hamlet program, 138
    students in, 154
    teachers in, 154
    U.S. Embassy in, 125, 188
    Veterans Legion, 133
    Village Self-Defense Corps, 134
    youth in, 137
    see also Vietnam War
Vietnam War, ix-x, xii, 85, 125-147,
        149-159, 163-164, 182-183,
        188-189, 192-193, 202
Vietnam Workers Party, 129
Vietnamese Communism (Turner), 209
Village Voice, 189
"Vince" (case officer in Saigon), 153
Vo Nguyen Giap, 186
Voice of the People of Thailand
    (radio station), 86
Vu Ngoc Nha, 150, 154-155, 157

Walden, Jerrold L., 204
Walk East on Beacon Street (film), 8
Wall Street Journal, 182, 210
War Comes to Long An (Race), 208
War Conspiracy, The (Scott), 209
Washington, D.C., 3-4, 7, 32-43, 121,
    160
    police trained by CIA, 63
Washington Plans an Aggressive War
    (Stavins), 209
Washington Post, 63, 180, 192, 201,
    205-207, 209-210
Wellesley College, 161
Wells, William "Wild Willie," 191
West Berlin, Federal Republic of
    Germany
    CIA station, 23
Western Enterprises Company, Taiwan,
    25-26, 214 (defined)

Western Europe
    CIA operations in, 24-25, 28-29
    see also specific countries
Westmoreland, William Childs, 141,
    209
White House, the, 61
White Paper? Whitewash! (Agee), 210
Williamsburg, Virginia, 12-13
Winchy, Eugene G., 209
Winter, Gordon, 206
Winters, Jim, 208
Wise, David, 204
Without Cloak and Dagger (Copeland),
    207
Wolf, Louis, [vi]
Women's Liberation Association,
    Vietnam, 128, 135, 137
working class, 166
World War II, 1, 4, 11-12, 42, 129
Wound Within, The (Kendrick), 208

Yan Ming Mountain, Taiwan, 45
Yao, the, 71, 78-80
YMCA, Washington, D.C., 4
Yokosuka, Japan, 31
youth movement, 62
Yunnan Province, China, 26

Index compiled by Daniel Tsang

Typesetting by

New Mississippi, Inc.
P. O. Box 3568
Jackson, MS 39207